MIGHTY MOUSE™

SAVING THE DAY

MIGHTY MOUSE™
SAVING THE DAY

WRITTEN BY **SHOLLY FISCH**

ART BY **IGOR LIMA**

COLOR BY **MOHAN**

LETTERING BY **TOM NAPOLITANO**

COLLECTION COVER BY **IGOR LIMA**
AND **PETE PANTAZIS**

EDITS BY **ANTHONY MARQUES**

COLLECTION DESIGN BY **GEOFF HARKINS**

DYNAMITE®

Nick Barrucci, CEO / Publisher
Juan Collado, President / COO

Joe Rybandt, Executive Editor
Matt Idelson, Senior Editor
Anthony Marques, Associate Editor
Kevin Ketner, Assistant Editor

Jason Ullmeyer, Art Director
Geoff Harkins, Senior Graphic Designer
Cathleen Heard, Graphic Designer
Alexis Persson, Graphic Designer
Chris Caniano, Digital Associate
Rachel Kilbury, Digital Assistant

Brandon Dante Primavera, V.P. of IT and Operations
Rich Young, Director of Business Development

Alan Payne, V.P. of Sales and Marketing
Janie Mackenzie, Marketing Coordinator
Pat O'Connell, Sales Manager

 www.DYNAMITE.com
Facebook /Dynamitecomics
Twitter @dynamitecomics

ISBN13: 978-1-5241-0525-9
First Printing   10 9 8 7 6 5 4 3 2 1

MIGHTY MOUSE™, VOLUME 1. Contains materials originally published in magazine form as MIGHTY MOUSE™, Volume 1, #1-5. Published by Dynamite Entertainment. 113 Gaither Dr., STE 205, Mt. Laurel, NJ 08054. TM & © 2017 CBS Operations Inc. Mighty Mouse and related marks are trademarks of CBS Operations Inc. All Rights Reserved. Dynamite, Dynamite Entertainment & its logo are ® 2017 Dynamite. All Rights Reserved. All names, characters, events, and locales in this publication are entirely fictional. Any resemblance to actual persons (living or dead), events or places, without satiric intent, is coincidental. No portion of this book may be reproduced by any means (digital or print) without the written permission of the publisher except for review purposes. The scanning, uploading and distribution of this book via the Internet or via any other means without the permission of the Dynamite Entertainment is illegal and punishable by law. Please purchase only authorized electronic editions, and do not participate in or encourage electronic piracy of copyrighted materials. **Printed in China.**

For information regarding press, media rights, foreign rights, licensing, promotions, and advertising e-mail: marketing@dynamite.com

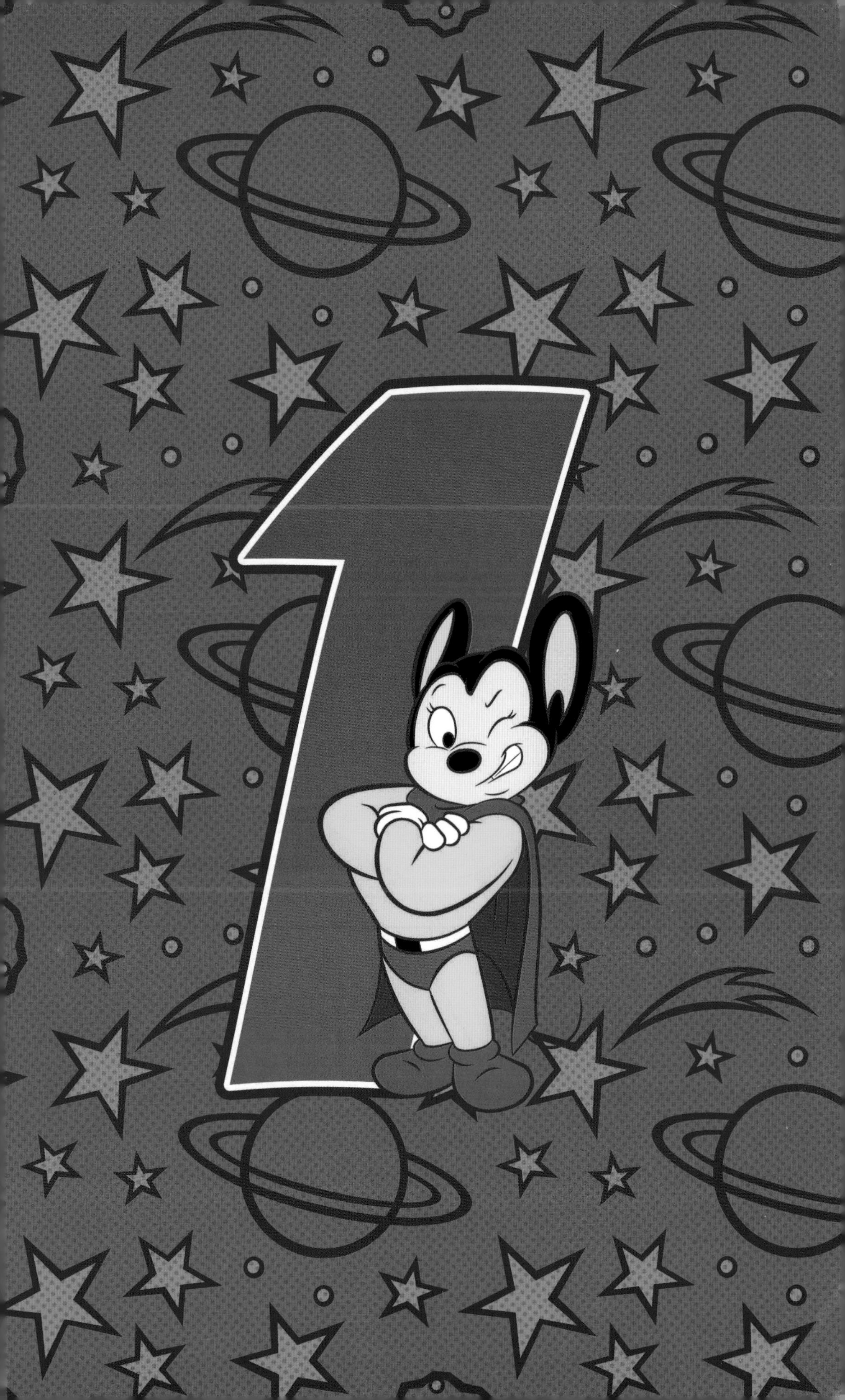
1

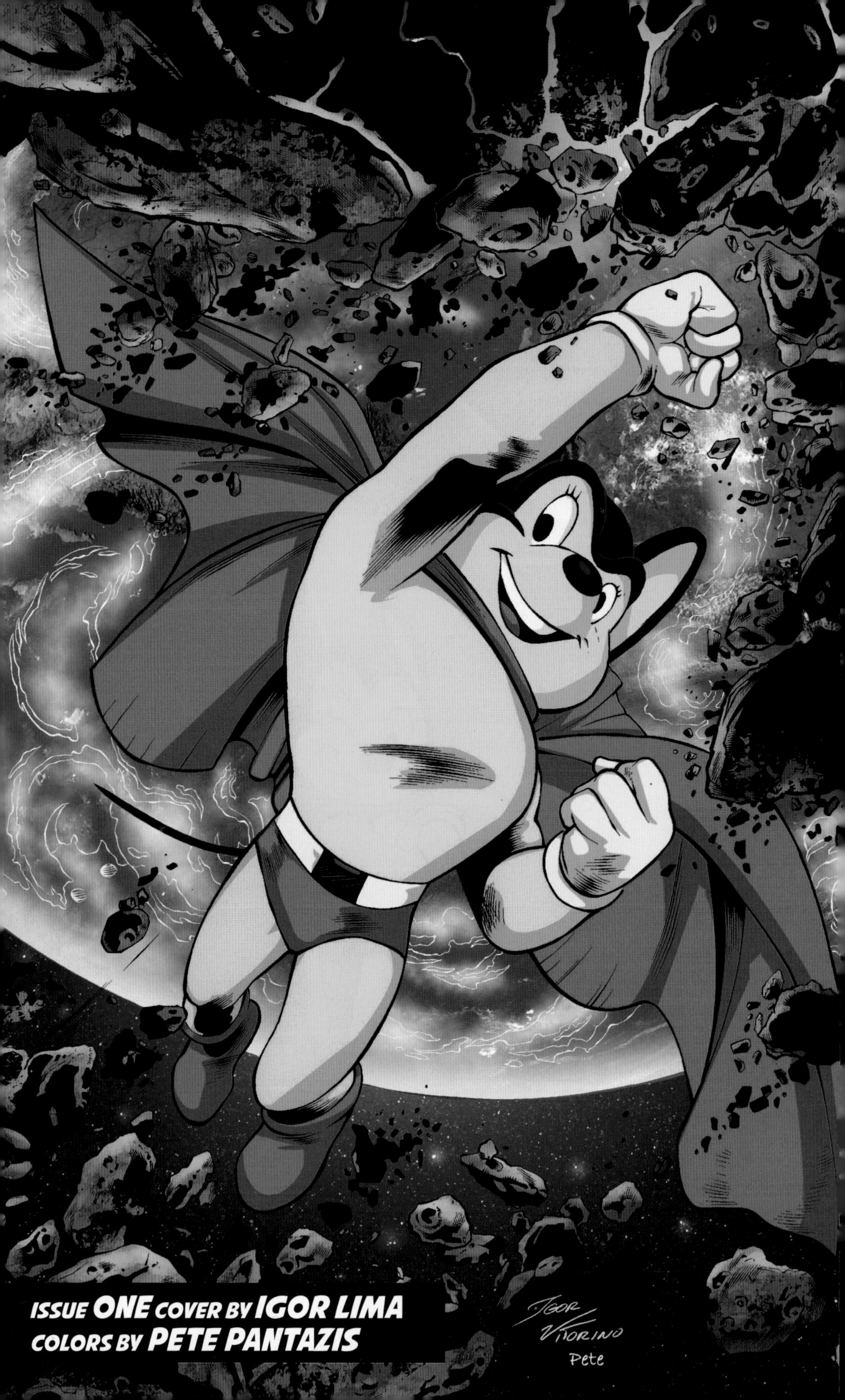
IGOR VITORINO
Pete

ISSUE ONE COVER BY IGOR LIMA
COLORS BY PETE PANTAZIS

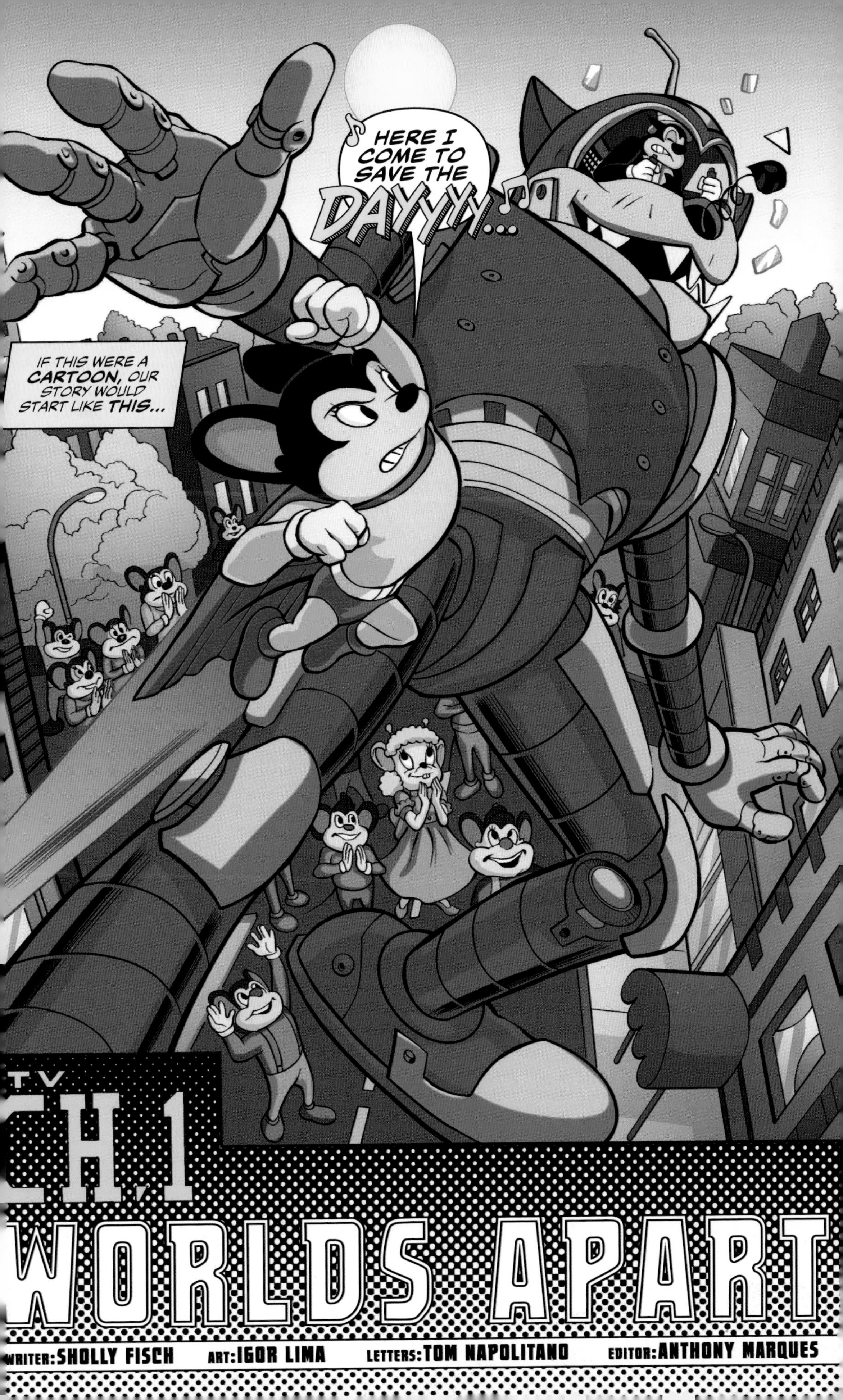
HERE I COME TO SAVE THE DAYYYY...
IF THIS WERE A CARTOON, OUR STORY WOULD START LIKE THIS...
TV CH. 1
WORLDS APART
WRITER: SHOLLY FISCH ART: IGOR LIMA LETTERS: TOM NAPOLITANO EDITOR: ANTHONY MARQUES

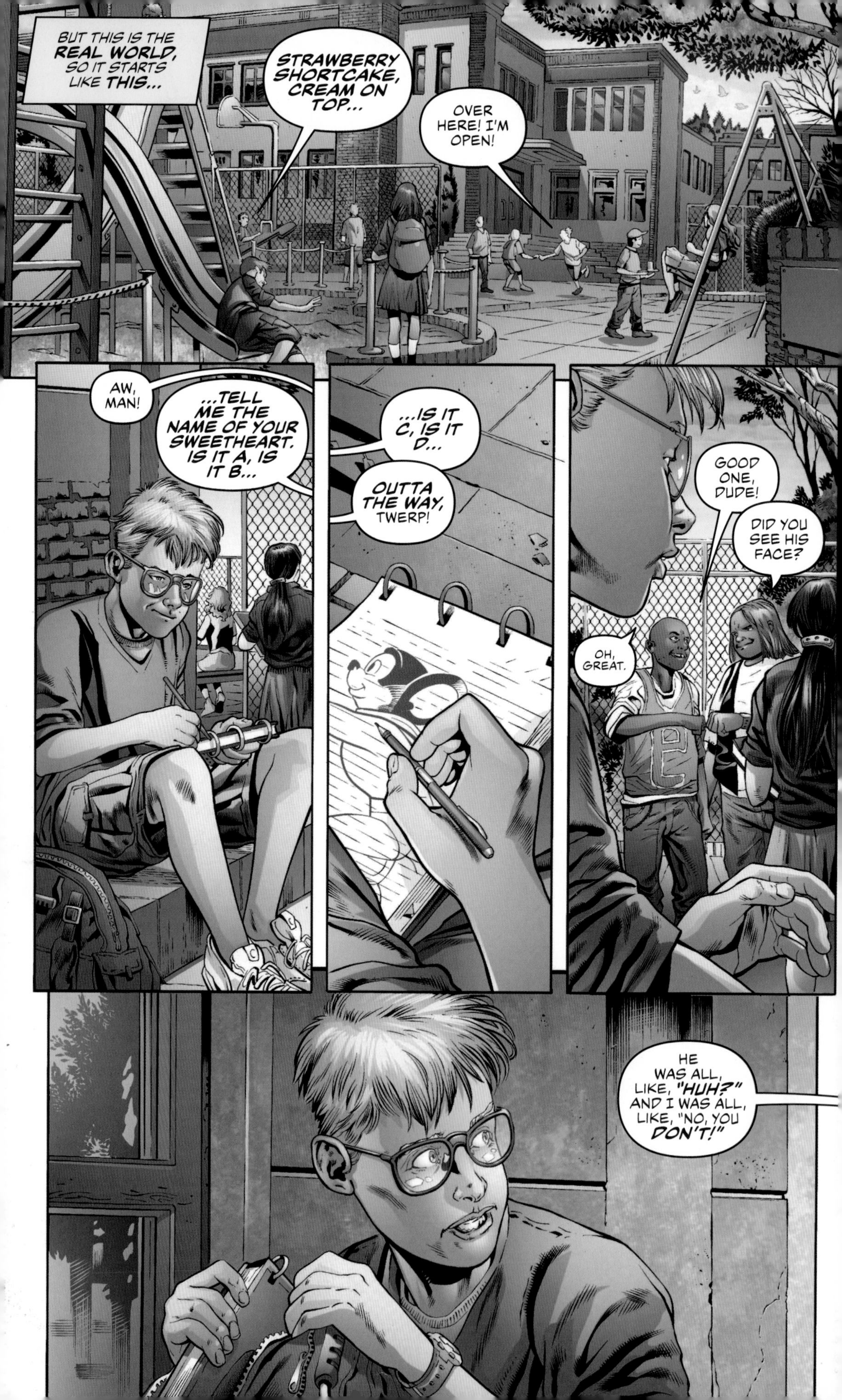

BUT THIS IS THE REAL WORLD, SO IT STARTS LIKE THIS...
STRAWBERRY SHORTCAKE, CREAM ON TOP...
OVER HERE! I'M OPEN!
AW, MAN!
...TELL ME THE NAME OF YOUR SWEETHEART. IS IT A, IS IT B...
...IS IT C, IS IT D...
OUTTA THE WAY, TWERP!
GOOD ONE, DUDE!
DID YOU SEE HIS FACE?
OH, GREAT.
HE WAS ALL, LIKE, "HUH?" AND I WAS ALL, LIKE, "NO, YOU DON'T!"

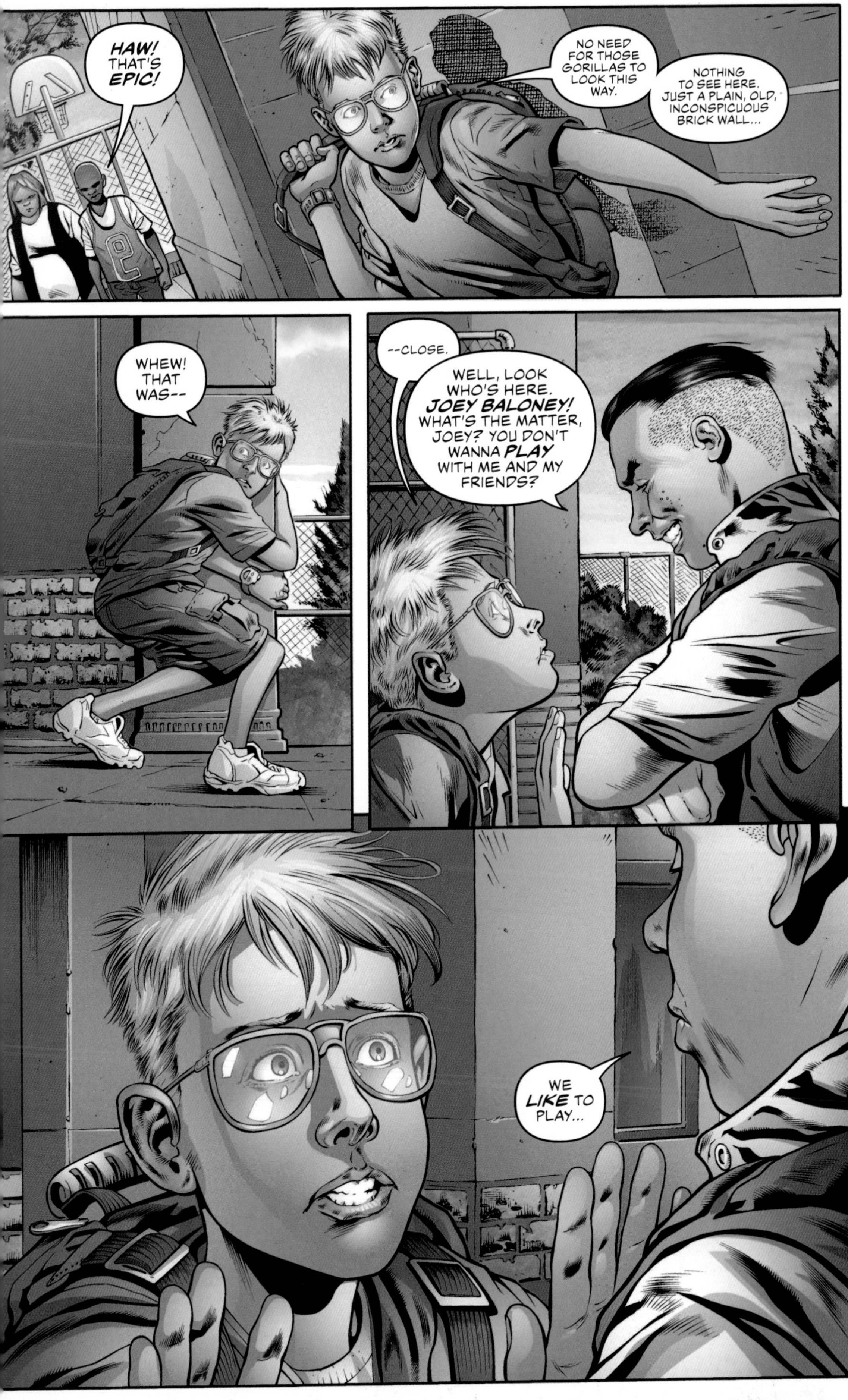
HAW! THAT'S EPIC!
NO NEED FOR THOSE GORILLAS TO LOOK THIS WAY.
NOTHING TO SEE HERE. JUST A PLAIN, OLD, INCONSPICUOUS BRICK WALL...
WHEW! THAT WAS--
--CLOSE.
WELL, LOOK WHO'S HERE. JOEY BALONEY! WHAT'S THE MATTER, JOEY? YOU DON'T WANNA PLAY WITH ME AND MY FRIENDS?
WE LIKE TO PLAY...

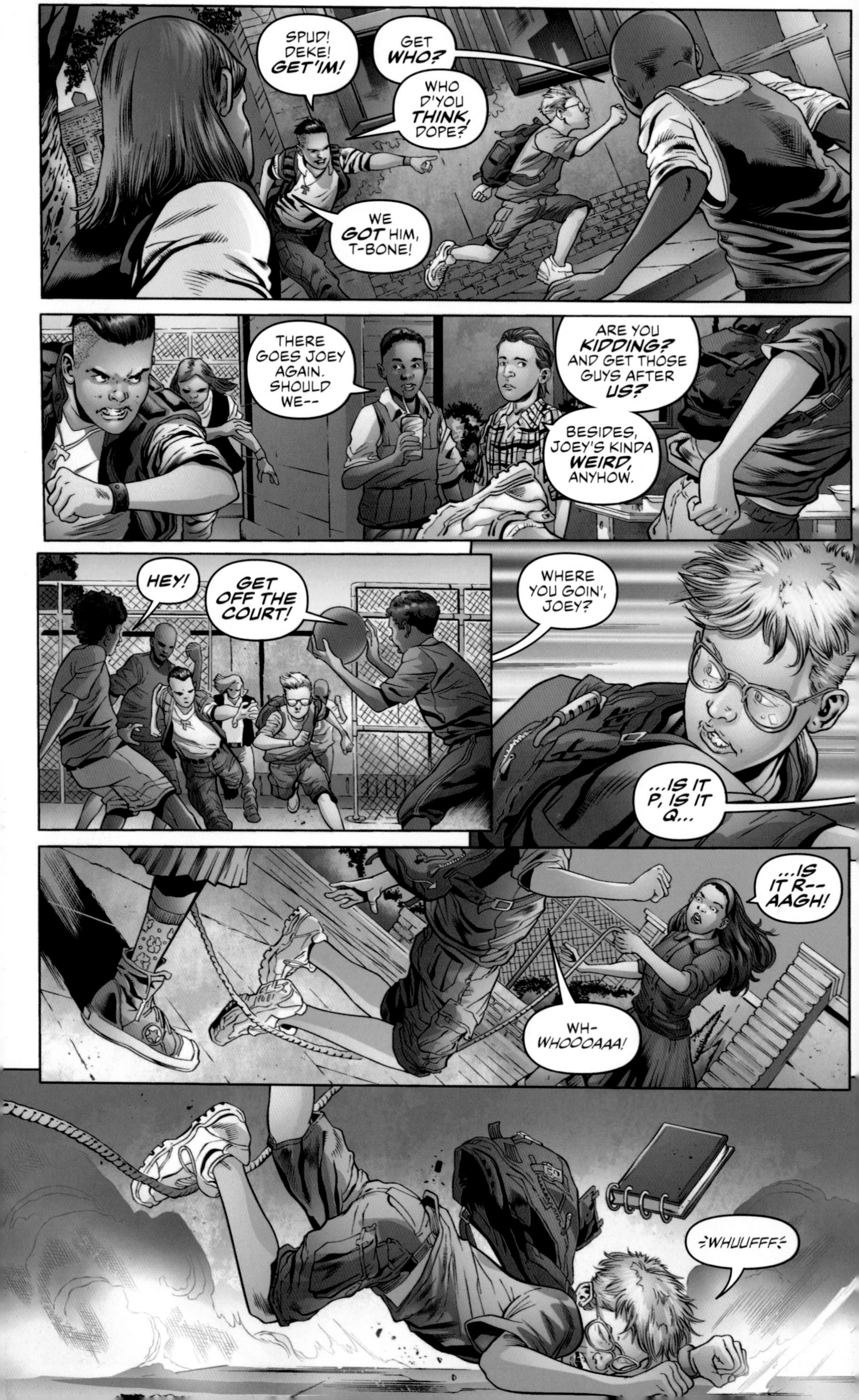
SPUD! DEKE! GET 'IM!
GET WHO?
WHO D'YOU THINK, DOPE?
WE GOT HIM, T-BONE!
THERE GOES JOEY AGAIN. SHOULD WE--
ARE YOU KIDDING? AND GET THOSE GUYS AFTER US?
BESIDES, JOEY'S KINDA WEIRD, ANYHOW.
HEY!
GET OFF THE COURT!
WHERE YOU GOIN', JOEY?
...IS IT P, IS IT Q...
...IS IT R--AAGH!
WH-WHOOOAAA!
WHUUFFF

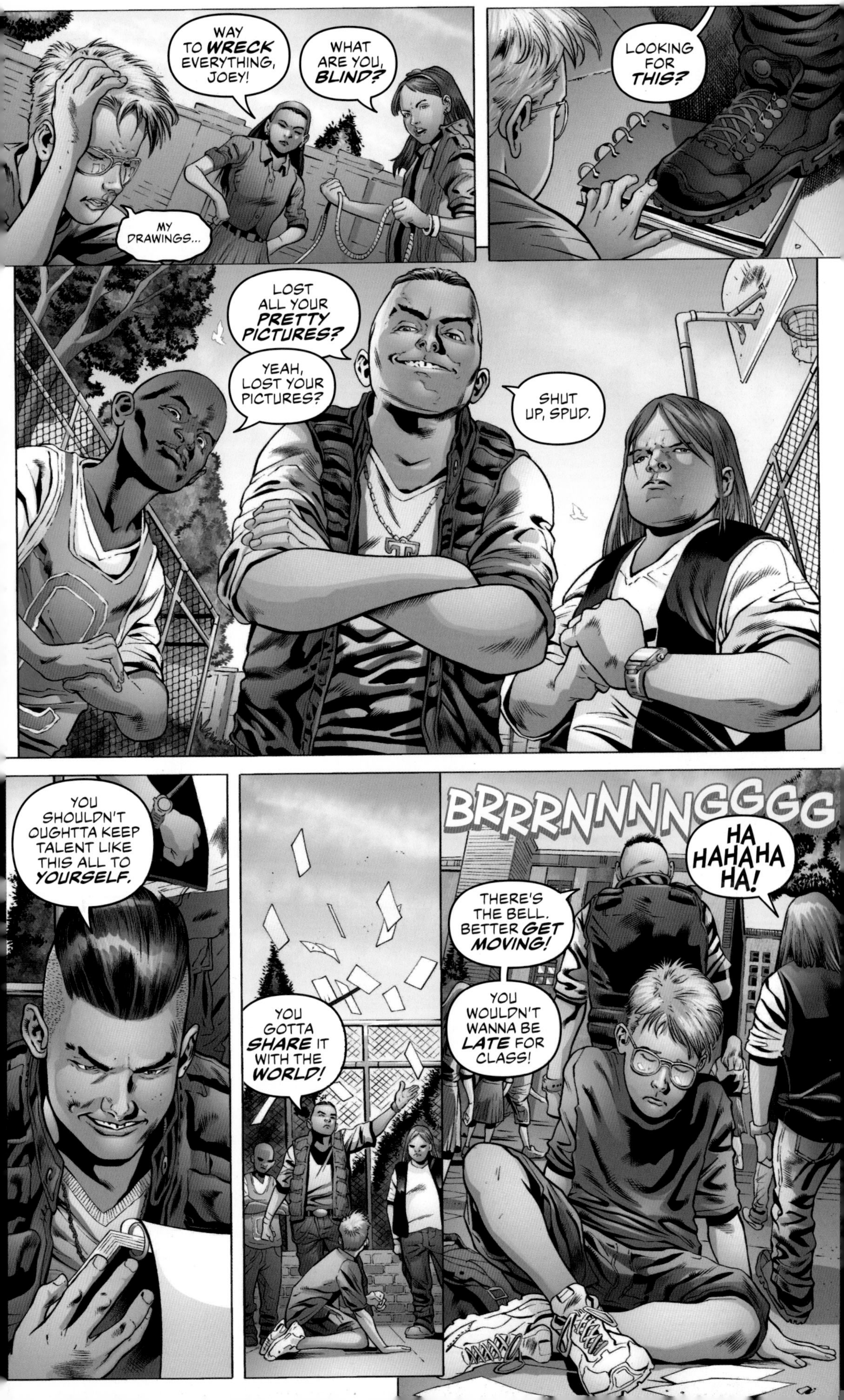
WAY TO WRECK EVERYTHING, JOEY!
WHAT ARE YOU, BLIND?
MY DRAWINGS...
LOOKING FOR THIS?
LOST ALL YOUR PRETTY PICTURES?
YEAH, LOST YOUR PICTURES?
SHUT UP, SPUD.
YOU SHOULDN'T OUGHTTA KEEP TALENT LIKE THIS ALL TO YOURSELF.
YOU GOTTA SHARE IT WITH THE WORLD!
BRRRNNNNGGGG
HA HAHAHA HA!
THERE'S THE BELL. BETTER GET MOVING!
YOU WOULDN'T WANNA BE LATE FOR CLASS!

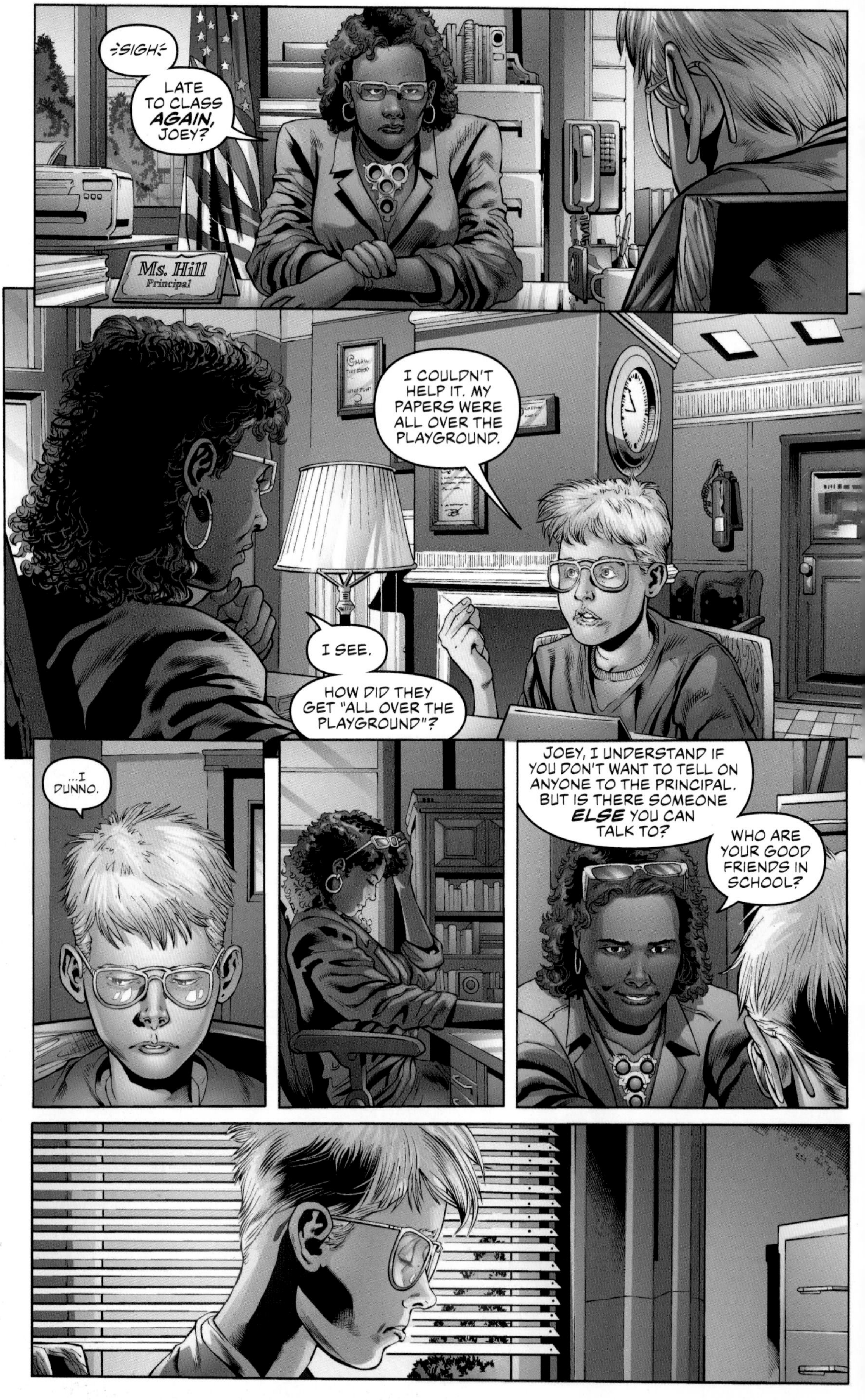

SIGH
LATE TO CLASS AGAIN, JOEY?
Ms. Hill
Principal
I COULDN'T HELP IT. MY PAPERS WERE ALL OVER THE PLAYGROUND.
I SEE.
HOW DID THEY GET "ALL OVER THE PLAYGROUND"?
...I DUNNO.
JOEY, I UNDERSTAND IF YOU DON'T WANT TO TELL ON ANYONE TO THE PRINCIPAL. BUT IS THERE SOMEONE ELSE YOU CAN TALK TO?
WHO ARE YOUR GOOD FRIENDS IN SCHOOL?

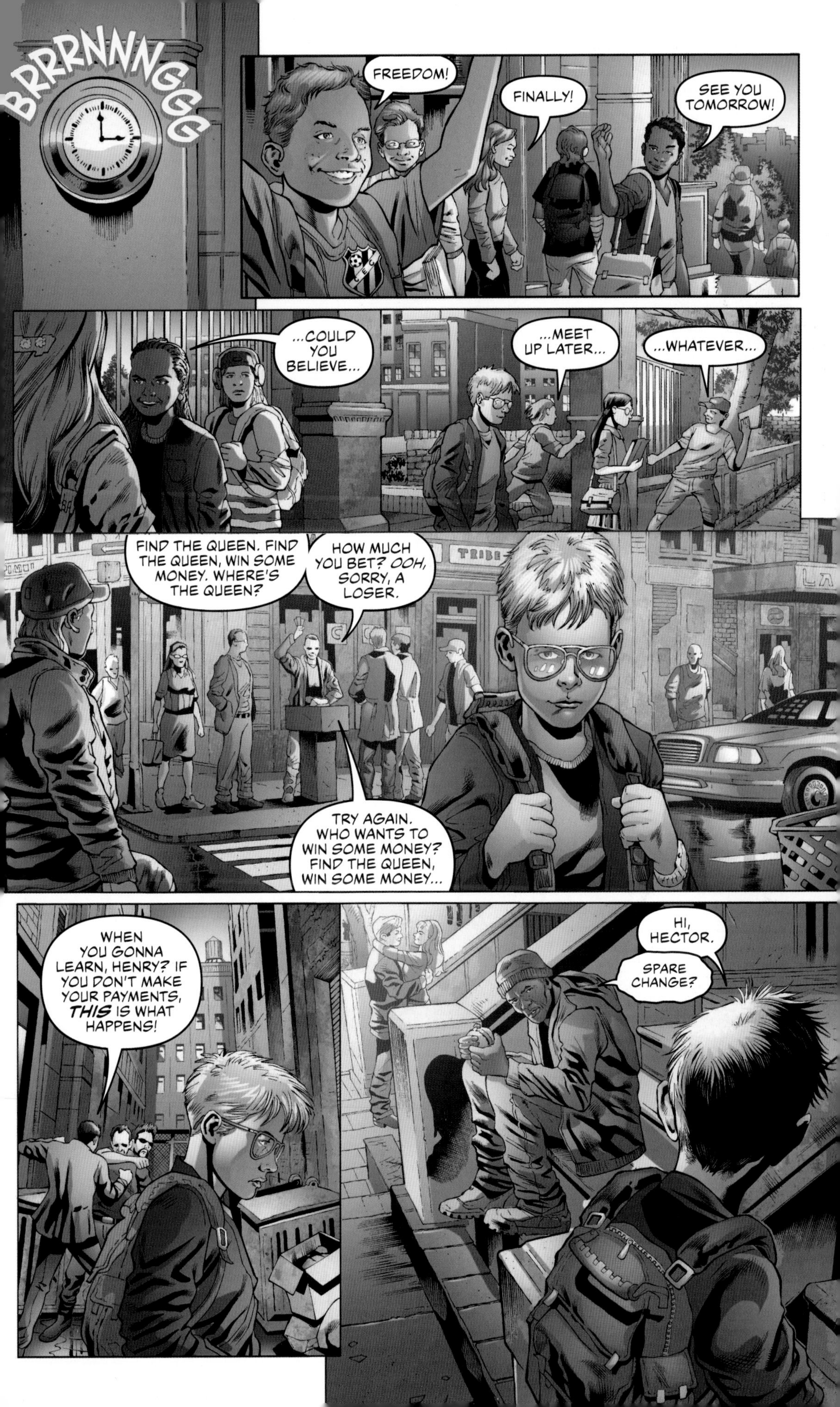
BRRRNNNGGG
FREEDOM!
FINALLY!
SEE YOU TOMORROW!
...COULD YOU BELIEVE...
...MEET UP LATER...
...WHATEVER...
FIND THE QUEEN. FIND THE QUEEN, WIN SOME MONEY. WHERE'S THE QUEEN?
HOW MUCH YOU BET? OOH, SORRY, A LOSER.
TRIBE
TRY AGAIN. WHO WANTS TO WIN SOME MONEY? FIND THE QUEEN, WIN SOME MONEY...
WHEN YOU GONNA LEARN, HENRY? IF YOU DON'T MAKE YOUR PAYMENTS, THIS IS WHAT HAPPENS!
HI, HECTOR.
SPARE CHANGE?

MOM! I'M HOME!

OH.

Joey —
I have to work a double shift tonight. Dinner's in the fridge. No junk food, and NO cartoons before your homework's done!
Love you,
Mom

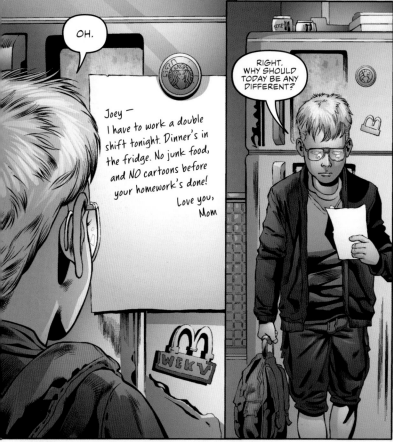

RIGHT. WHY SHOULD TODAY BE ANY DIFFERENT?

I'LL GET RIGHT ON THAT, MOM.

NO JUNK FOOD.

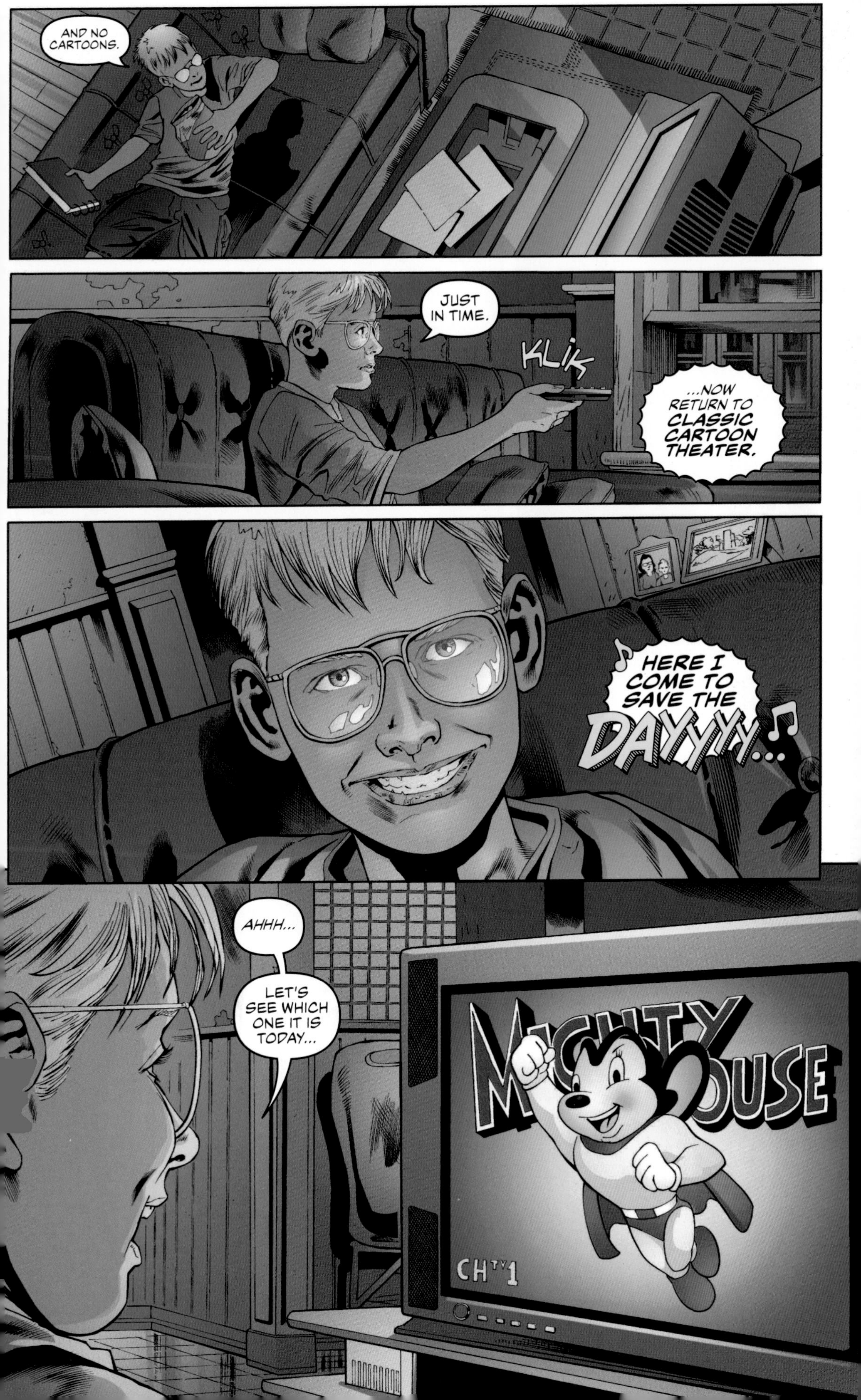
AND NO CARTOONS.
JUST IN TIME.
KLIK
...NOW RETURN TO CLASSIC CARTOON THEATER.
HERE I COME TO SAVE THE DAYYYY...
AHHH...
LET'S SEE WHICH ONE IT IS TODAY...
MIGHTY MOUSE
CH TV 1

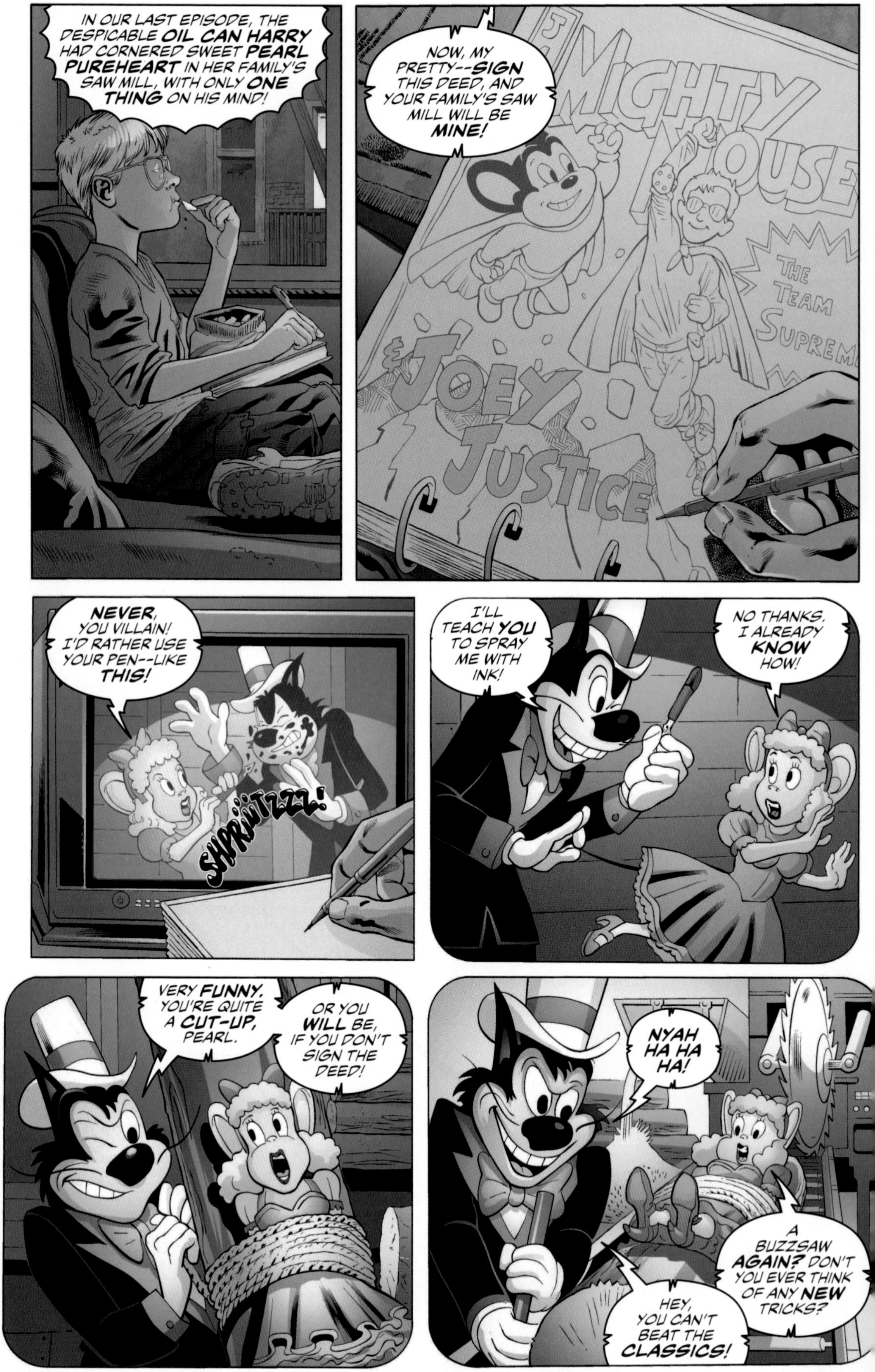

IN OUR LAST EPISODE, THE DESPICABLE OIL CAN HARRY HAD CORNERED SWEET PEARL PUREHEART IN HER FAMILY'S SAW MILL, WITH ONLY ONE THING ON HIS MIND!
NOW, MY PRETTY--SIGN THIS DEED, AND YOUR FAMILY'S SAW MILL WILL BE MINE!
MIGHTY MOUSE
& JOEY JUSTICE
THE TEAM SUPREME
NEVER, YOU VILLAIN! I'D RATHER USE YOUR PEN--LIKE THIS!
SHPRÜÜTZZZ!
I'LL TEACH YOU TO SPRAY ME WITH INK!
NO THANKS. I ALREADY KNOW HOW!
VERY FUNNY. YOU'RE QUITE A CUT-UP, PEARL.
OR YOU WILL BE, IF YOU DON'T SIGN THE DEED!
NYAH HA HA HA!
A BUZZSAW AGAIN? DON'T YOU EVER THINK OF ANY NEW TRICKS?
HEY, YOU CAN'T BEAT THE CLASSICS!

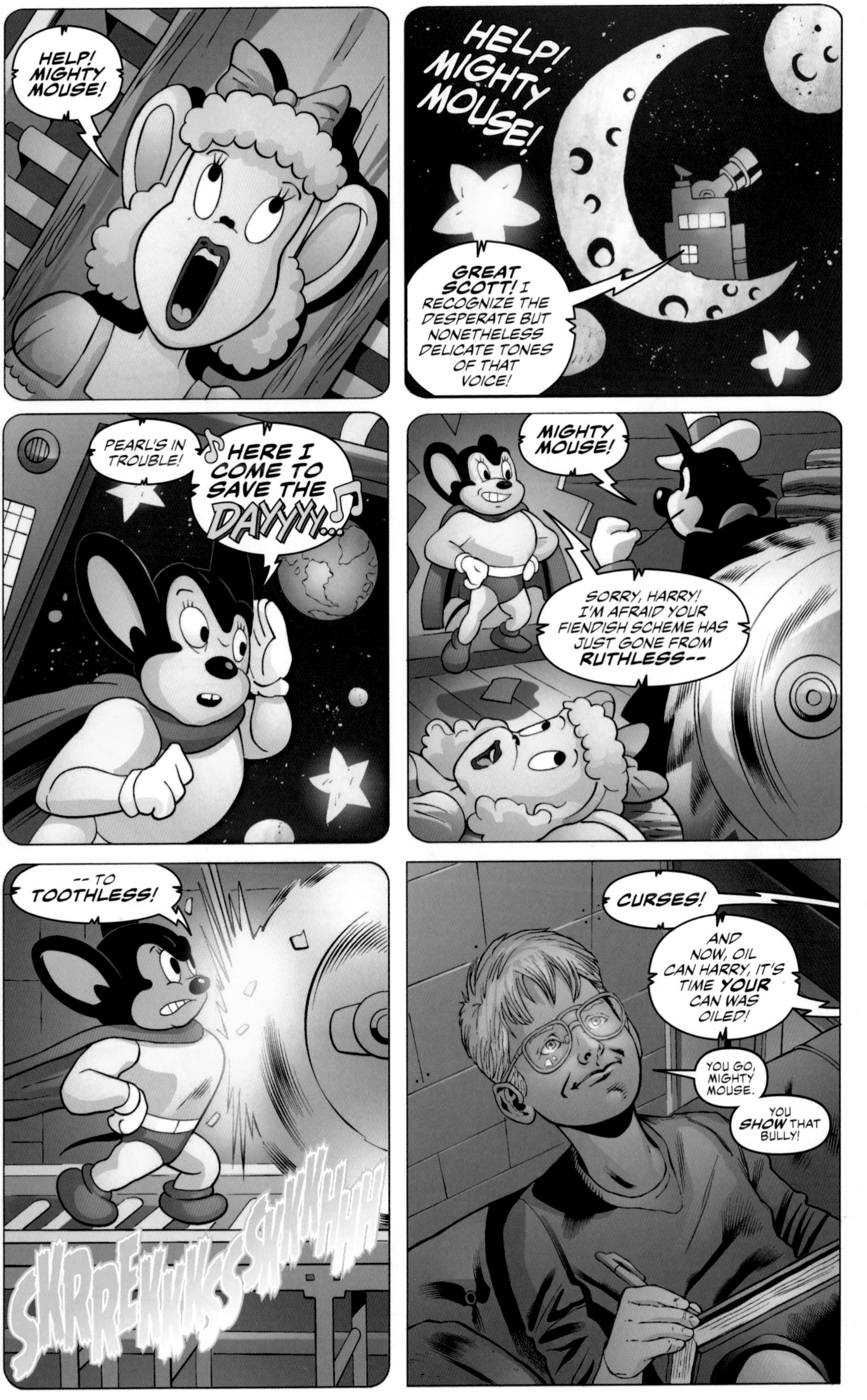
HELP! MIGHTY MOUSE!
HELP! MIGHTY MOUSE!
GREAT SCOTT! I RECOGNIZE THE DESPERATE BUT NONETHELESS DELICATE TONES OF THAT VOICE!
PEARL'S IN TROUBLE!
HERE I COME TO SAVE THE DAYYYY...
MIGHTY MOUSE!
SORRY, HARRY! I'M AFRAID YOUR FIENDISH SCHEME HAS JUST GONE FROM RUTHLESS--
-- TO TOOTHLESS!
SKRREKKKSSSKKKHHHH
CURSES!
AND NOW, OIL CAN HARRY, IT'S TIME YOUR CAN WAS OILED!
YOU GO, MIGHTY MOUSE.
YOU SHOW THAT BULLY!

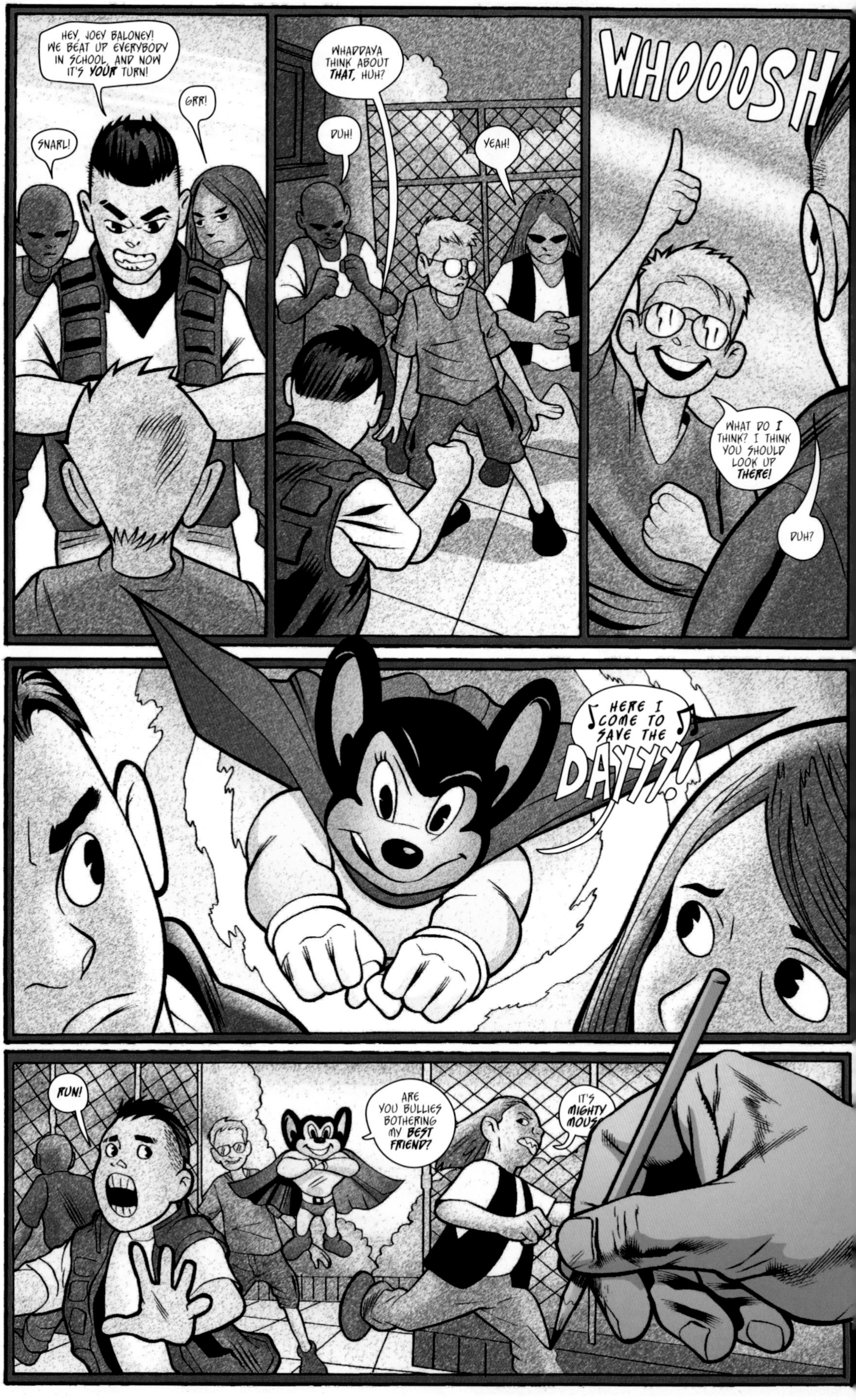

HEY, JOEY BALONEY! WE BEAT UP EVERYBODY IN SCHOOL, AND NOW IT'S YOUR TURN!
SNARL!
GRR!
WHADDAYA THINK ABOUT THAT, HUH?
DUH!
YEAH!
WHOOOSH
WHAT DO I THINK? I THINK YOU SHOULD LOOK UP THERE!
DUH?
HERE I COME TO SAVE THE DAYYY!
RUN!
ARE YOU BULLIES BOTHERING MY BEST FRIEND?
IT'S MIGHTY MOUS

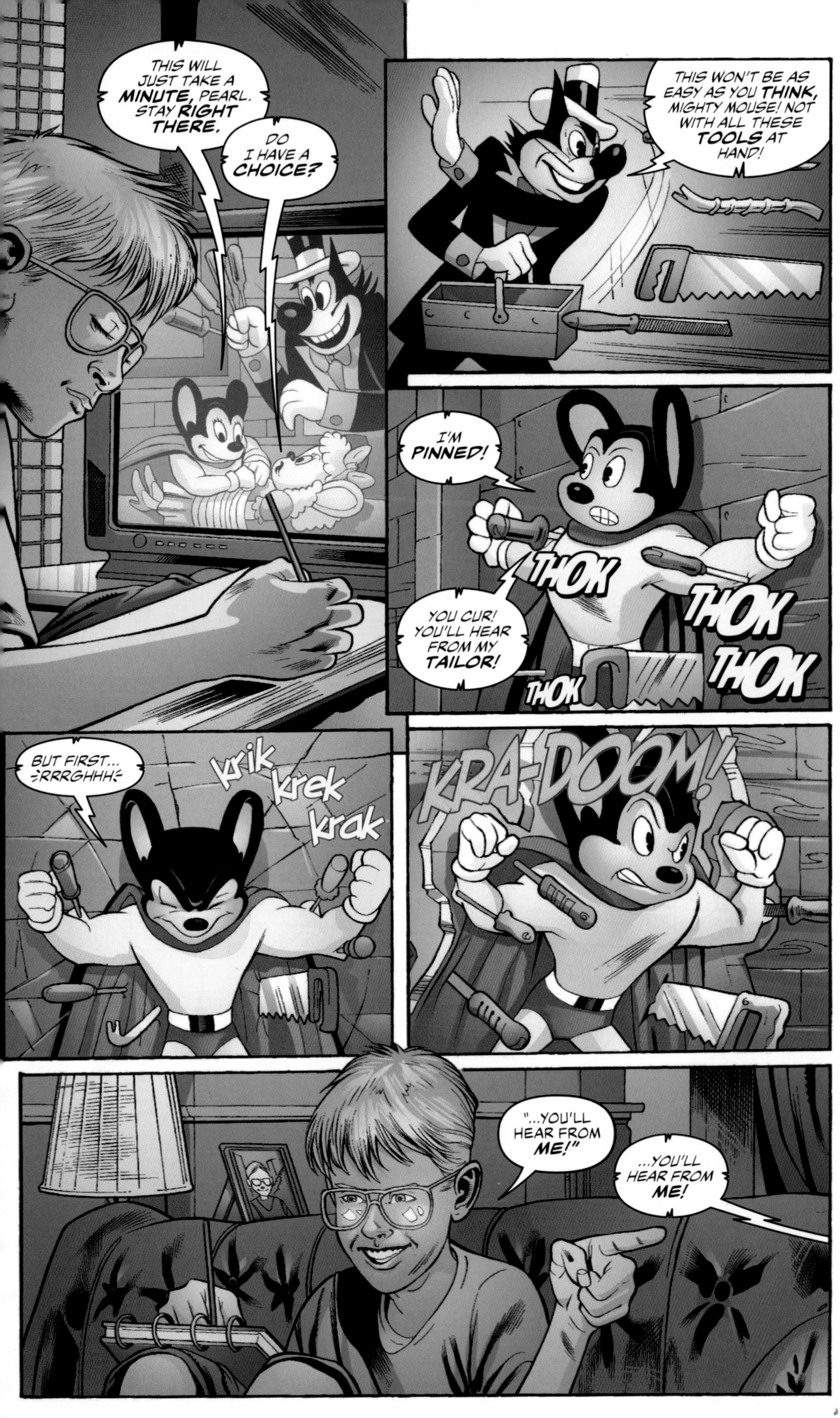
THIS WILL JUST TAKE A MINUTE, PEARL. STAY RIGHT THERE.
DO I HAVE A CHOICE?
THIS WON'T BE AS EASY AS YOU THINK, MIGHTY MOUSE! NOT WITH ALL THESE TOOLS AT HAND!
I'M PINNED!
THOK
YOU CUR! YOU'LL HEAR FROM MY TAILOR!
THOK
THOK
THOK
BUT FIRST... RRRGHHH
krik
krek
krak
KRA-DOOM!
"...YOU'LL HEAR FROM ME!"
...YOU'LL HEAR FROM ME!

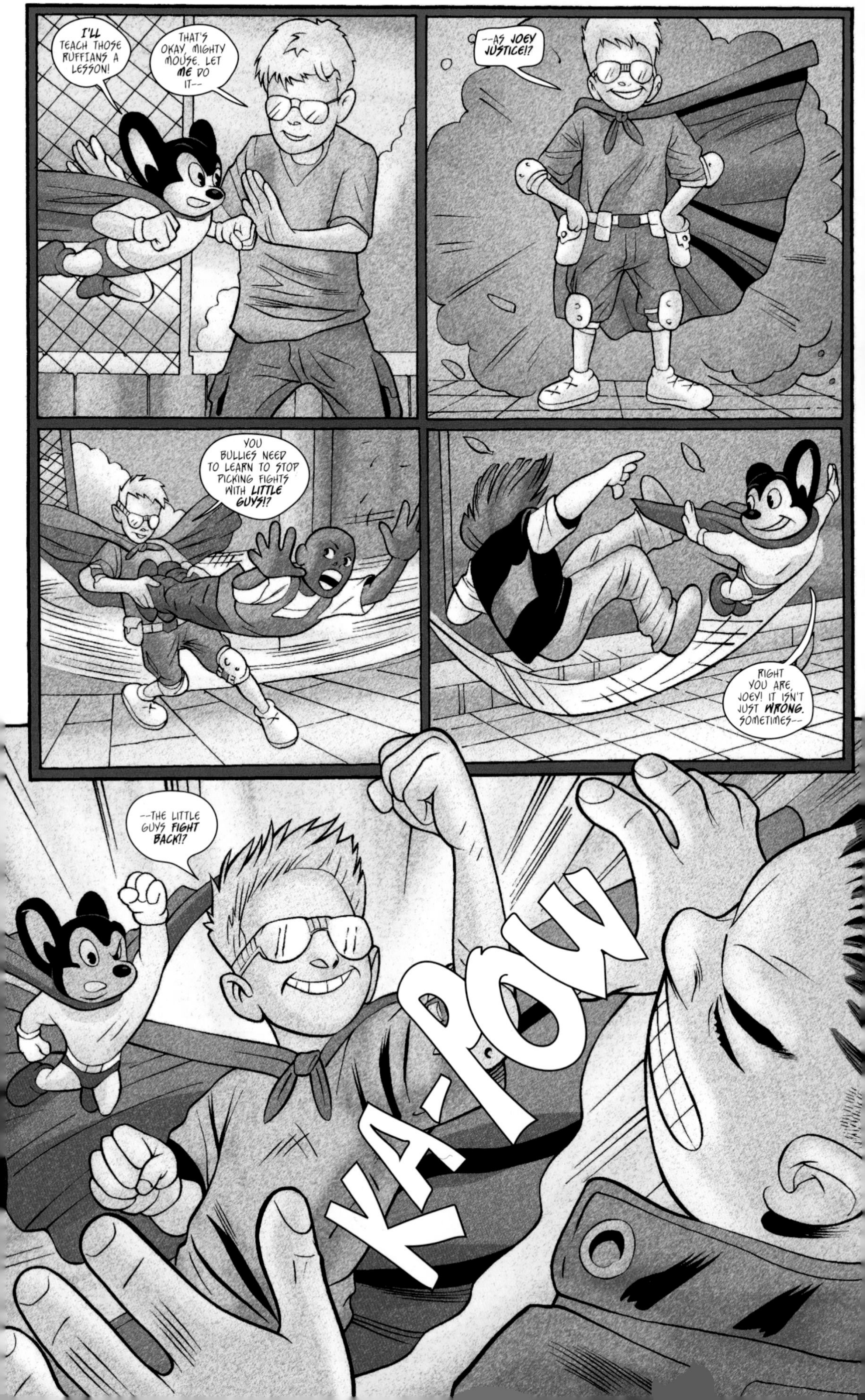
I'LL TEACH THOSE RUFFIANS A LESSON!
THAT'S OKAY, MIGHTY MOUSE. LET ME DO IT--
--AS JOEY JUSTICE!?
YOU BULLIES NEED TO LEARN TO STOP PICKING FIGHTS WITH LITTLE GUYS!?
RIGHT YOU ARE, JOEY! IT ISN'T JUST WRONG. SOMETIMES--
--THE LITTLE GUYS FIGHT BACK!?
KA-POW

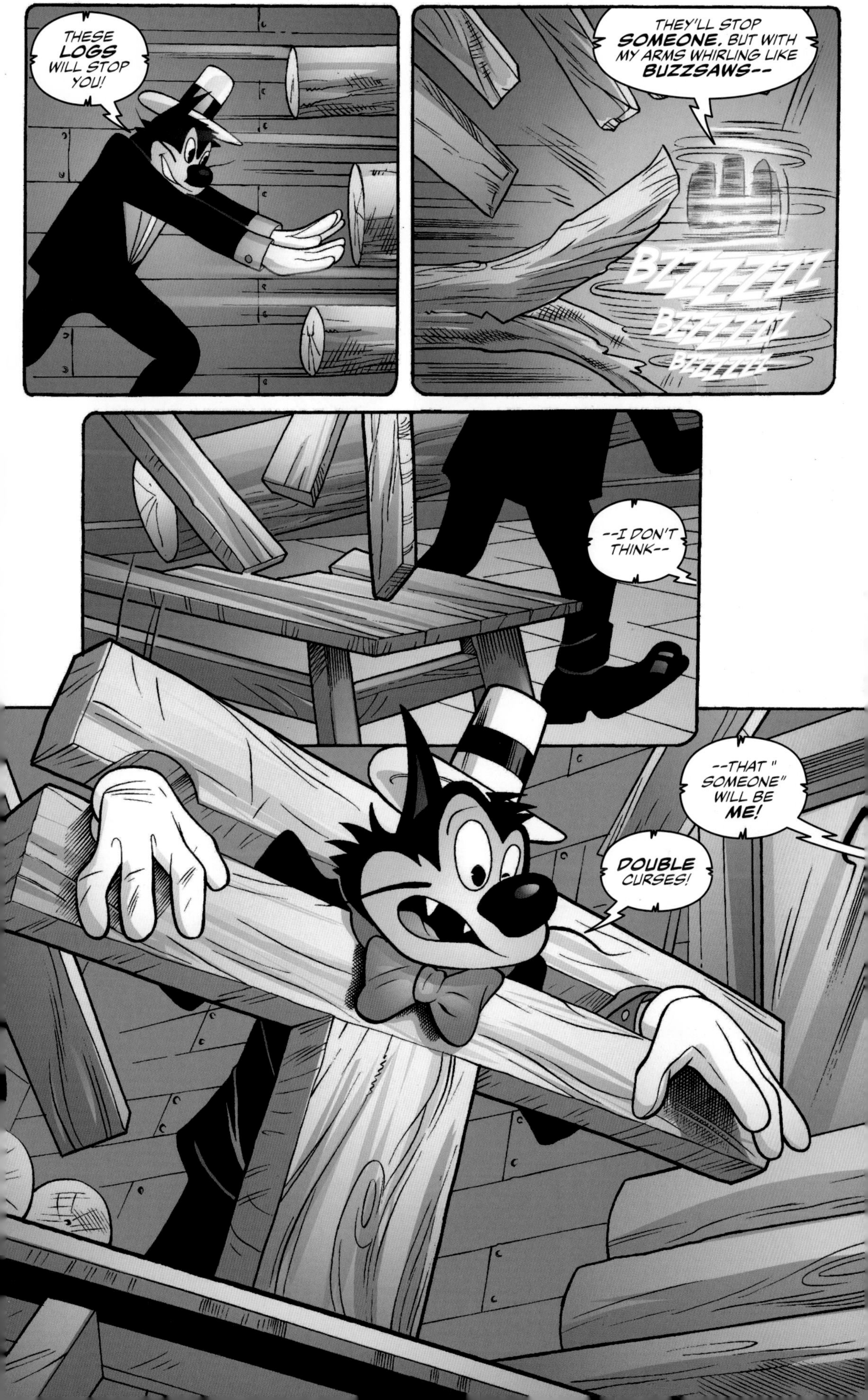
THESE LOGS WILL STOP YOU!
THEY'LL STOP SOMEONE. BUT WITH MY ARMS WHIRLING LIKE BUZZSAWS--
BZZZZZZZ
BZZZZZZ
BZZZZZ
--I DON'T THINK--
--THAT "SOMEONE" WILL BE ME!
DOUBLE CURSES!

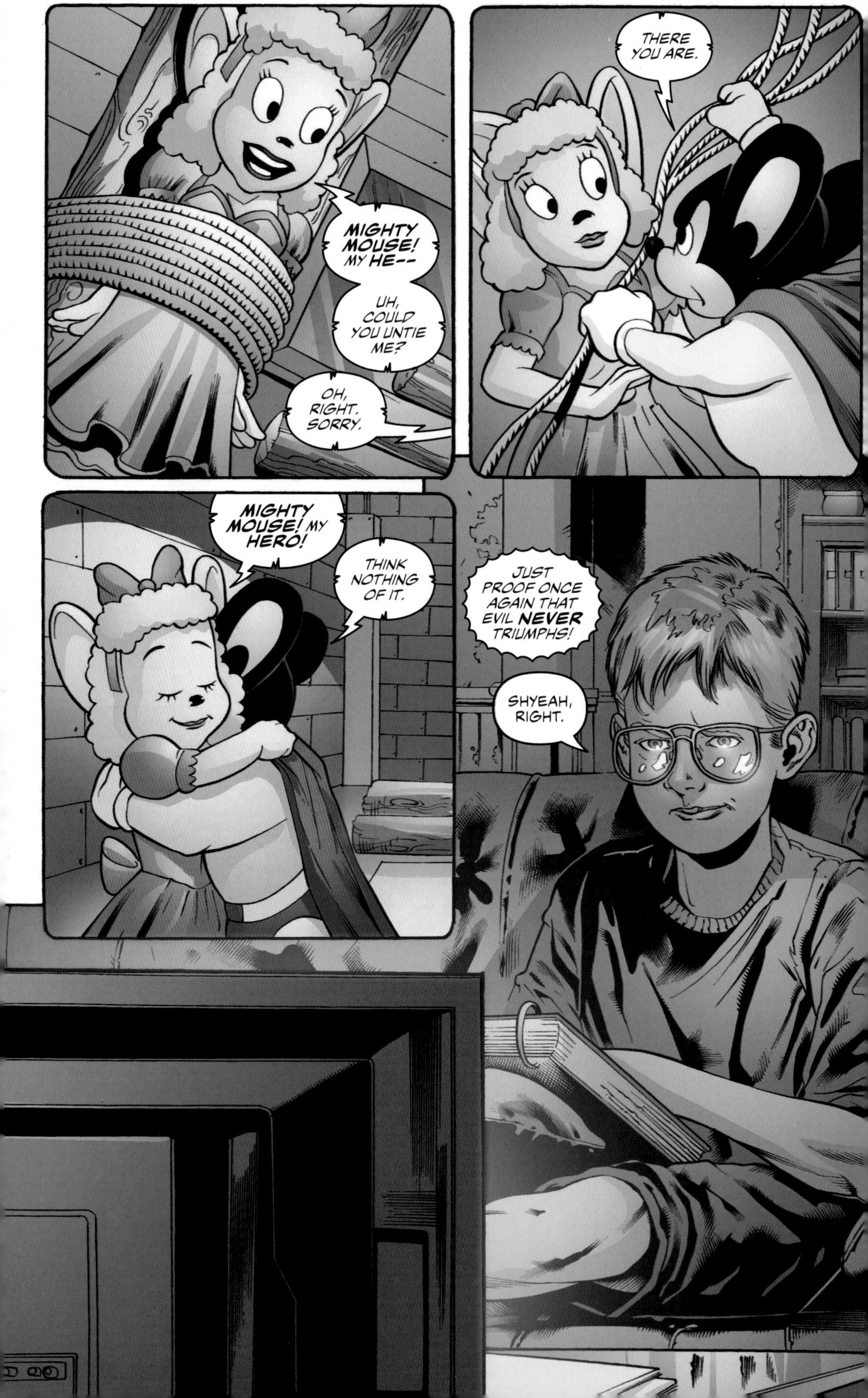
MIGHTY MOUSE! MY HE--
UH, COULD YOU UNTIE ME?
OH, RIGHT. SORRY.
THERE YOU ARE.
MIGHTY MOUSE! MY HERO!
THINK NOTHING OF IT.
JUST PROOF ONCE AGAIN THAT EVIL NEVER TRIUMPHS!
SHYEAH, RIGHT.

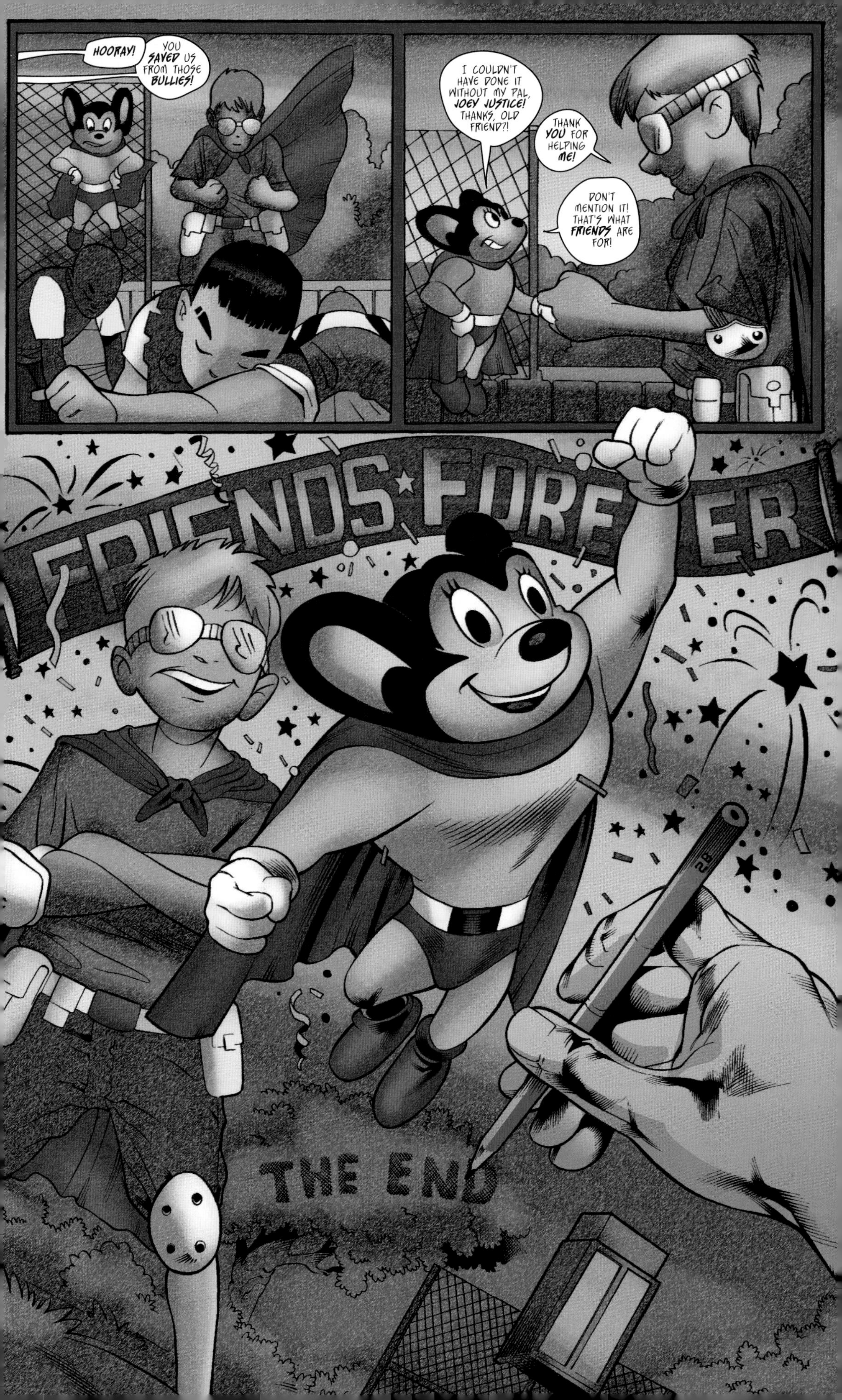

HOORAY!
YOU SAVED US FROM THOSE BULLIES!
I COULDN'T HAVE DONE IT WITHOUT MY PAL, JOEY JUSTICE! THANKS, OLD FRIEND?!
THANK YOU FOR HELPING ME!
DON'T MENTION IT! THAT'S WHAT FRIENDS ARE FOR!
FRIENDS FOREVER
2B
THE END

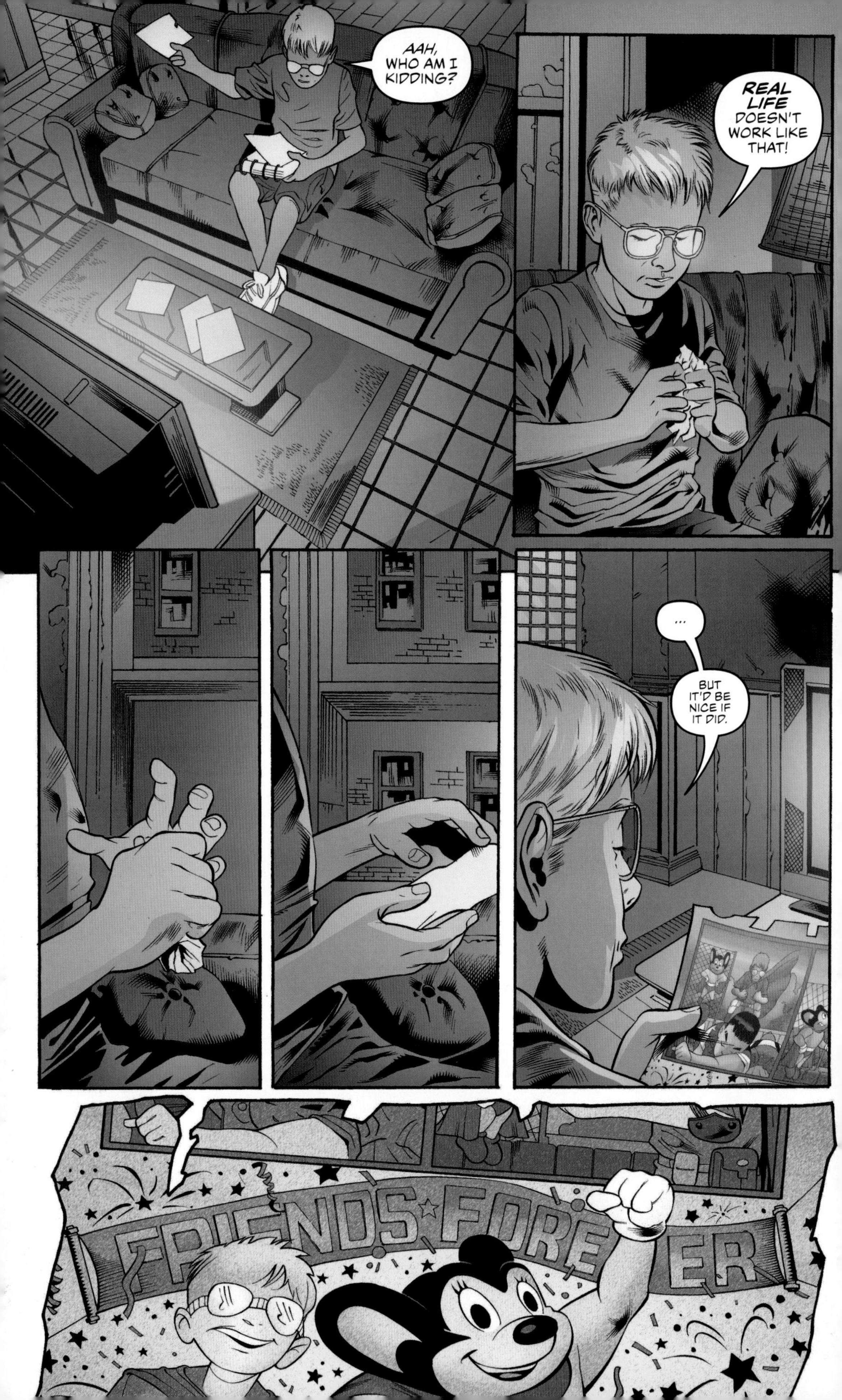
AAH, WHO AM I KIDDING?
REAL LIFE DOESN'T WORK LIKE THAT!
...
BUT IT'D BE NICE IF IT DID.
FRIENDS FOREVER

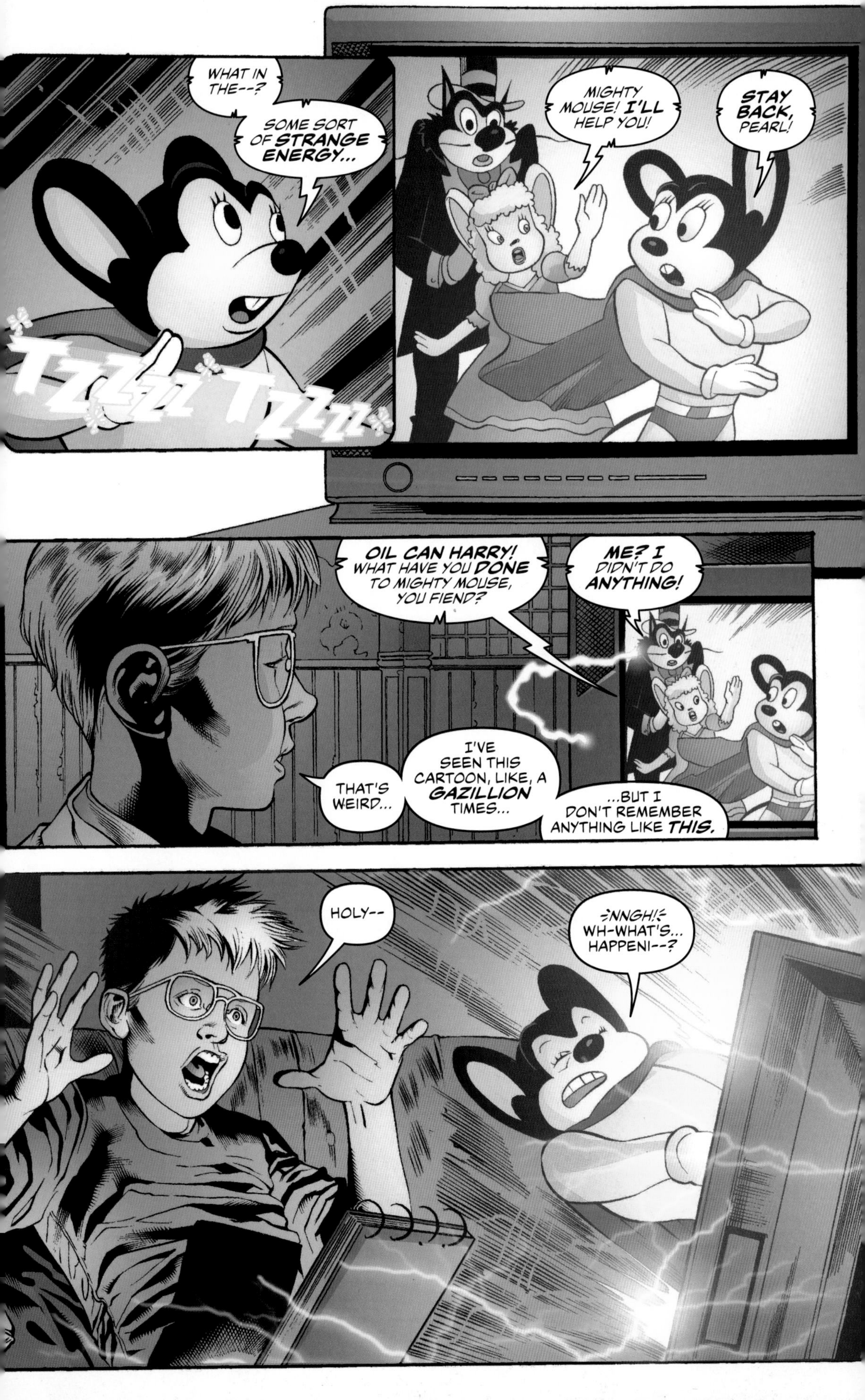

WHAT IN THE--?
SOME SORT OF STRANGE ENERGY...
TZZZZ TZZZZZ
MIGHTY MOUSE! I'LL HELP YOU!
STAY BACK, PEARL!
OIL CAN HARRY! WHAT HAVE YOU DONE TO MIGHTY MOUSE, YOU FIEND?
ME? I DIDN'T DO ANYTHING!
THAT'S WEIRD...
I'VE SEEN THIS CARTOON, LIKE, A GAZILLION TIMES...
...BUT I DON'T REMEMBER ANYTHING LIKE THIS.
HOLY--
NNGH! WH-WHAT'S... HAPPENI--?

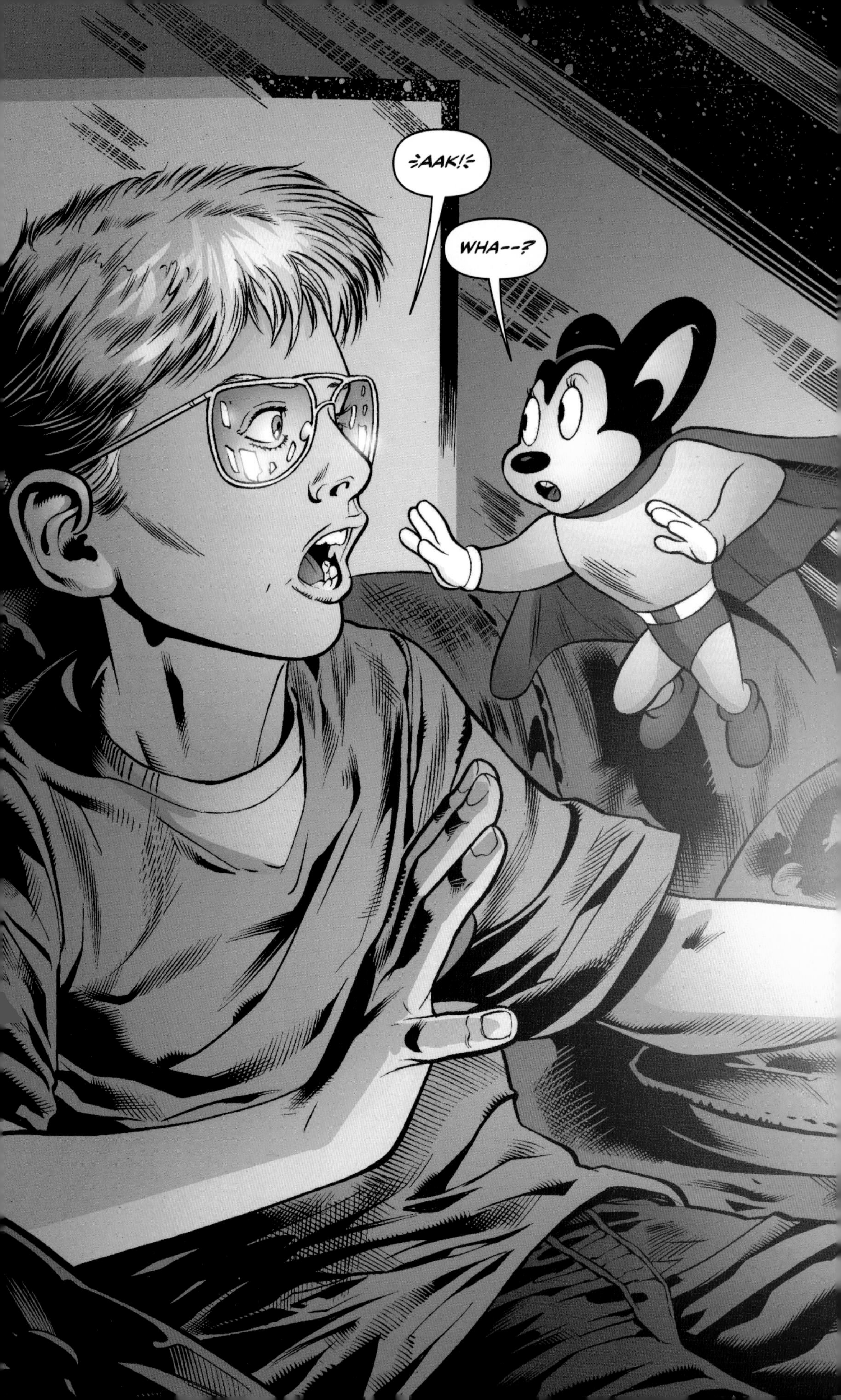

AAK!
WHA--?

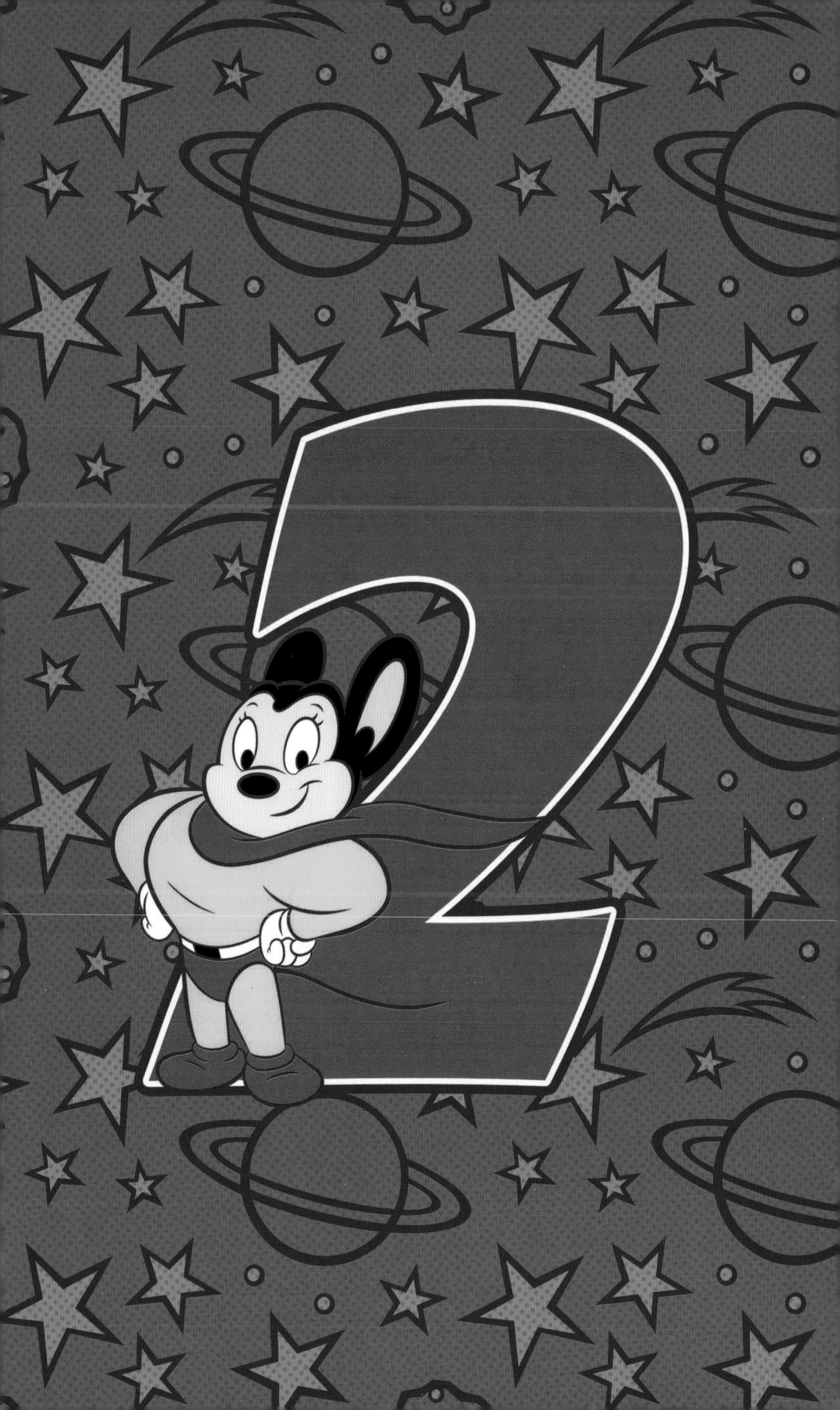

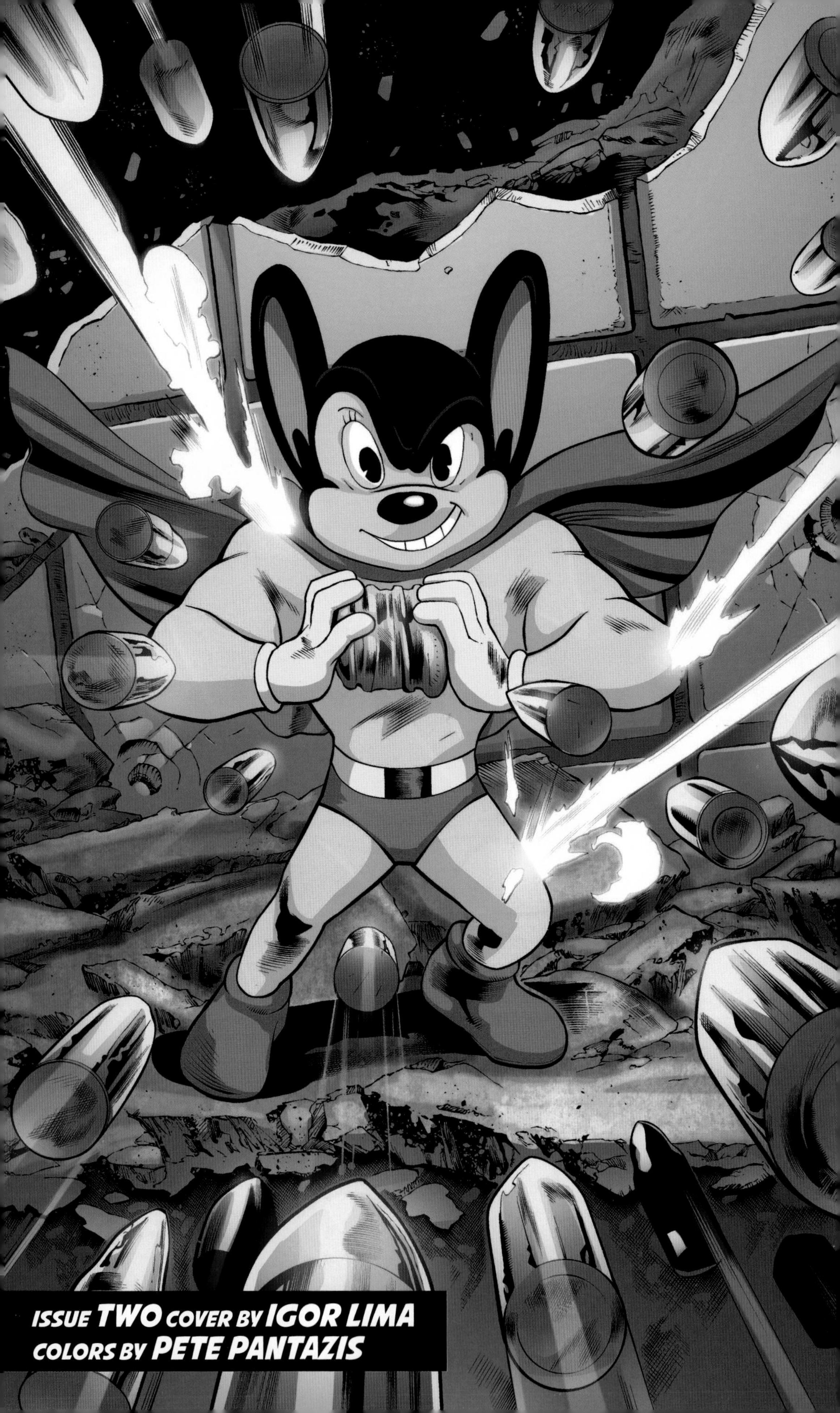

ISSUE TWO COVER BY IGOR LIMA
COLORS BY PETE PANTAZIS

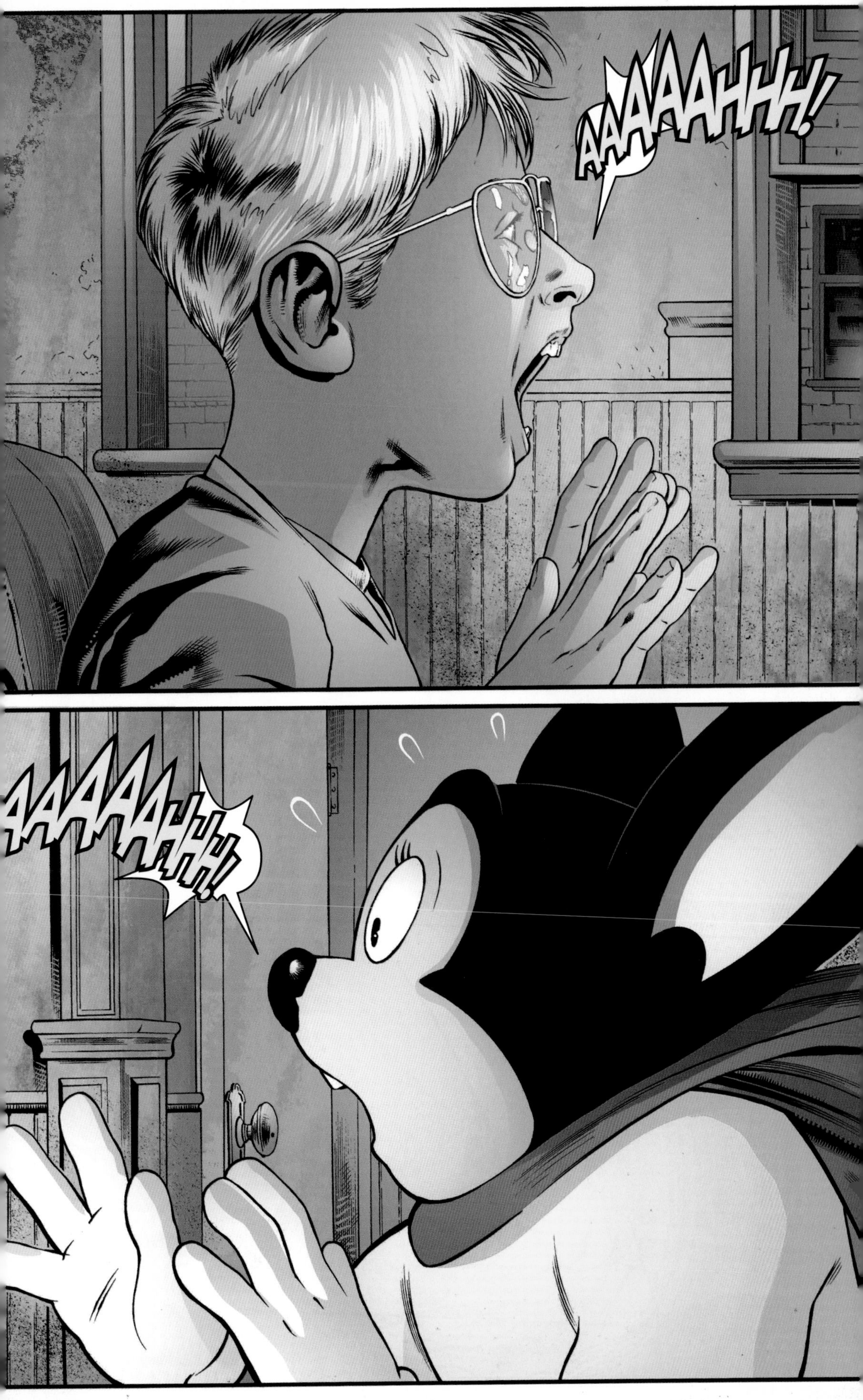
AAAAAHHH!
AAAAAAHHH!

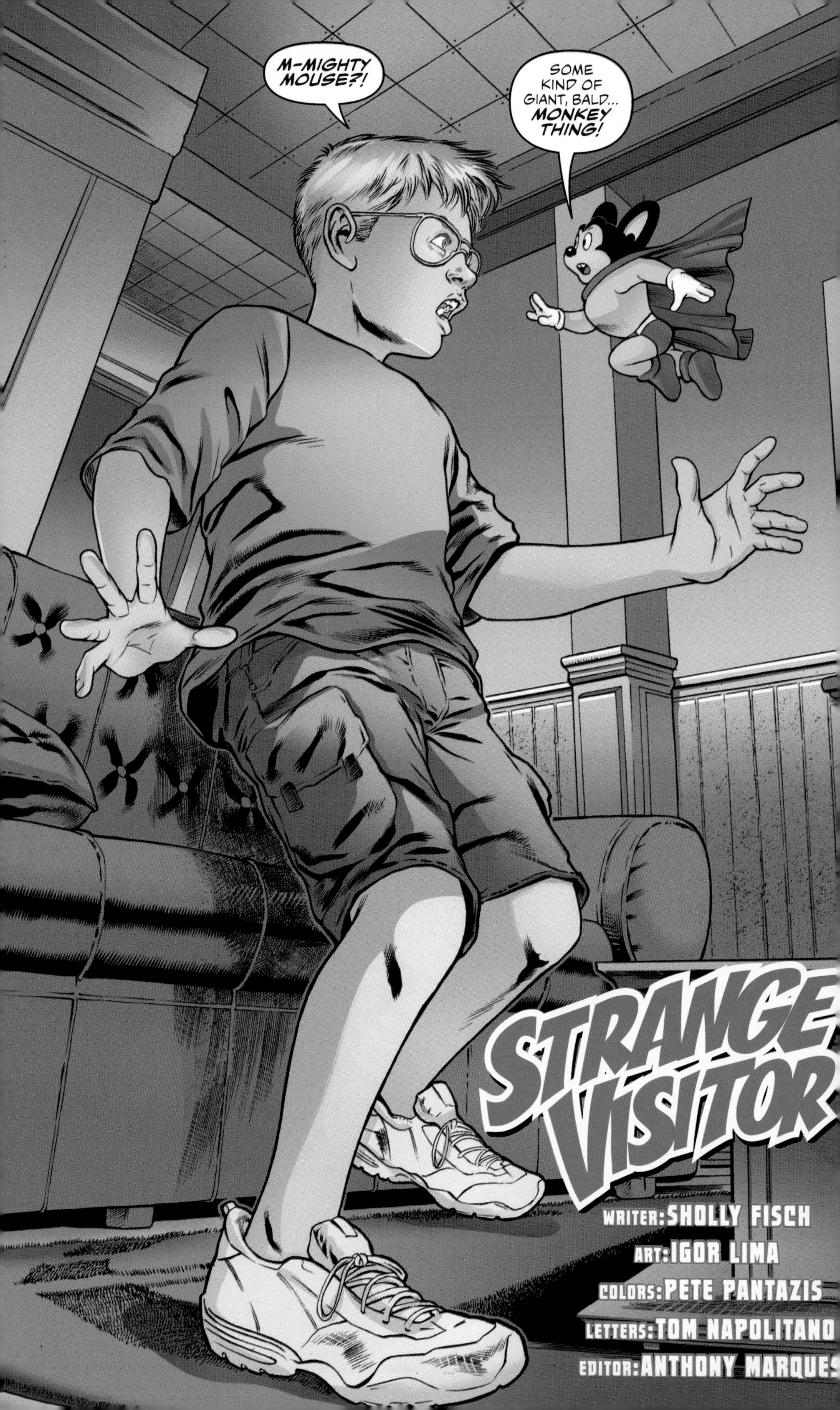
M-MIGHTY MOUSE?!
SOME KIND OF GIANT, BALD... MONKEY THING!
STRANGE VISITOR
WRITER: SHOLLY FISCH
ART: IGOR LIMA
COLORS: PETE PANTAZIS
LETTERS: TOM NAPOLITANO
EDITOR: ANTHONY MARQUES

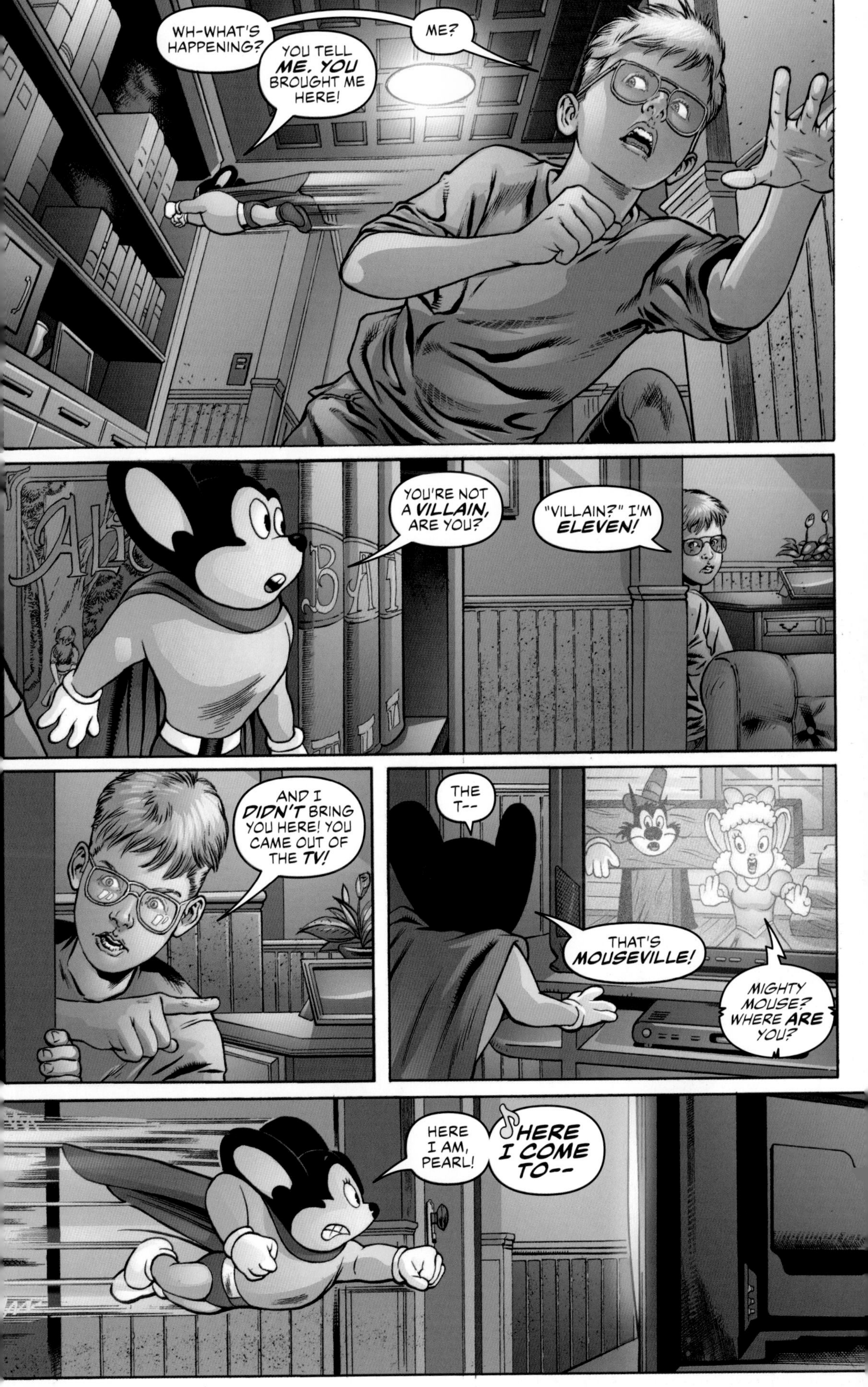
WH-WHAT'S HAPPENING?
ME?
YOU TELL ME, YOU BROUGHT ME HERE!
YOU'RE NOT A VILLAIN, ARE YOU?
"VILLAIN?" I'M ELEVEN!
AND I DIDN'T BRING YOU HERE! YOU CAME OUT OF THE TV!
THE T--
THAT'S MOUSEVILLE!
MIGHTY MOUSE? WHERE ARE YOU?
HERE I AM, PEARL!
HERE I COME TO--

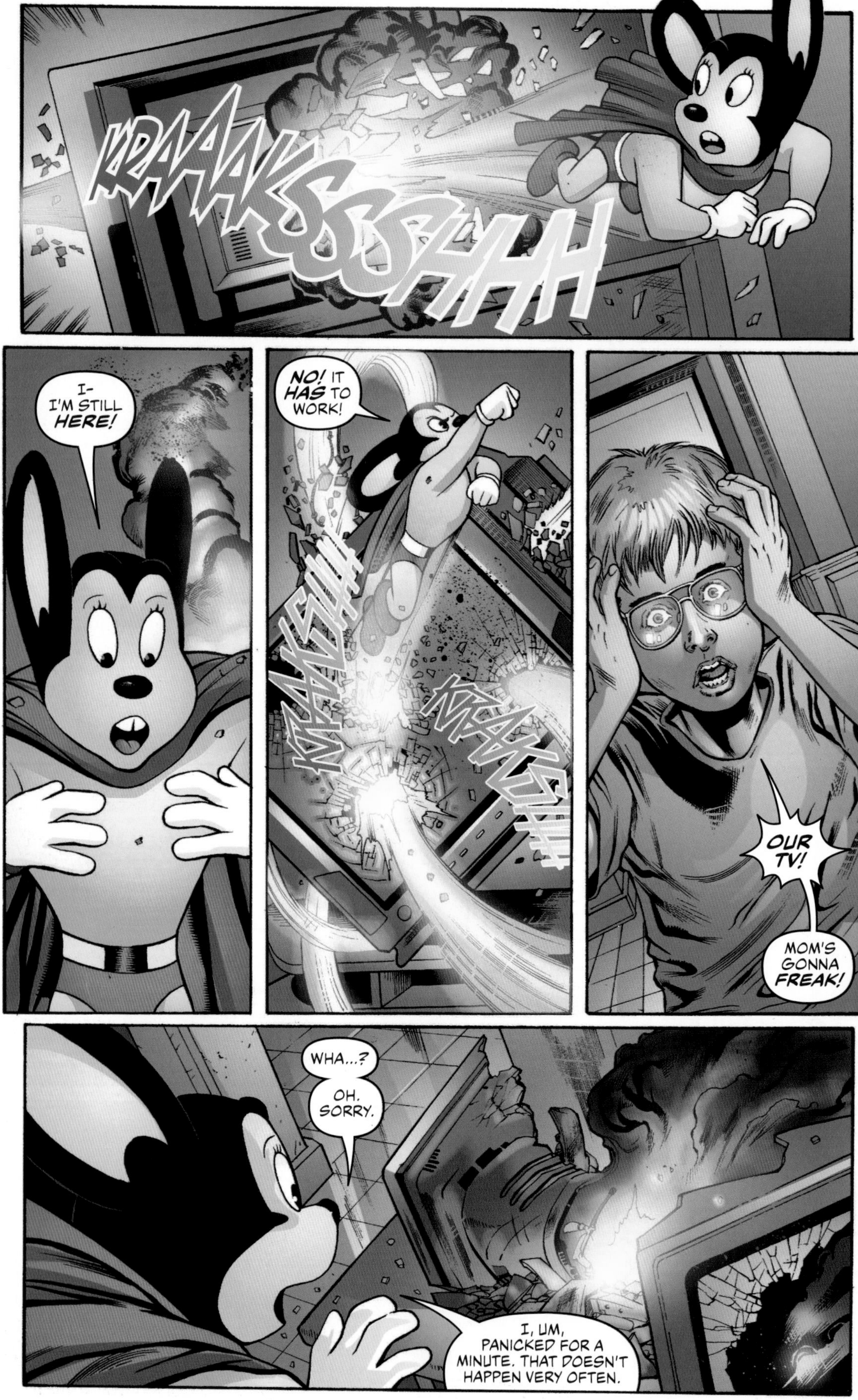
KRAAAKSSSHHH
I- I'M STILL HERE!
NO! IT HAS TO WORK!
KRAAKSHH
KRAAKSHHH
OUR TV!
MOM'S GONNA FREAK!
WHA...?
OH. SORRY.
I, UM, PANICKED FOR A MINUTE. THAT DOESN'T HAPPEN VERY OFTEN.

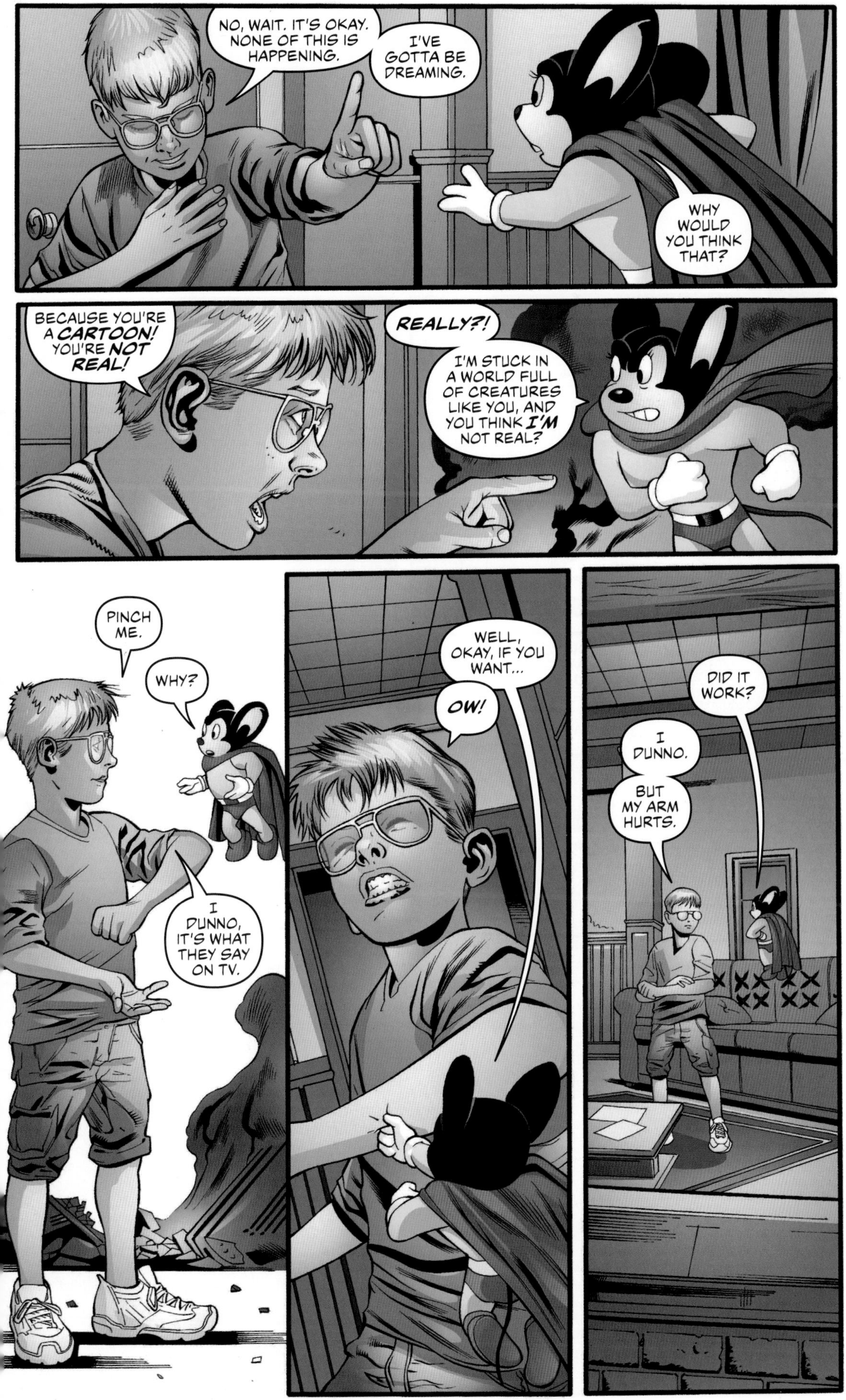
NO, WAIT. IT'S OKAY. NONE OF THIS IS HAPPENING.
I'VE GOTTA BE DREAMING.
WHY WOULD YOU THINK THAT?
BECAUSE YOU'RE A CARTOON! YOU'RE NOT REAL!
REALLY?!
I'M STUCK IN A WORLD FULL OF CREATURES LIKE YOU, AND YOU THINK I'M NOT REAL?
PINCH ME.
WHY?
I DUNNO, IT'S WHAT THEY SAY ON TV.
WELL, OKAY, IF YOU WANT...
OW!
DID IT WORK?
I DUNNO.
BUT MY ARM HURTS.

LISTEN, UH...
JOEY.
I'M MIGHTY MOUSE.
I KNOW.
YOU... DO?
SURE! I'VE SEEN ALL YOUR CARTOONS.
I HAVE CARTOONS?
TERRIFIC CARTOONS! AND NOT JUST THAT! I'VE GOT POSTERS OF YOU. ACTION FIGURES. SOME GUYS EVEN PUBLISHED A COMIC BOOK.
I CAN SHOW YOU IF YOU COME TO MY ROOM, AND--
...WHAT?
OH, THAT'S, UH, NOTHING.

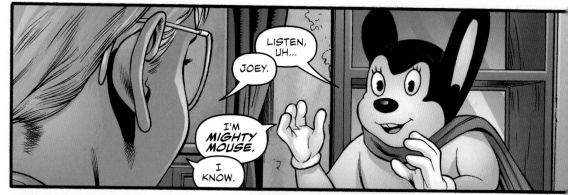

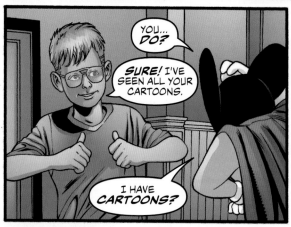

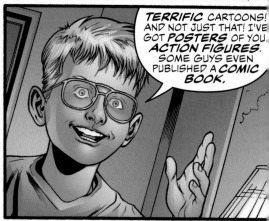

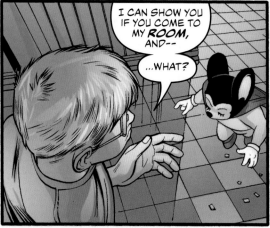

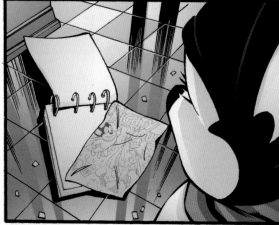

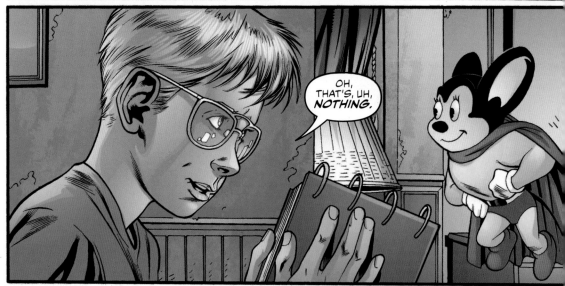

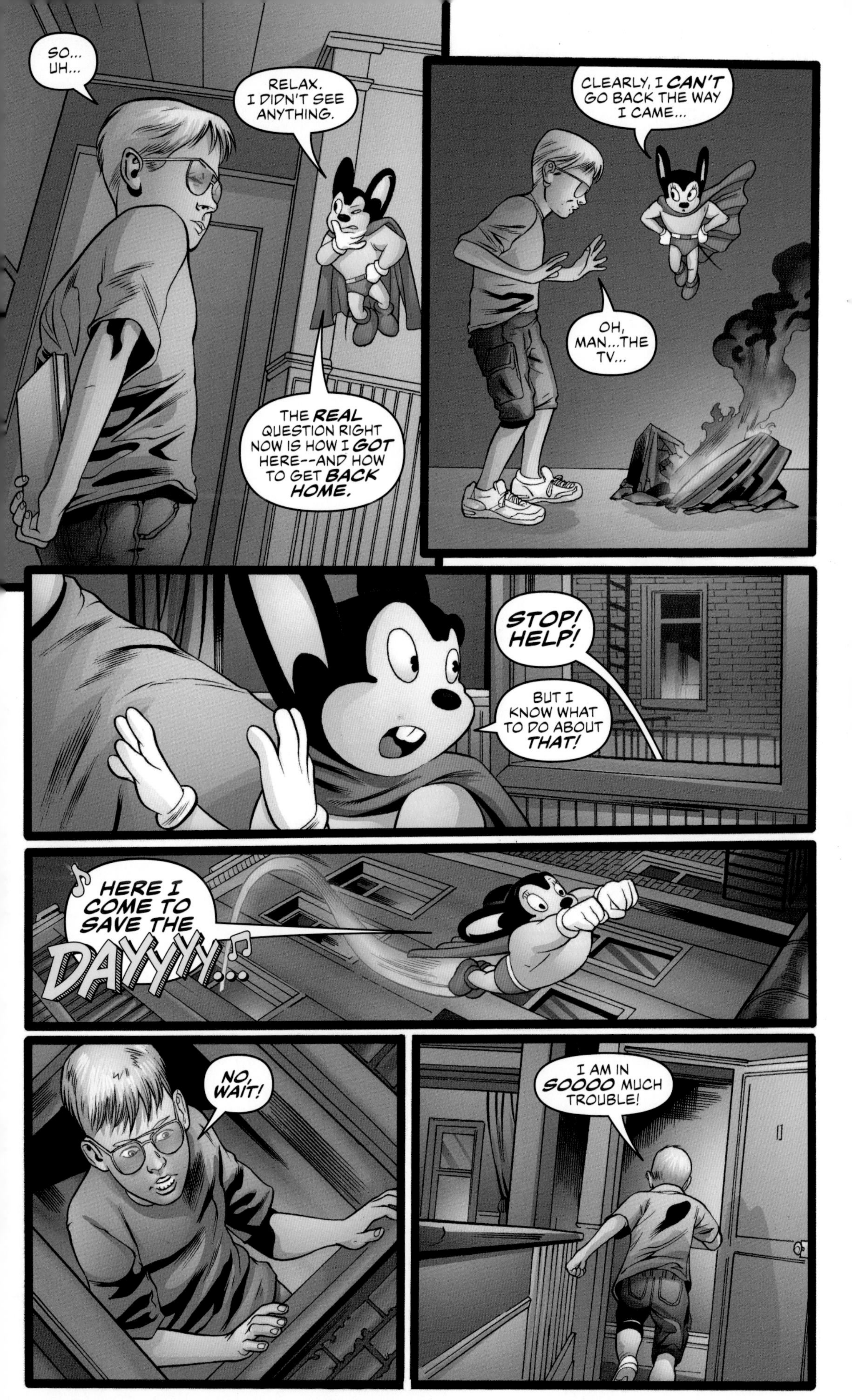
SO... UH...
RELAX. I DIDN'T SEE ANYTHING.
THE REAL QUESTION RIGHT NOW IS HOW I GOT HERE--AND HOW TO GET BACK HOME.
CLEARLY, I CAN'T GO BACK THE WAY I CAME...
OH, MAN...THE TV...
STOP! HELP!
BUT I KNOW WHAT TO DO ABOUT THAT!
HERE I COME TO SAVE THE
DAYYYY...
NO, WAIT!
I AM IN SOOOO MUCH TROUBLE!

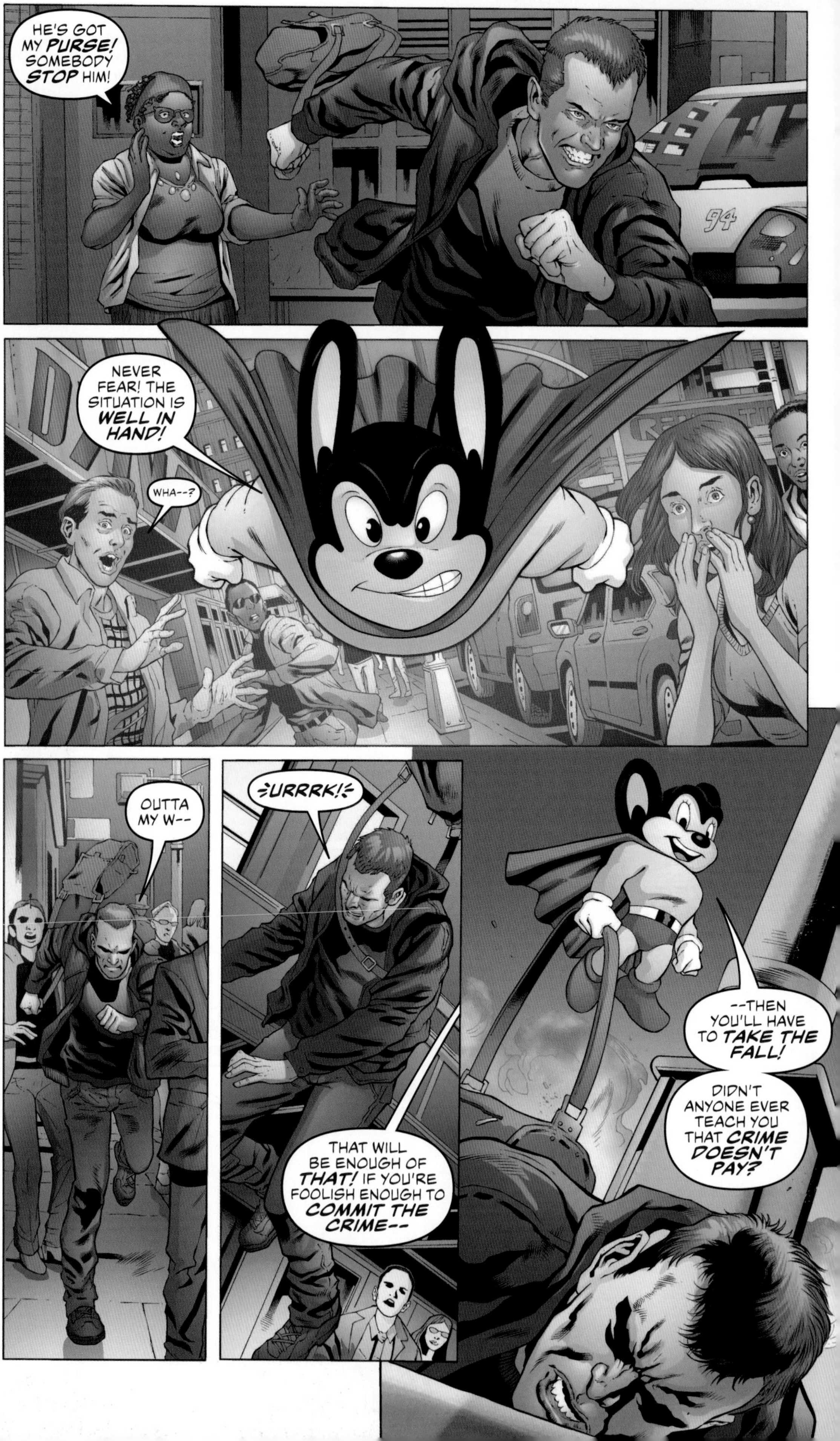
HE'S GOT MY PURSE! SOMEBODY STOP HIM!
NEVER FEAR! THE SITUATION IS WELL IN HAND!
WHA--?
OUTTA MY W--
URRRK!
THAT WILL BE ENOUGH OF THAT! IF YOU'RE FOOLISH ENOUGH TO COMMIT THE CRIME--
--THEN YOU'LL HAVE TO TAKE THE FALL!
DIDN'T ANYONE EVER TEACH YOU THAT CRIME DOESN'T PAY?

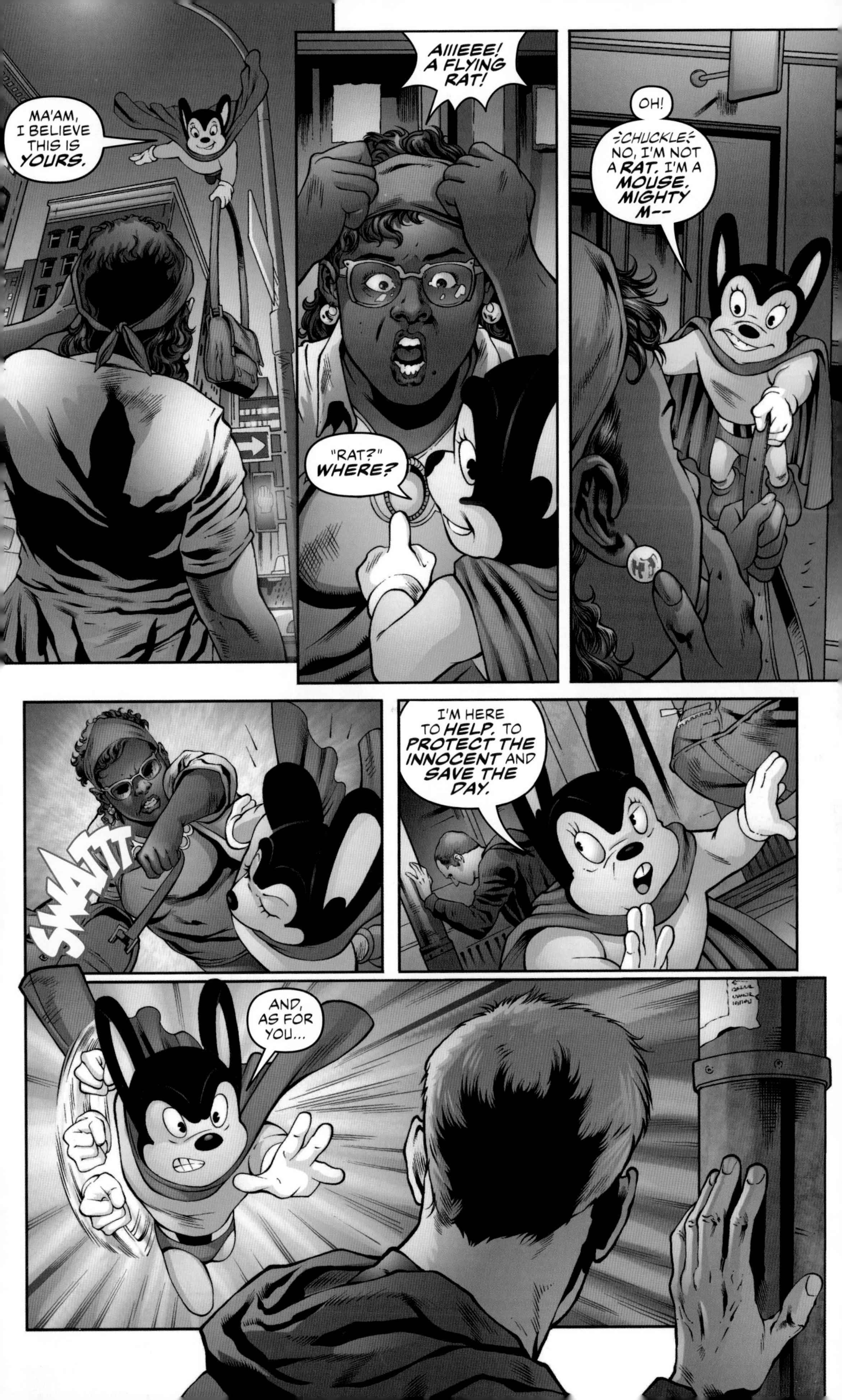

MA'AM, I BELIEVE THIS IS YOURS.
AIIIEEE! A FLYING RAT!
"RAT?" WHERE?
OH!
=CHUCKLE= NO, I'M NOT A RAT. I'M A MOUSE. MIGHTY M--
SWATTT
I'M HERE TO HELP. TO PROTECT THE INNOCENT AND SAVE THE DAY.
AND, AS FOR YOU...

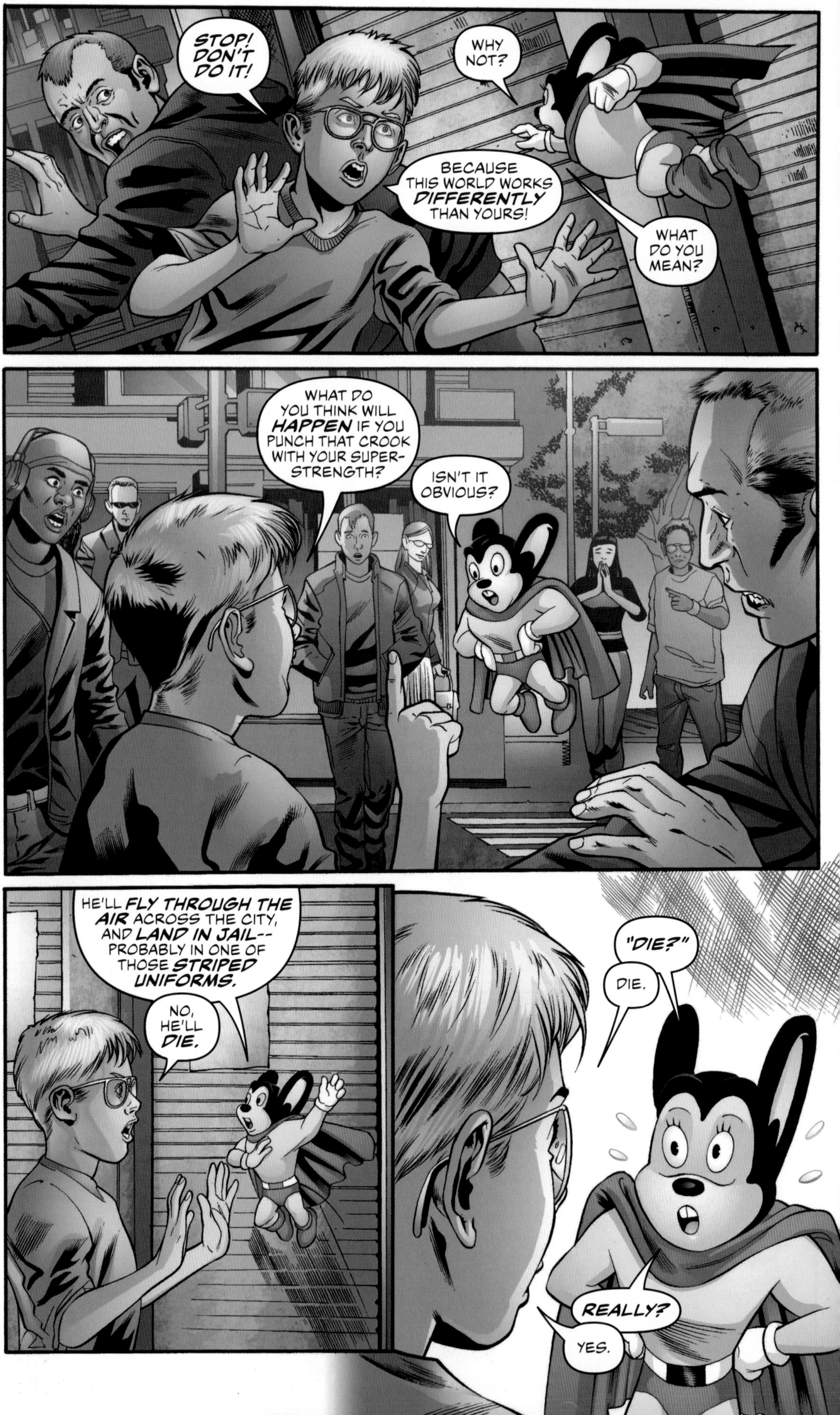
STOP! DON'T DO IT!
WHY NOT?
BECAUSE THIS WORLD WORKS DIFFERENTLY THAN YOURS!
WHAT DO YOU MEAN?
WHAT DO YOU THINK WILL HAPPEN IF YOU PUNCH THAT CROOK WITH YOUR SUPER-STRENGTH?
ISN'T IT OBVIOUS?
HE'LL FLY THROUGH THE AIR ACROSS THE CITY, AND LAND IN JAIL-- PROBABLY IN ONE OF THOSE STRIPED UNIFORMS.
NO, HE'LL DIE.
"DIE?"
DIE.
REALLY?
YES.

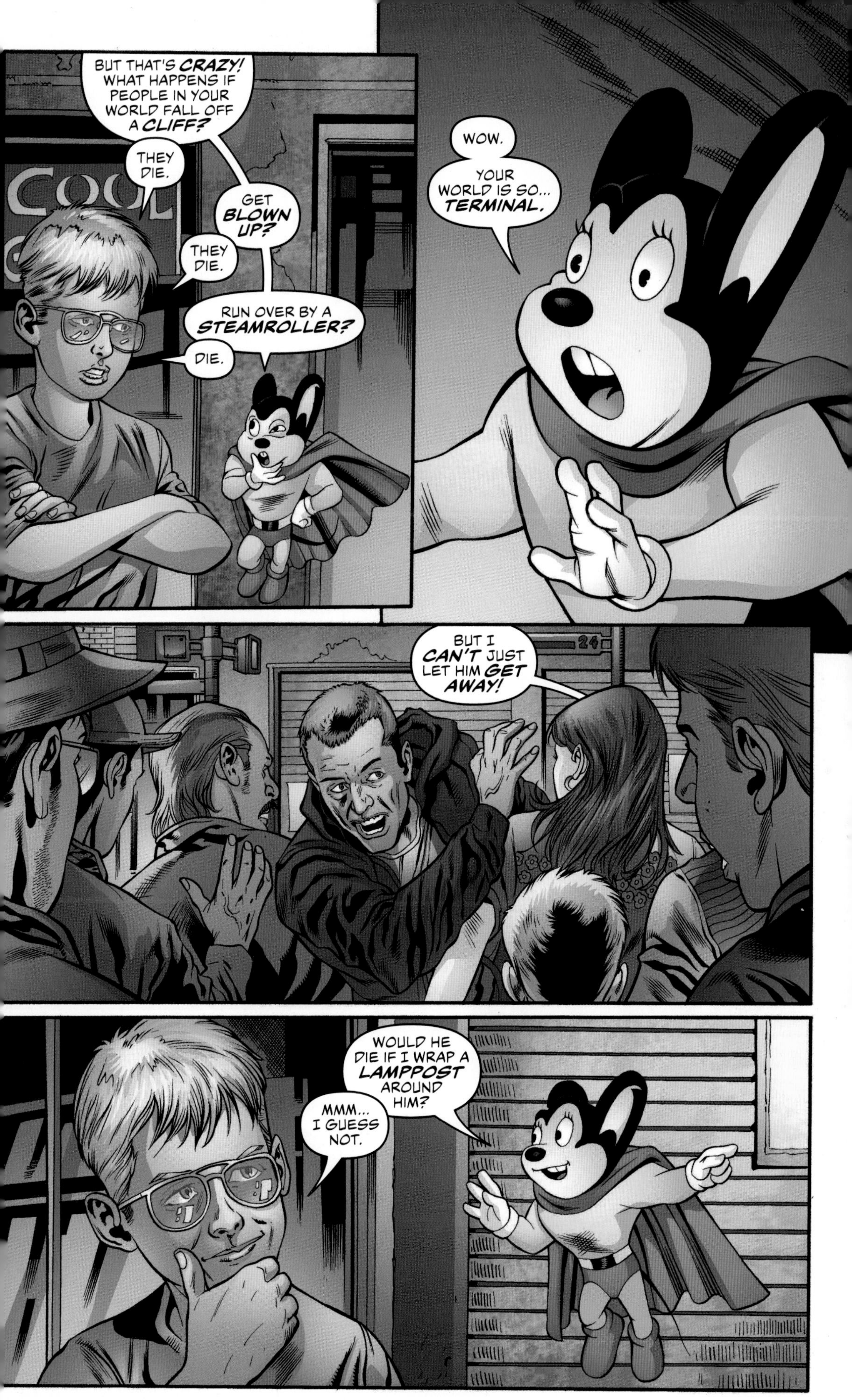
BUT THAT'S CRAZY! WHAT HAPPENS IF PEOPLE IN YOUR WORLD FALL OFF A CLIFF?
THEY DIE.
GET BLOWN UP?
THEY DIE.
RUN OVER BY A STEAMROLLER?
DIE.
WOW.
YOUR WORLD IS SO... TERMINAL.
BUT I CAN'T JUST LET HIM GET AWAY!
WOULD HE DIE IF I WRAP A LAMPPOST AROUND HIM?
MMM... I GUESS NOT.

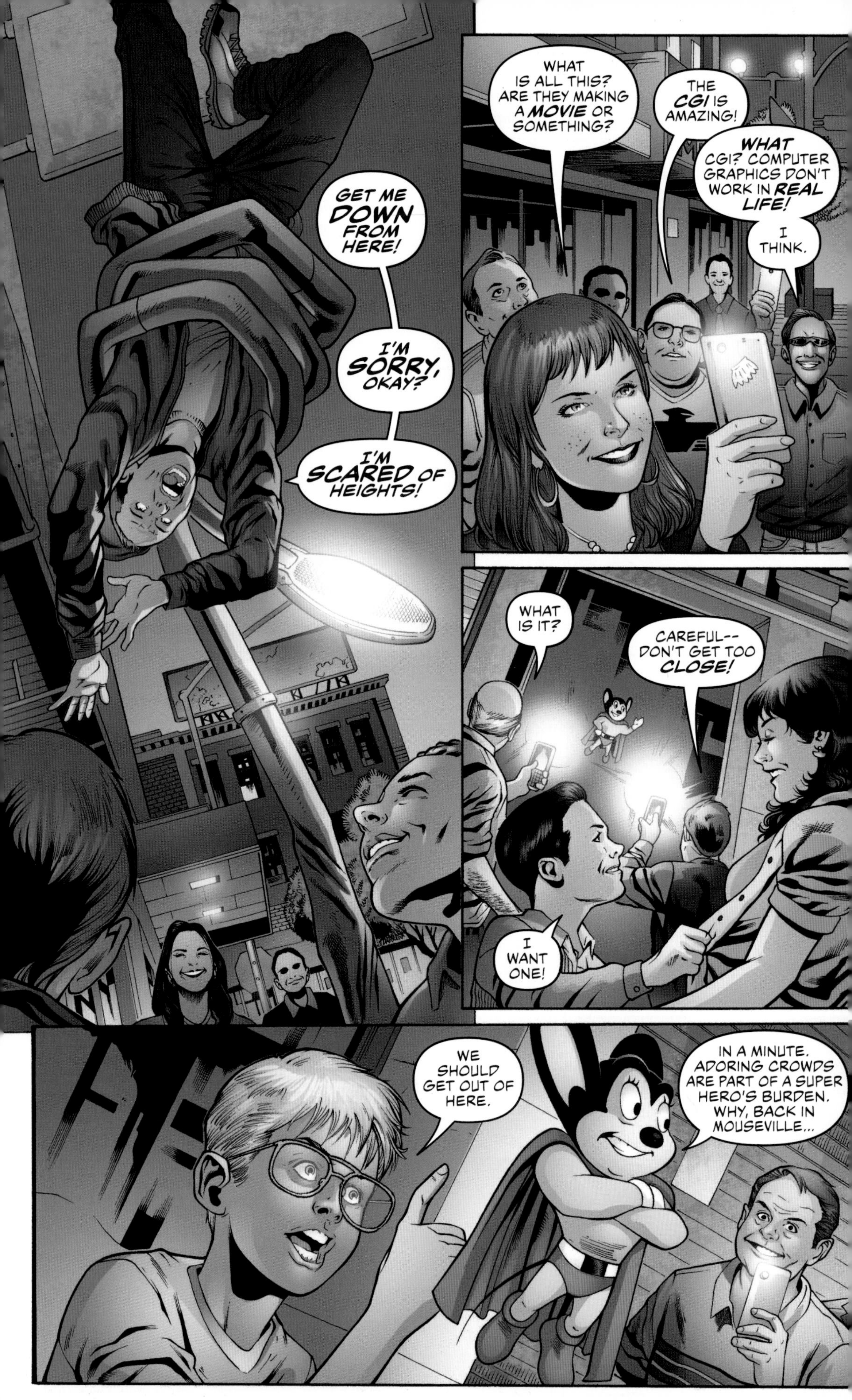

GET ME DOWN FROM HERE!
I'M SORRY, OKAY?
I'M SCARED OF HEIGHTS!
WHAT IS ALL THIS? ARE THEY MAKING A MOVIE OR SOMETHING?
THE CGI IS AMAZING!
WHAT CGI? COMPUTER GRAPHICS DON'T WORK IN REAL LIFE!
I THINK.
WHAT IS IT?
CAREFUL-- DON'T GET TOO CLOSE!
I WANT ONE!
WE SHOULD GET OUT OF HERE.
IN A MINUTE. ADORING CROWDS ARE PART OF A SUPER HERO'S BURDEN. WHY, BACK IN MOUSEVILLE...

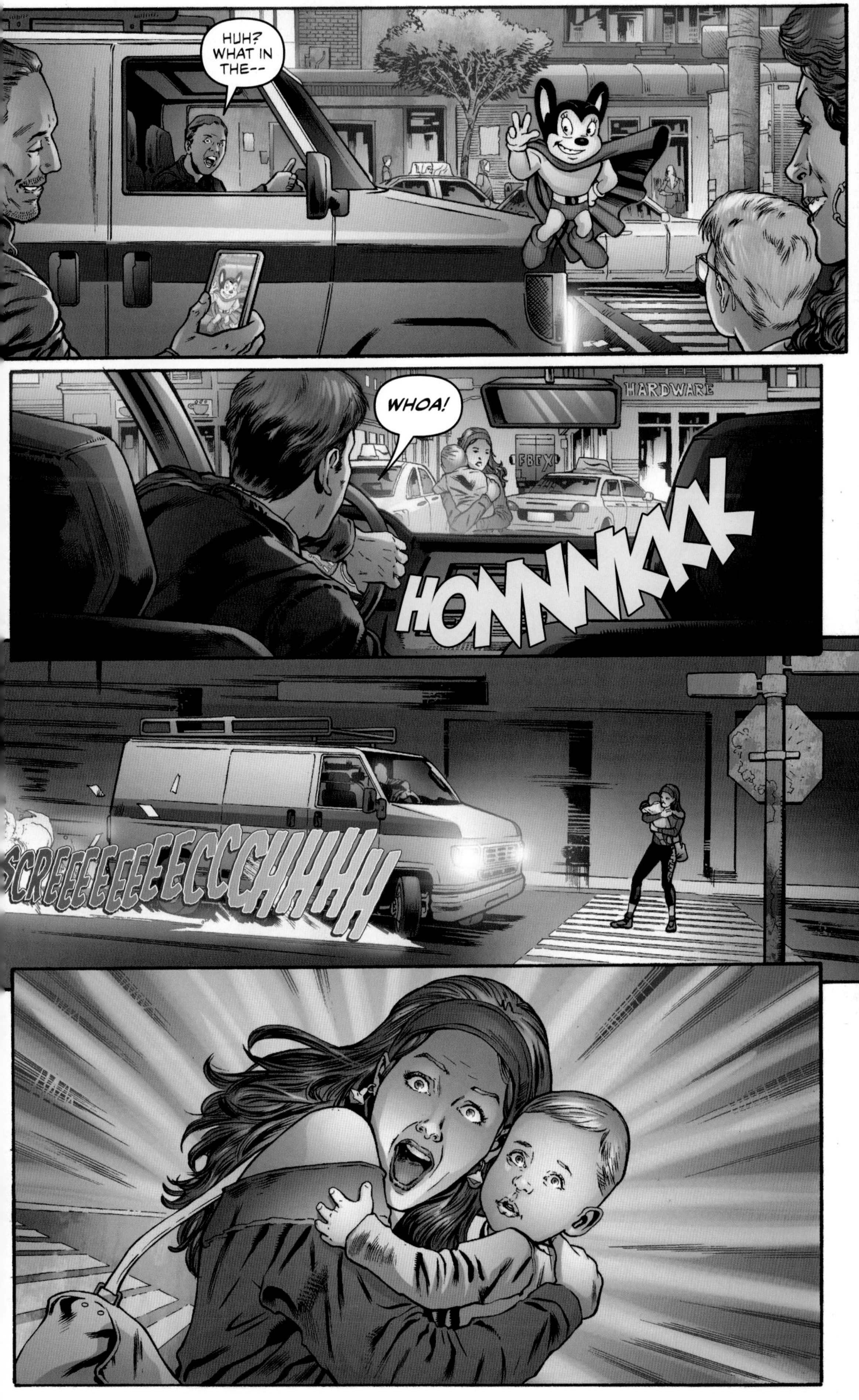
HUH? WHAT IN THE--
WHOA!
HARDWARE
HONNNKKK
SCREEEEEEEEECCCHHHHH

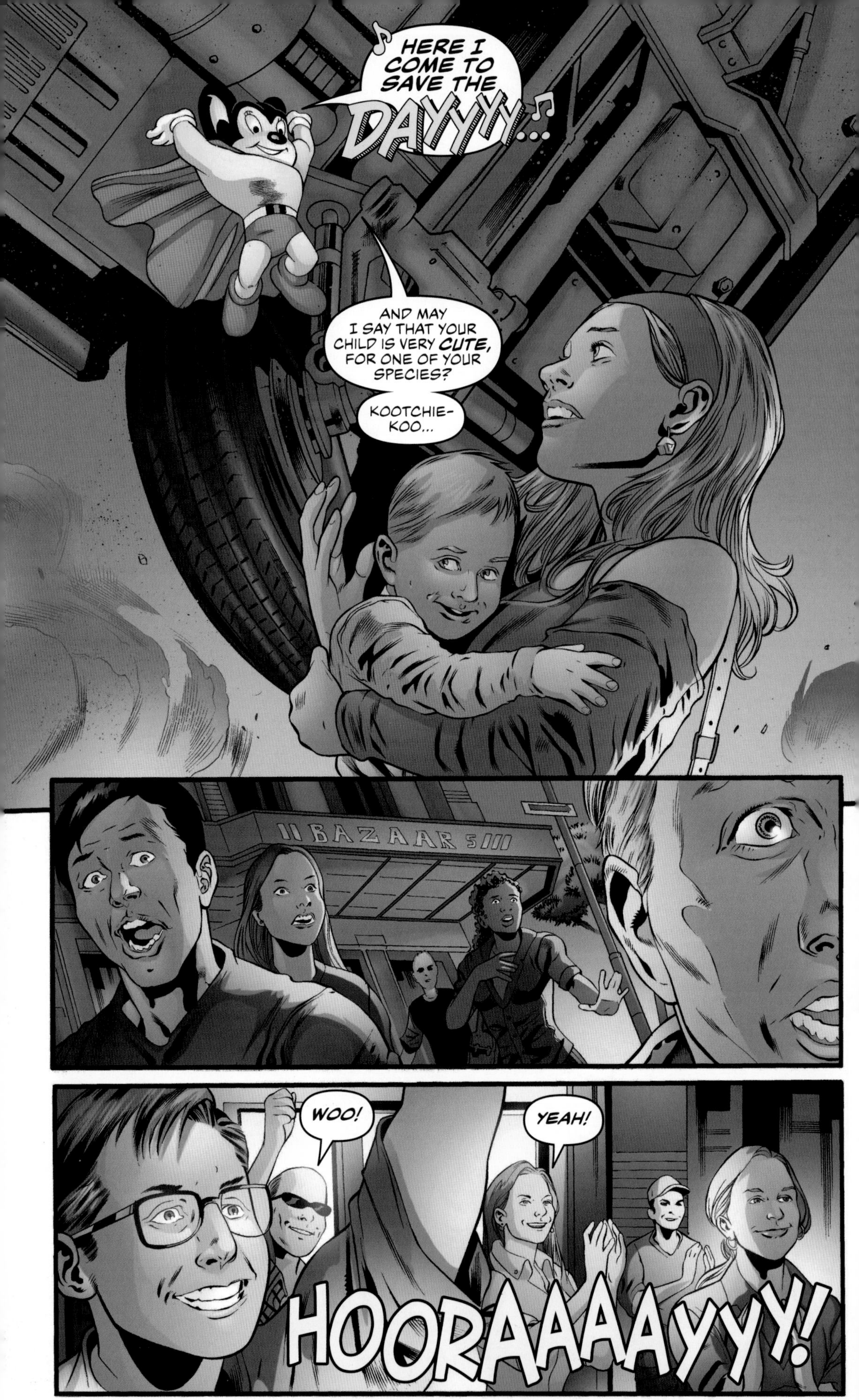

HERE I COME TO SAVE THE DAYYYY...
AND MAY I SAY THAT YOUR CHILD IS VERY CUTE, FOR ONE OF YOUR SPECIES?
KOOTCHIE-KOO...
BAZAAR
WOO!
YEAH!
HOORAAAAYYY!

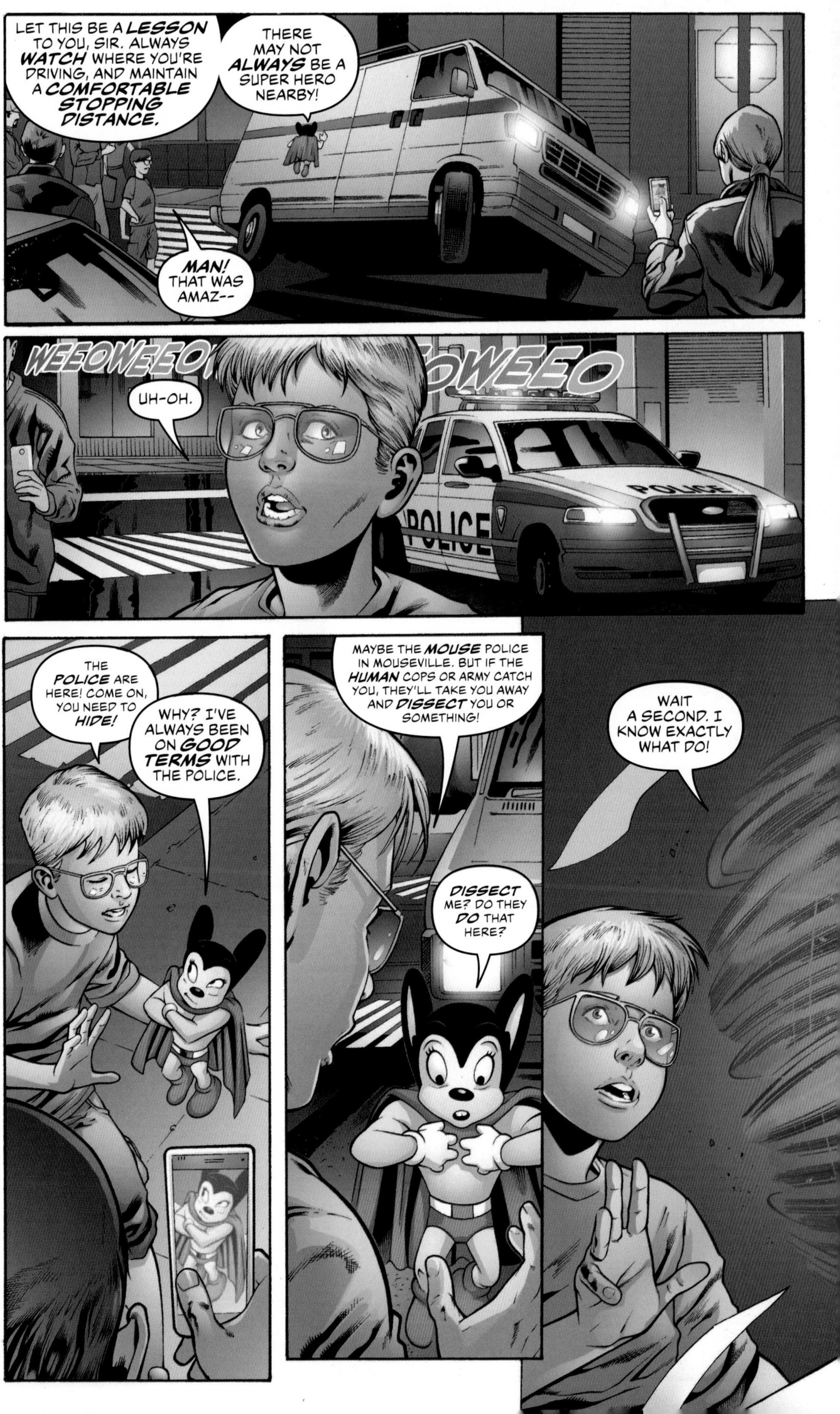
LET THIS BE A LESSON TO YOU, SIR. ALWAYS WATCH WHERE YOU'RE DRIVING, AND MAINTAIN A COMFORTABLE STOPPING DISTANCE.
THERE MAY NOT ALWAYS BE A SUPER HERO NEARBY!
MAN! THAT WAS AMAZ--
WEEOWEEO
OWEEO
UH-OH.
POLICE
THE POLICE ARE HERE! COME ON, YOU NEED TO HIDE!
WHY? I'VE ALWAYS BEEN ON GOOD TERMS WITH THE POLICE.
MAYBE THE MOUSE POLICE IN MOUSEVILLE. BUT IF THE HUMAN COPS OR ARMY CATCH YOU, THEY'LL TAKE YOU AWAY AND DISSECT YOU OR SOMETHING!
DISSECT ME? DO THEY DO THAT HERE?
WAIT A SECOND. I KNOW EXACTLY WHAT DO!

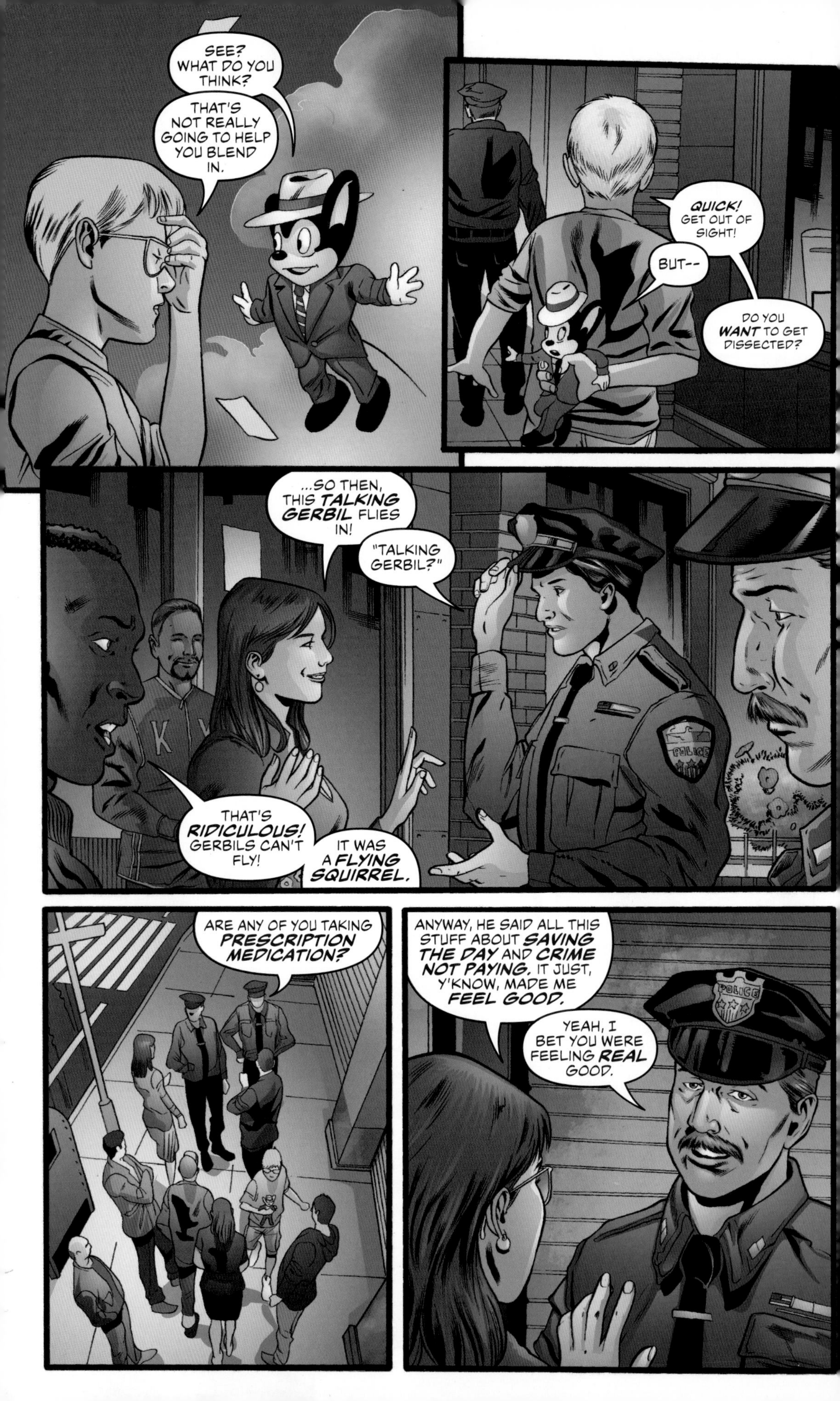
SEE? WHAT DO YOU THINK?
THAT'S NOT REALLY GOING TO HELP YOU BLEND IN.
QUICK! GET OUT OF SIGHT!
BUT--
DO YOU WANT TO GET DISSECTED?
...SO THEN, THIS TALKING GERBIL FLIES IN!
"TALKING GERBIL?"
THAT'S RIDICULOUS! GERBILS CAN'T FLY!
IT WAS A FLYING SQUIRREL.
ARE ANY OF YOU TAKING PRESCRIPTION MEDICATION?
ANYWAY, HE SAID ALL THIS STUFF ABOUT SAVING THE DAY AND CRIME NOT PAYING. IT JUST, Y'KNOW, MADE ME FEEL GOOD.
YEAH, I BET YOU WERE FEELING REAL GOOD.

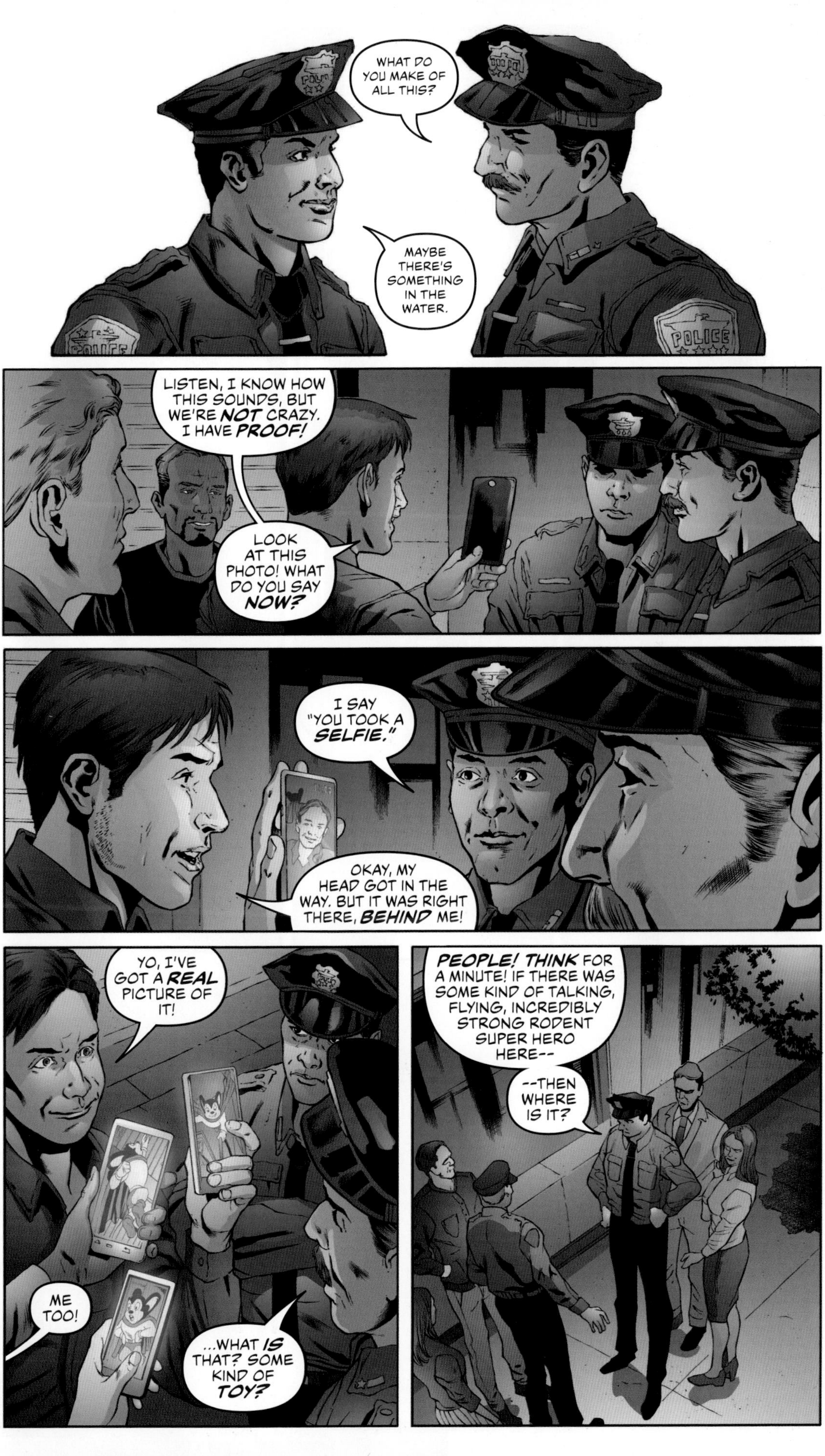
WHAT DO YOU MAKE OF ALL THIS?
MAYBE THERE'S SOMETHING IN THE WATER.
LISTEN, I KNOW HOW THIS SOUNDS, BUT WE'RE **NOT** CRAZY. I HAVE **PROOF!**
LOOK AT THIS PHOTO! WHAT DO YOU SAY **NOW?**
I SAY "YOU TOOK A **SELFIE.**"
OKAY, MY HEAD GOT IN THE WAY. BUT IT WAS RIGHT THERE, **BEHIND** ME!
YO, I'VE GOT A **REAL** PICTURE OF IT!
ME TOO!
...WHAT **IS** THAT? SOME KIND OF **TOY?**
PEOPLE! THINK FOR A MINUTE! IF THERE WAS SOME KIND OF TALKING, FLYING, INCREDIBLY STRONG RODENT SUPER HERO HERE--
--THEN WHERE IS IT?

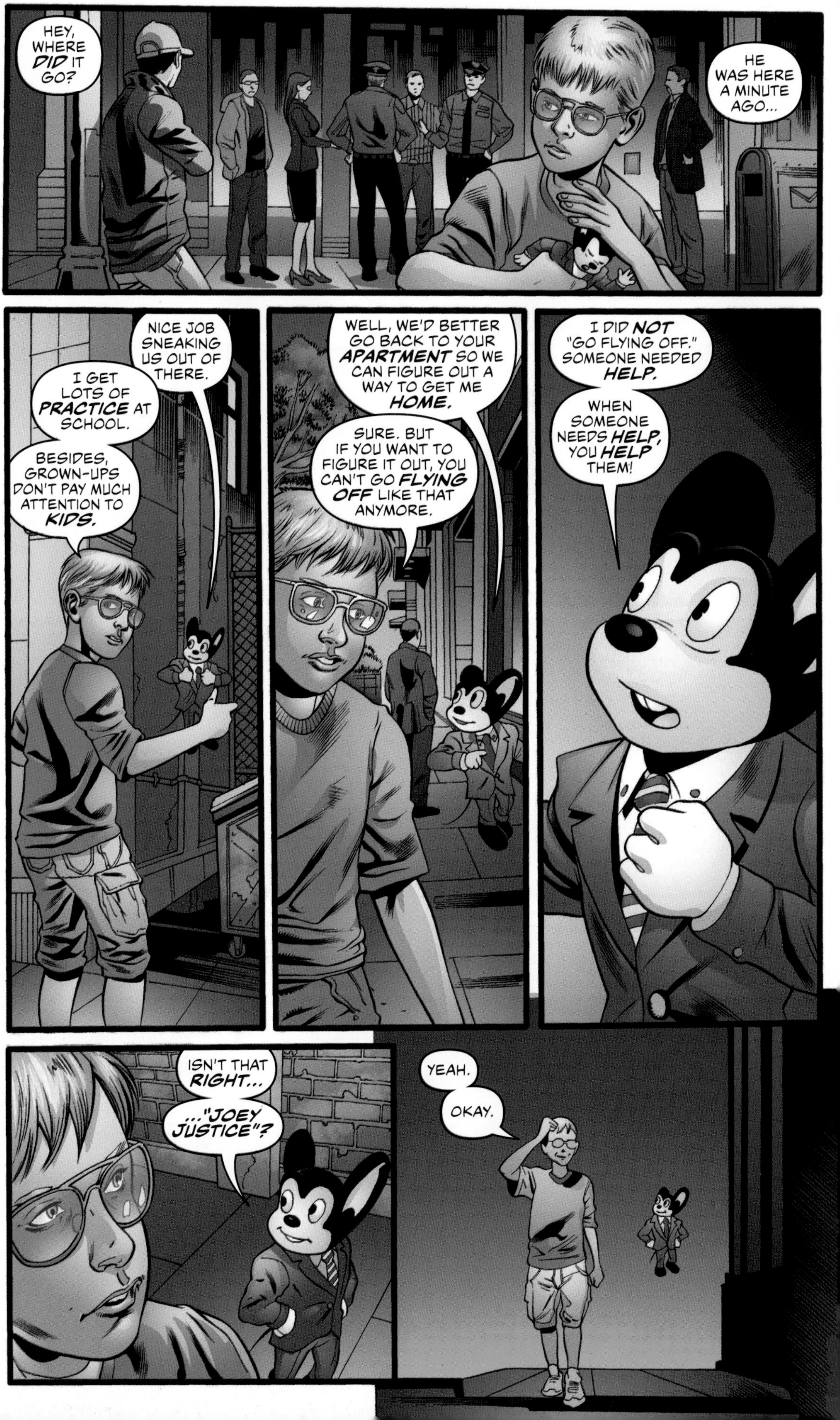
HEY, WHERE DID IT GO?
HE WAS HERE A MINUTE AGO...
NICE JOB SNEAKING US OUT OF THERE.
I GET LOTS OF PRACTICE AT SCHOOL.
BESIDES, GROWN-UPS DON'T PAY MUCH ATTENTION TO KIDS.
WELL, WE'D BETTER GO BACK TO YOUR APARTMENT SO WE CAN FIGURE OUT A WAY TO GET ME HOME.
SURE. BUT IF YOU WANT TO FIGURE IT OUT, YOU CAN'T GO FLYING OFF LIKE THAT ANYMORE.
I DID NOT "GO FLYING OFF." SOMEONE NEEDED HELP.
WHEN SOMEONE NEEDS HELP, YOU HELP THEM!
ISN'T THAT RIGHT...
..."JOEY JUSTICE"?
YEAH.
OKAY.

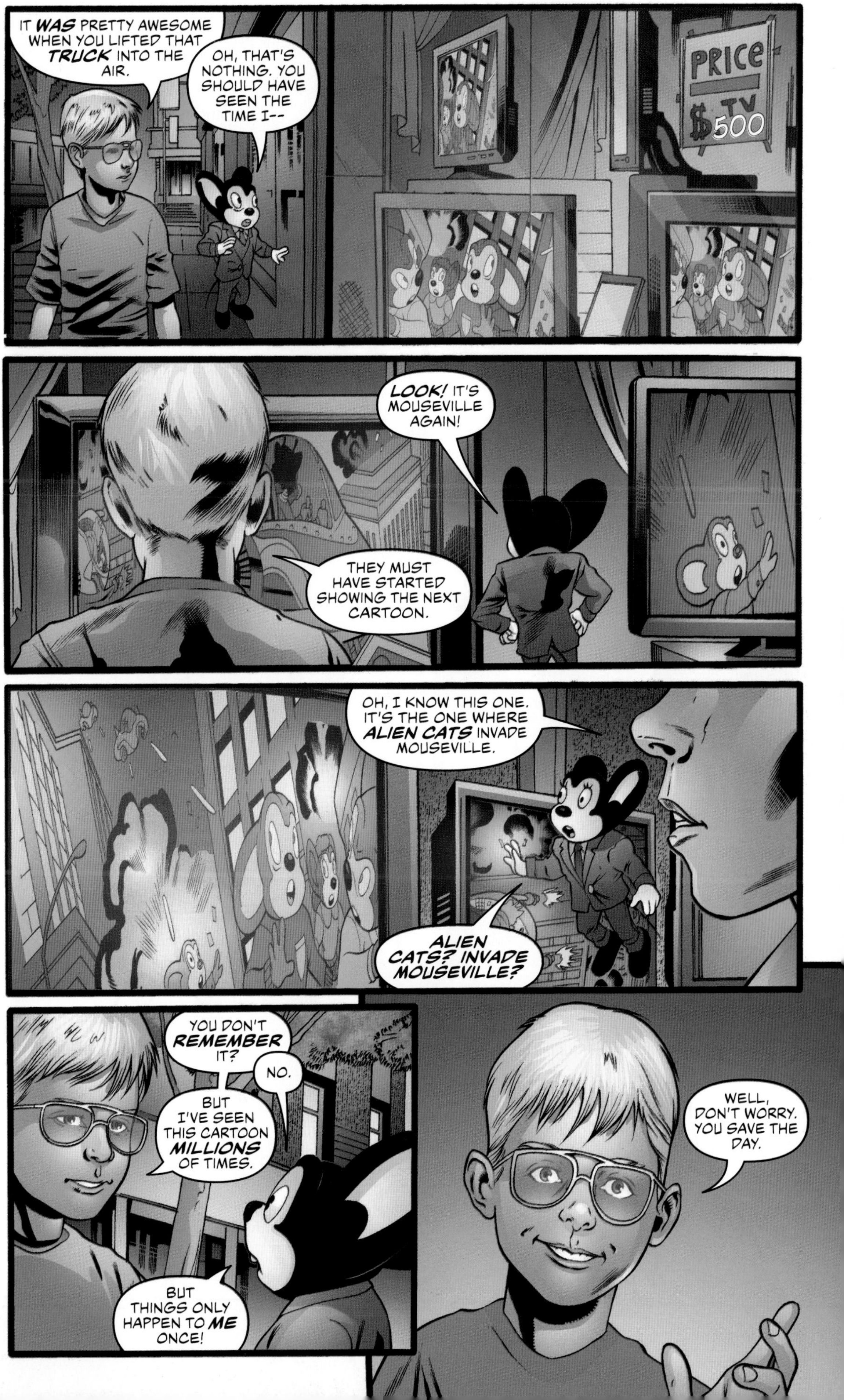

IT WAS PRETTY AWESOME WHEN YOU LIFTED THAT TRUCK INTO THE AIR.
OH, THAT'S NOTHING. YOU SHOULD HAVE SEEN THE TIME I--
PRICE TV $500
LOOK! IT'S MOUSEVILLE AGAIN!
THEY MUST HAVE STARTED SHOWING THE NEXT CARTOON.
OH, I KNOW THIS ONE. IT'S THE ONE WHERE ALIEN CATS INVADE MOUSEVILLE.
ALIEN CATS? INVADE MOUSEVILLE?
YOU DON'T REMEMBER IT?
NO.
BUT I'VE SEEN THIS CARTOON MILLIONS OF TIMES.
BUT THINGS ONLY HAPPEN TO ME ONCE!
WELL, DON'T WORRY. YOU SAVE THE DAY.

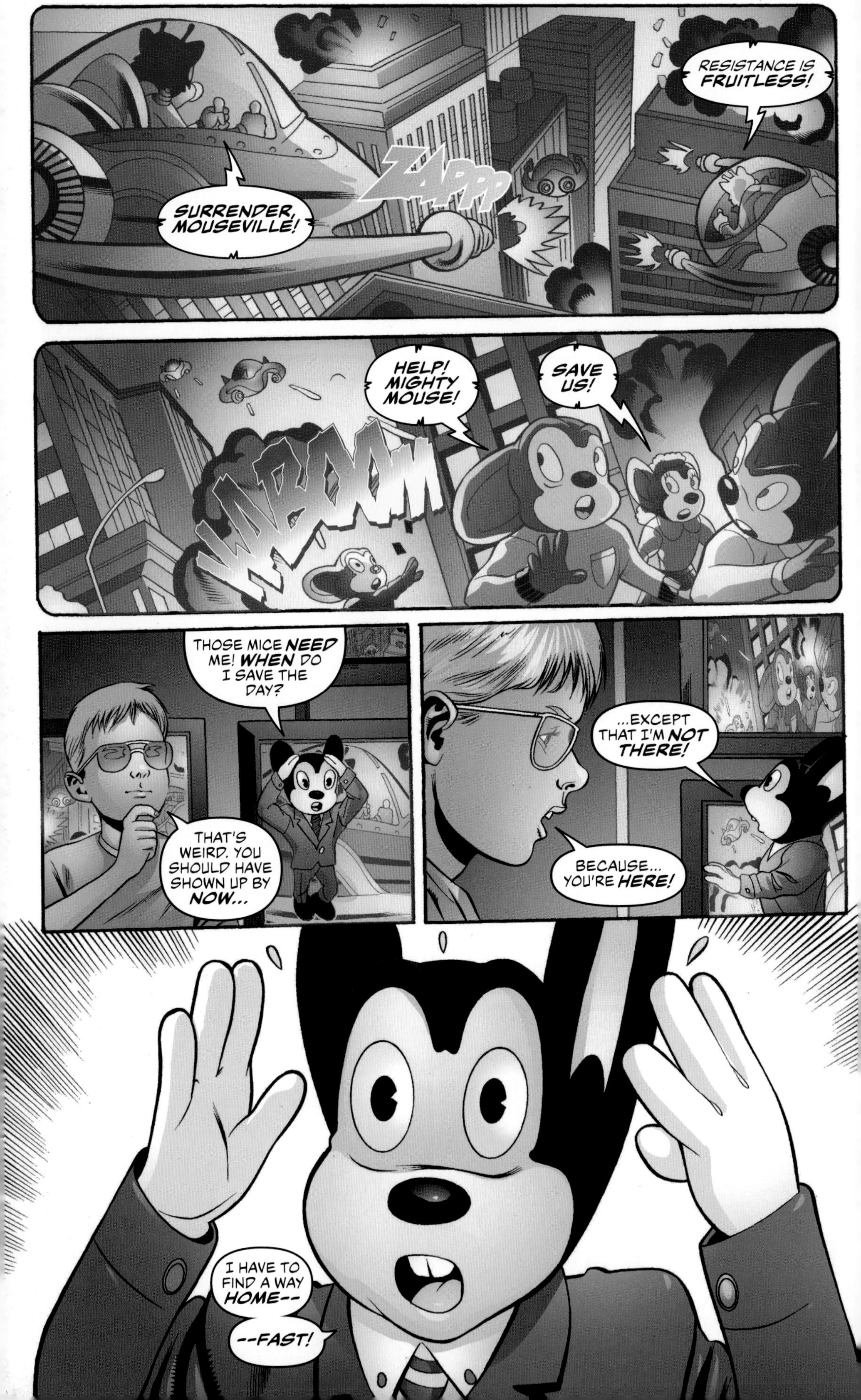

RESISTANCE IS FRUITLESS!
SURRENDER, MOUSEVILLE!
ZAPPP
HELP! MIGHTY MOUSE!
SAVE US!
WHBOOM
THOSE MICE NEED ME! WHEN DO I SAVE THE DAY?
THAT'S WEIRD. YOU SHOULD HAVE SHOWN UP BY NOW...
...EXCEPT THAT I'M NOT THERE!
BECAUSE... YOU'RE HERE!
I HAVE TO FIND A WAY HOME--
--FAST!

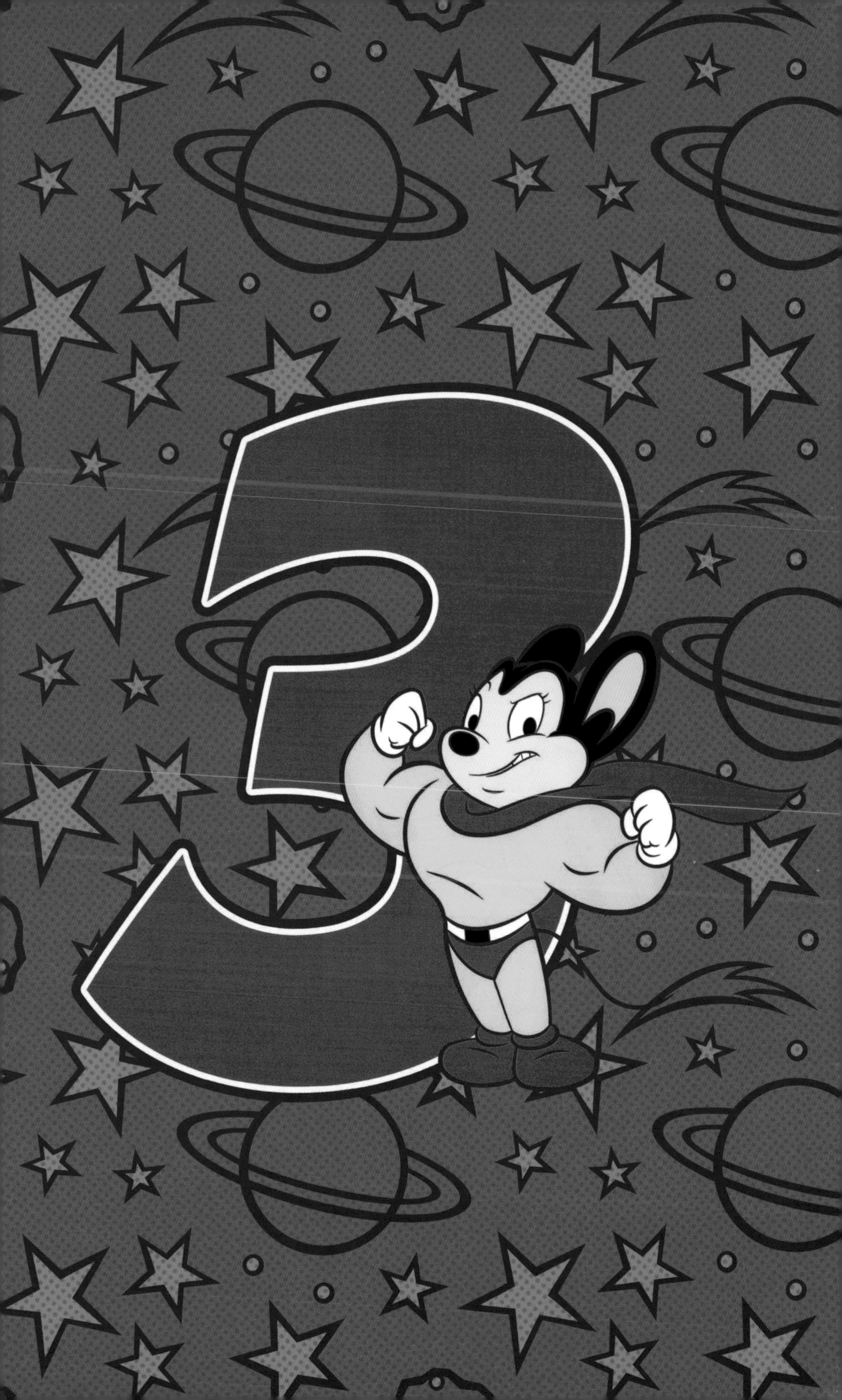

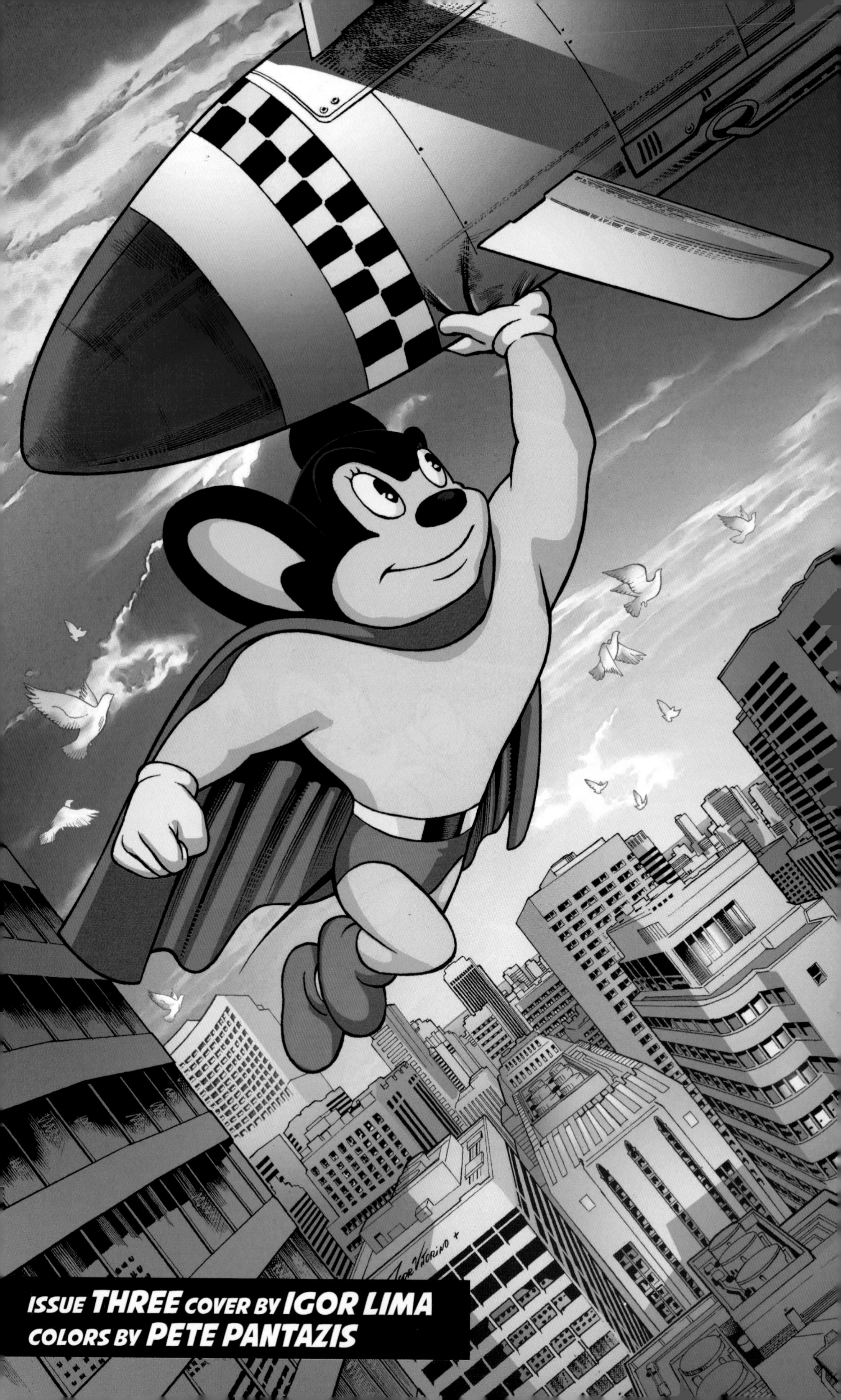

ISSUE THREE COVER BY IGOR LIMA
COLORS BY PETE PANTAZIS

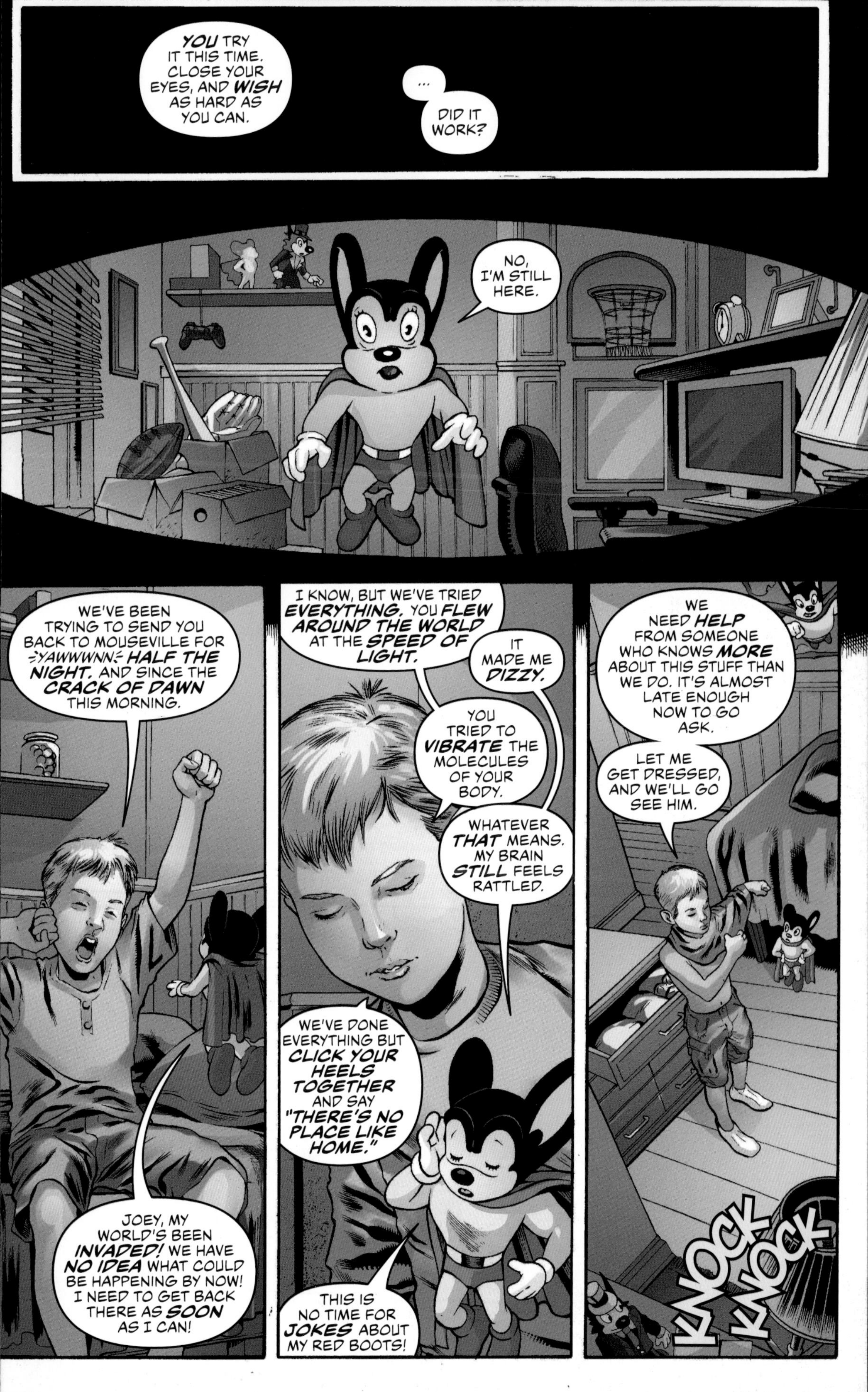
YOU TRY IT THIS TIME. CLOSE YOUR EYES, AND WISH AS HARD AS YOU CAN.
...
DID IT WORK?
NO, I'M STILL HERE.
WE'VE BEEN TRYING TO SEND YOU BACK TO MOUSEVILLE FOR =YAWWWNN= HALF THE NIGHT, AND SINCE THE CRACK OF DAWN THIS MORNING.
JOEY, MY WORLD'S BEEN INVADED! WE HAVE NO IDEA WHAT COULD BE HAPPENING BY NOW! I NEED TO GET BACK THERE AS SOON AS I CAN!
I KNOW, BUT WE'VE TRIED EVERYTHING. YOU FLEW AROUND THE WORLD AT THE SPEED OF LIGHT.
IT MADE ME DIZZY.
YOU TRIED TO VIBRATE THE MOLECULES OF YOUR BODY.
WHATEVER THAT MEANS. MY BRAIN STILL FEELS RATTLED.
WE'VE DONE EVERYTHING BUT CLICK YOUR HEELS TOGETHER AND SAY "THERE'S NO PLACE LIKE HOME."
THIS IS NO TIME FOR JOKES ABOUT MY RED BOOTS!
WE NEED HELP FROM SOMEONE WHO KNOWS MORE ABOUT THIS STUFF THAN WE DO. IT'S ALMOST LATE ENOUGH NOW TO GO ASK.
LET ME GET DRESSED, AND WE'LL GO SEE HIM.
KNOCK KNOCK

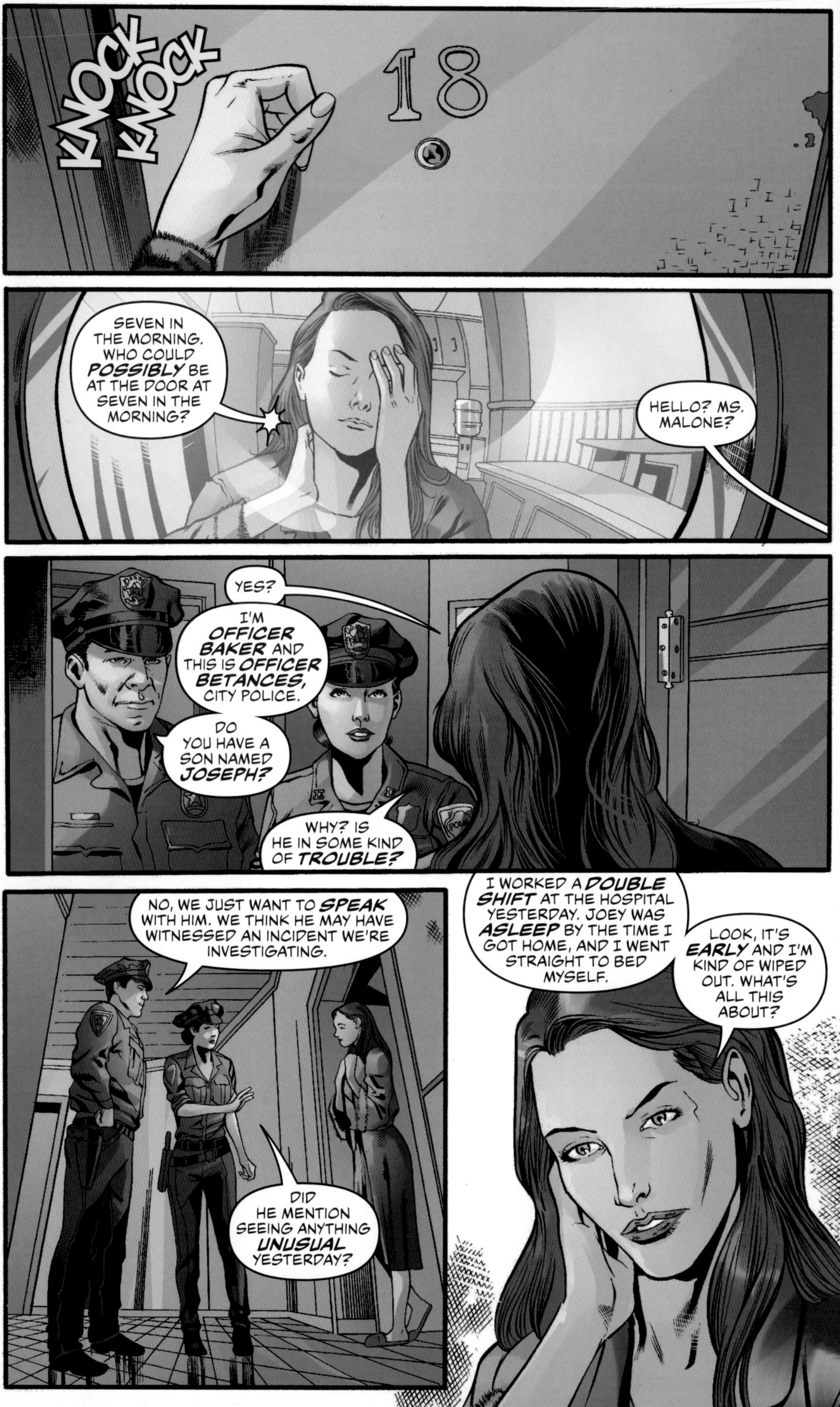

KNOCK KNOCK
18
SEVEN IN THE MORNING. WHO COULD POSSIBLY BE AT THE DOOR AT SEVEN IN THE MORNING?
HELLO? MS. MALONE?
YES?
I'M OFFICER BAKER AND THIS IS OFFICER BETANCES, CITY POLICE.
DO YOU HAVE A SON NAMED JOSEPH?
WHY? IS HE IN SOME KIND OF TROUBLE?
NO, WE JUST WANT TO SPEAK WITH HIM. WE THINK HE MAY HAVE WITNESSED AN INCIDENT WE'RE INVESTIGATING.
DID HE MENTION SEEING ANYTHING UNUSUAL YESTERDAY?
I WORKED A DOUBLE SHIFT AT THE HOSPITAL YESTERDAY. JOEY WAS ASLEEP BY THE TIME I GOT HOME, AND I WENT STRAIGHT TO BED MYSELF.
LOOK, IT'S EARLY AND I'M KIND OF WIPED OUT. WHAT'S ALL THIS ABOUT?

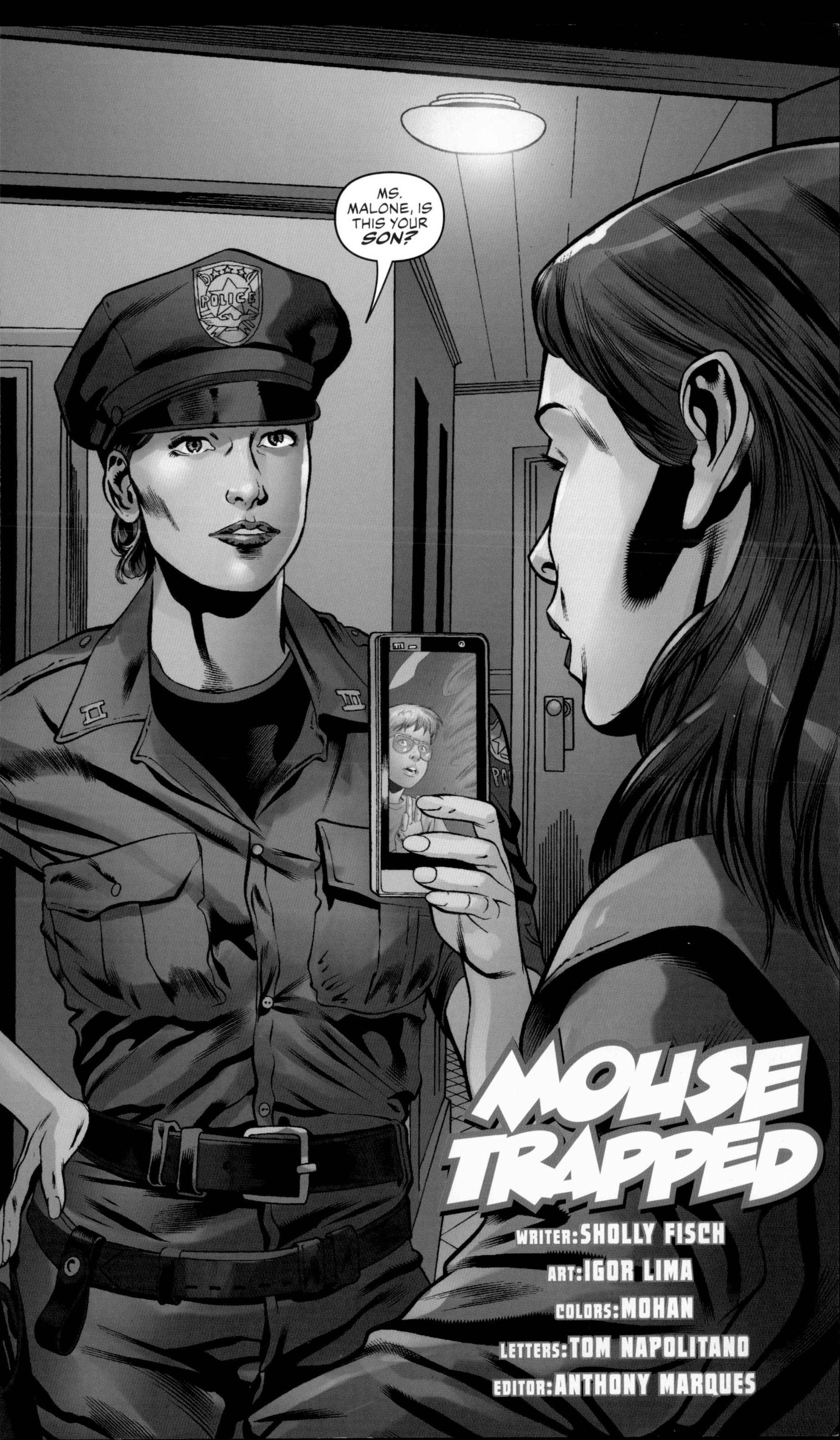
MS. MALONE, IS THIS YOUR SON?
POLICE
MOUSE TRAPPED
WRITER: SHOLLY FISCH
ART: IGOR LIMA
COLORS: MOHAN
LETTERS: TOM NAPOLITANO
EDITOR: ANTHONY MARQUES

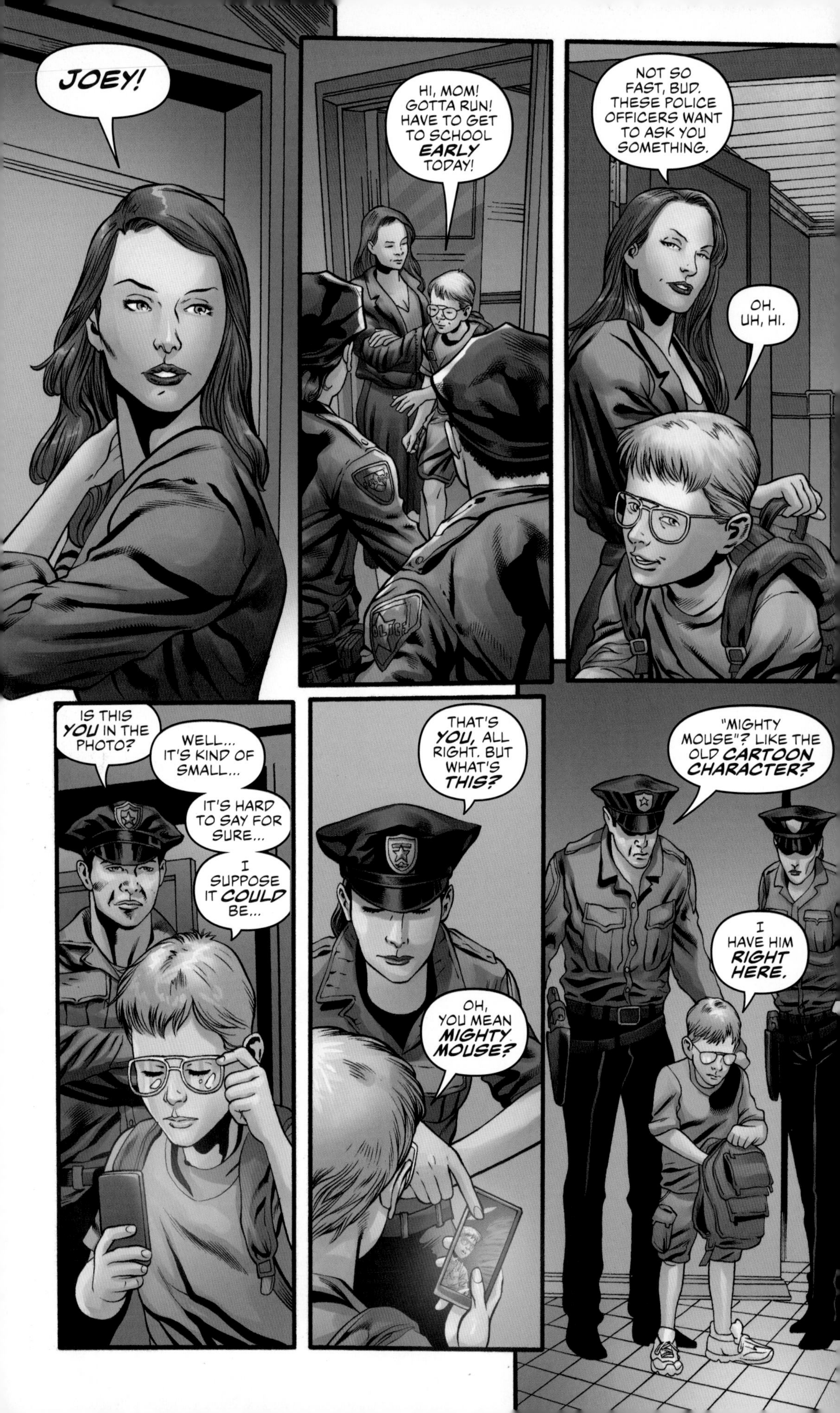
JOEY!
HI, MOM! GOTTA RUN! HAVE TO GET TO SCHOOL EARLY TODAY!
NOT SO FAST, BUD. THESE POLICE OFFICERS WANT TO ASK YOU SOMETHING.
OH. UH, HI.
IS THIS YOU IN THE PHOTO?
WELL... IT'S KIND OF SMALL...
IT'S HARD TO SAY FOR SURE...
I SUPPOSE IT COULD BE...
THAT'S YOU, ALL RIGHT. BUT WHAT'S THIS?
OH, YOU MEAN MIGHTY MOUSE?
"MIGHTY MOUSE"? LIKE THE OLD CARTOON CHARACTER?
I HAVE HIM RIGHT HERE.

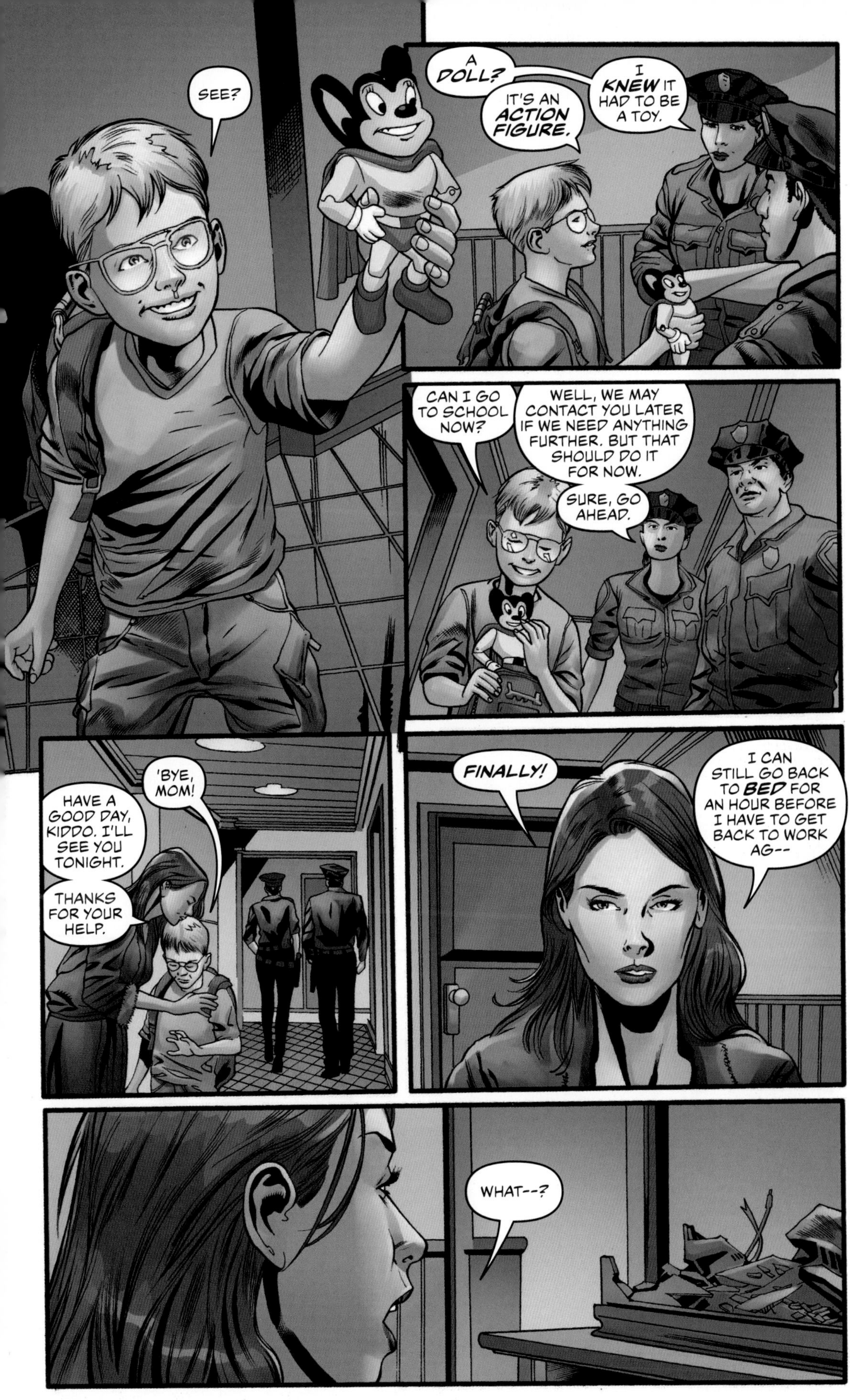
SEE?
A DOLL?
IT'S AN ACTION FIGURE.
I KNEW IT HAD TO BE A TOY.
CAN I GO TO SCHOOL NOW?
WELL, WE MAY CONTACT YOU LATER IF WE NEED ANYTHING FURTHER. BUT THAT SHOULD DO IT FOR NOW.
SURE, GO AHEAD.
'BYE, MOM!
HAVE A GOOD DAY, KIDDO. I'LL SEE YOU TONIGHT.
THANKS FOR YOUR HELP.
FINALLY!
I CAN STILL GO BACK TO BED FOR AN HOUR BEFORE I HAVE TO GET BACK TO WORK AG--
WHAT--?

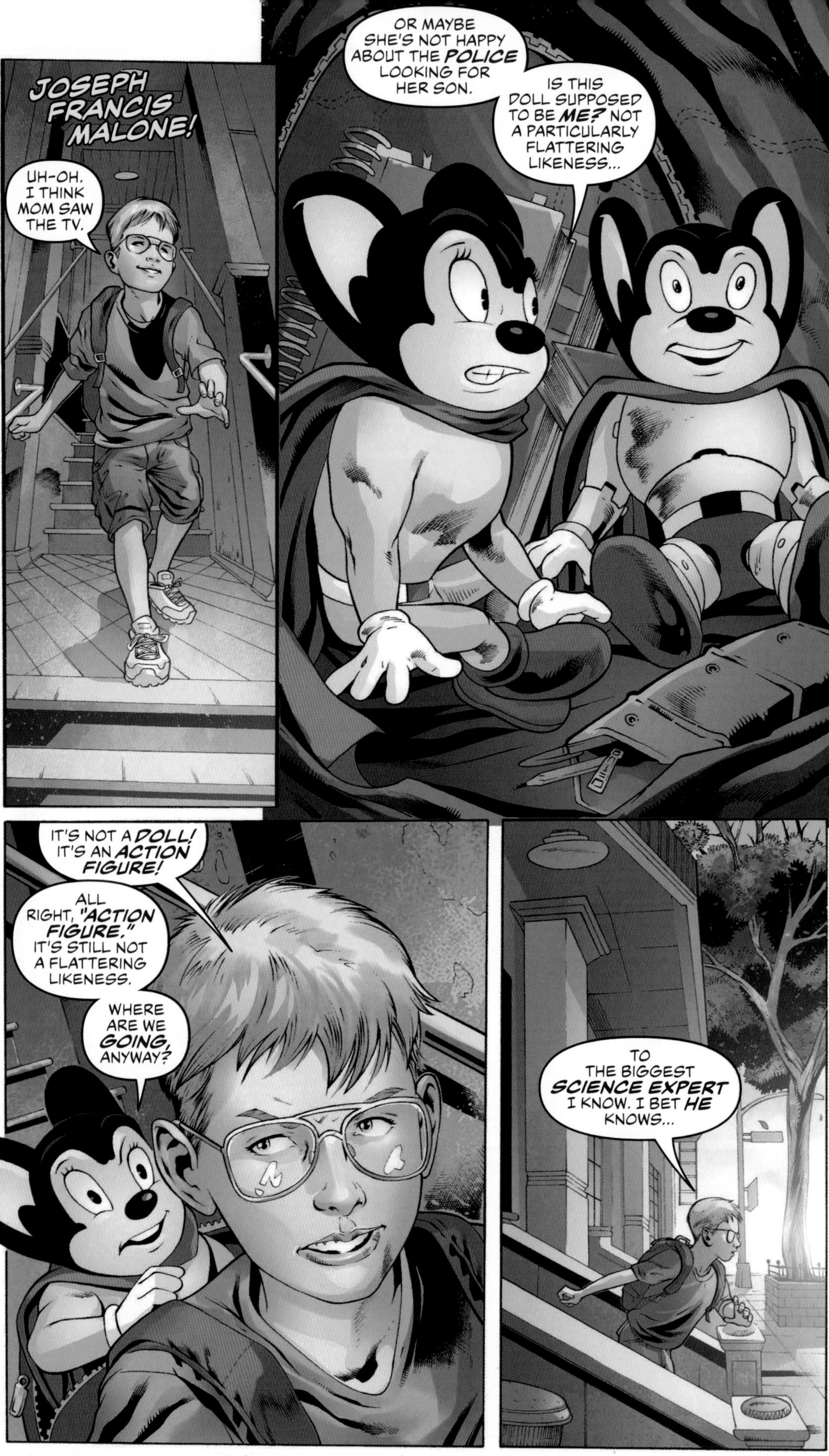
JOSEPH FRANCIS MALONE!
UH-OH. I THINK MOM SAW THE TV.
OR MAYBE SHE'S NOT HAPPY ABOUT THE POLICE LOOKING FOR HER SON.
IS THIS DOLL SUPPOSED TO BE ME? NOT A PARTICULARLY FLATTERING LIKENESS...
IT'S NOT A DOLL! IT'S AN ACTION FIGURE!
ALL RIGHT, "ACTION FIGURE." IT'S STILL NOT A FLATTERING LIKENESS.
WHERE ARE WE GOING, ANYWAY?
TO THE BIGGEST SCIENCE EXPERT I KNOW. I BET HE KNOWS...

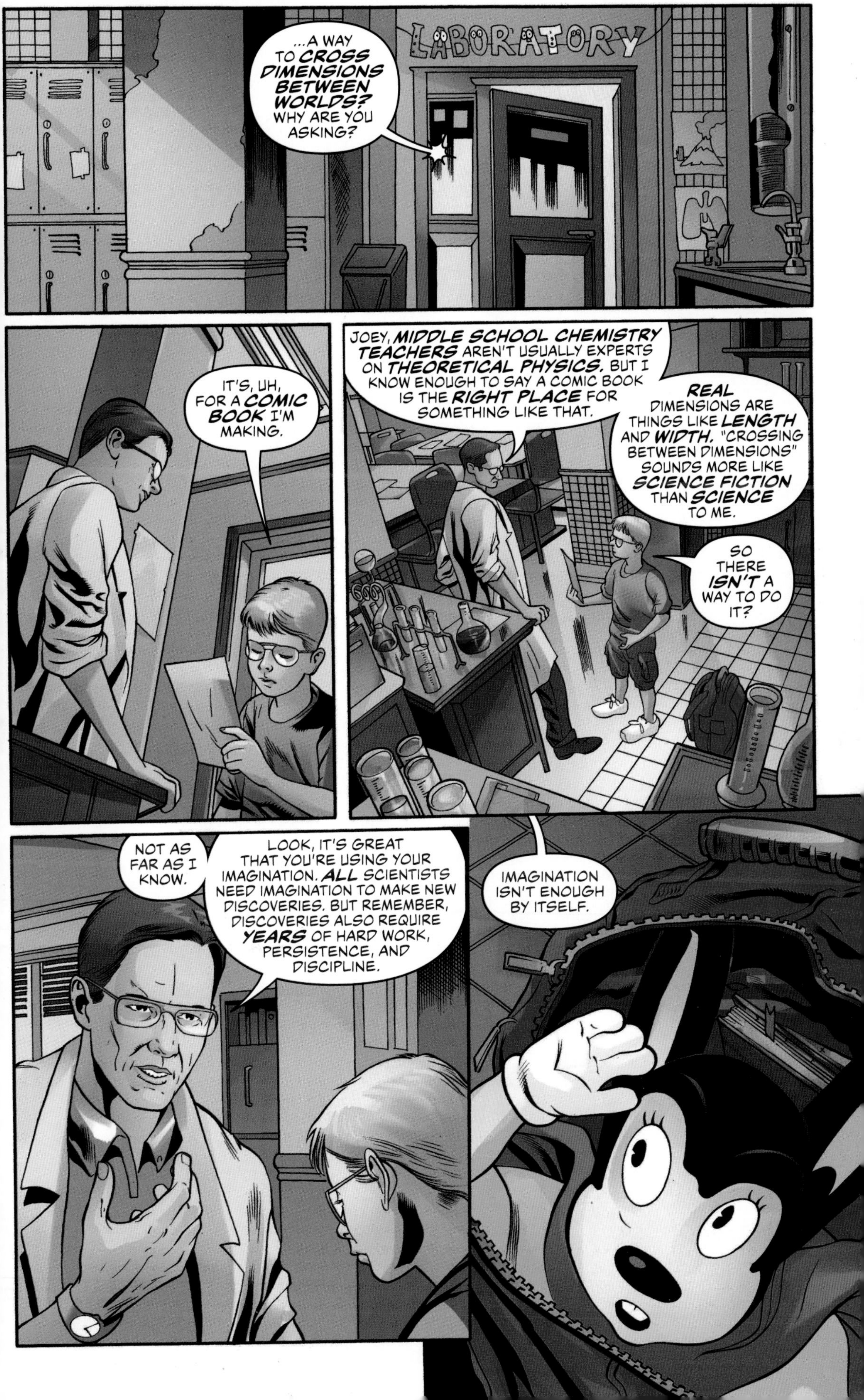
LABORATORY
...A WAY TO CROSS DIMENSIONS BETWEEN WORLDS? WHY ARE YOU ASKING?
IT'S, UH, FOR A COMIC BOOK I'M MAKING.
JOEY, MIDDLE SCHOOL CHEMISTRY TEACHERS AREN'T USUALLY EXPERTS ON THEORETICAL PHYSICS, BUT I KNOW ENOUGH TO SAY A COMIC BOOK IS THE RIGHT PLACE FOR SOMETHING LIKE THAT.
REAL DIMENSIONS ARE THINGS LIKE LENGTH AND WIDTH. "CROSSING BETWEEN DIMENSIONS" SOUNDS MORE LIKE SCIENCE FICTION THAN SCIENCE TO ME.
SO THERE ISN'T A WAY TO DO IT?
NOT AS FAR AS I KNOW.
LOOK, IT'S GREAT THAT YOU'RE USING YOUR IMAGINATION. ALL SCIENTISTS NEED IMAGINATION TO MAKE NEW DISCOVERIES. BUT REMEMBER, DISCOVERIES ALSO REQUIRE YEARS OF HARD WORK, PERSISTENCE, AND DISCIPLINE.
IMAGINATION ISN'T ENOUGH BY ITSELF.

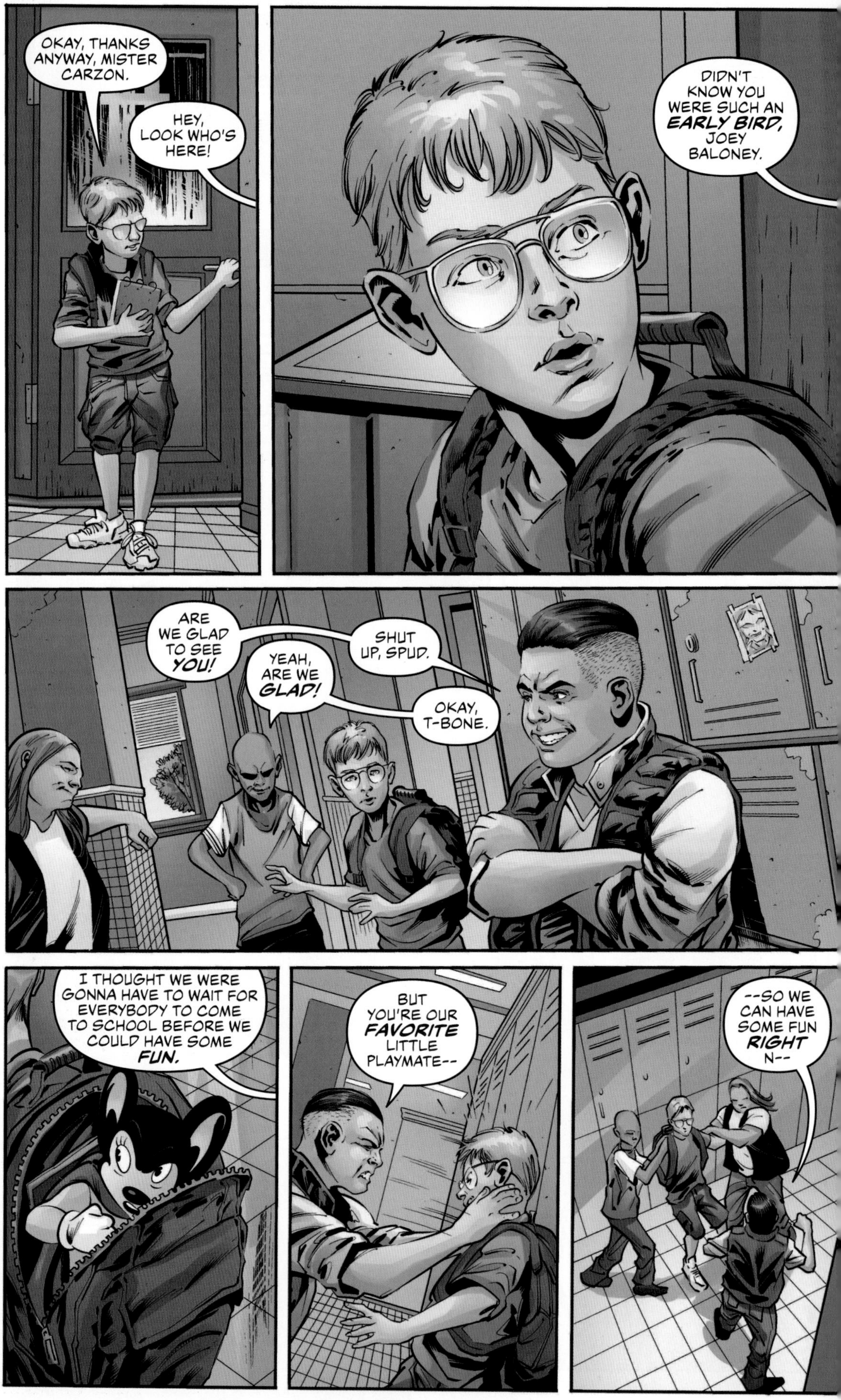
OKAY, THANKS ANYWAY, MISTER CARZON.
HEY, LOOK WHO'S HERE!
DIDN'T KNOW YOU WERE SUCH AN EARLY BIRD, JOEY BALONEY.
ARE WE GLAD TO SEE YOU!
SHUT UP, SPUD.
YEAH, ARE WE GLAD!
OKAY, T-BONE.
I THOUGHT WE WERE GONNA HAVE TO WAIT FOR EVERYBODY TO COME TO SCHOOL BEFORE WE COULD HAVE SOME FUN.
BUT YOU'RE OUR FAVORITE LITTLE PLAYMATE--
--SO WE CAN HAVE SOME FUN RIGHT N--

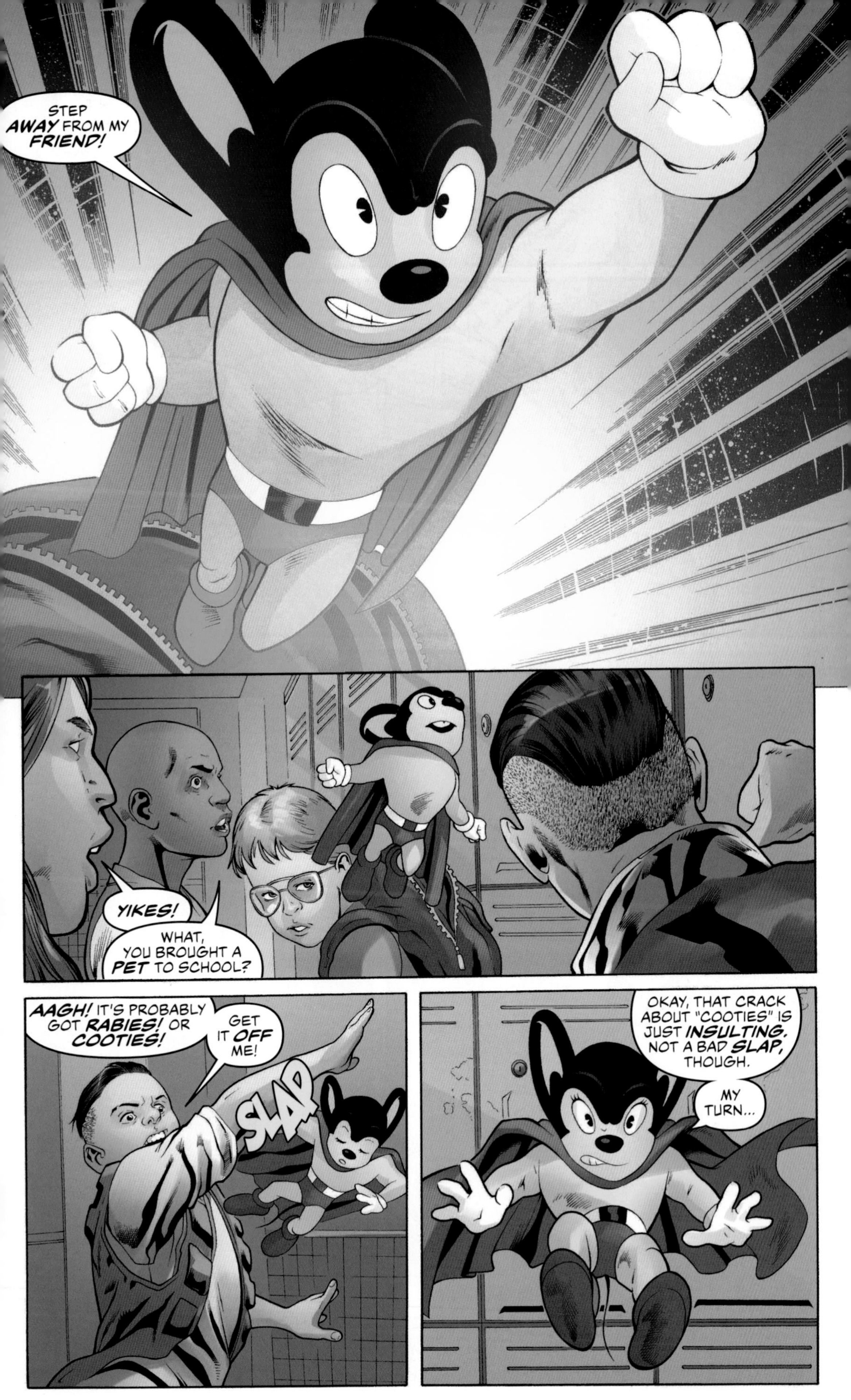
STEP AWAY FROM MY FRIEND!
YIKES!
WHAT, YOU BROUGHT A PET TO SCHOOL?
AAGH! IT'S PROBABLY GOT RABIES! OR COOTIES!
GET IT OFF ME!
SLAP
OKAY, THAT CRACK ABOUT "COOTIES" IS JUST INSULTING. NOT A BAD SLAP, THOUGH.
MY TURN...

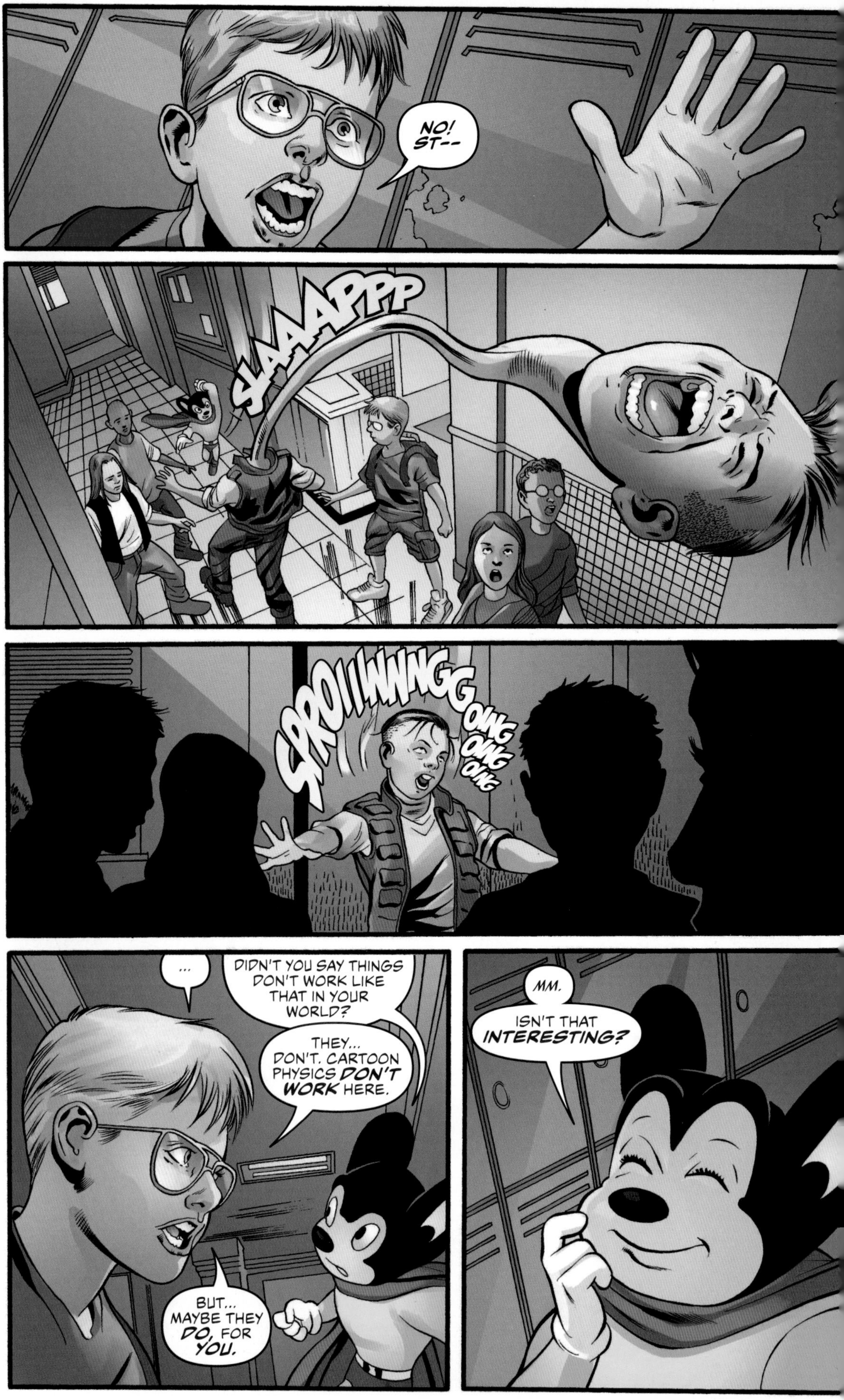
NO! ST--
SLAAAPPP
SPROIIINNNGG
OING
OING
OING
...
DIDN'T YOU SAY THINGS DON'T WORK LIKE THAT IN YOUR WORLD?
THEY... DON'T. CARTOON PHYSICS DON'T WORK HERE.
BUT... MAYBE THEY DO, FOR YOU.
MM.
ISN'T THAT INTERESTING?

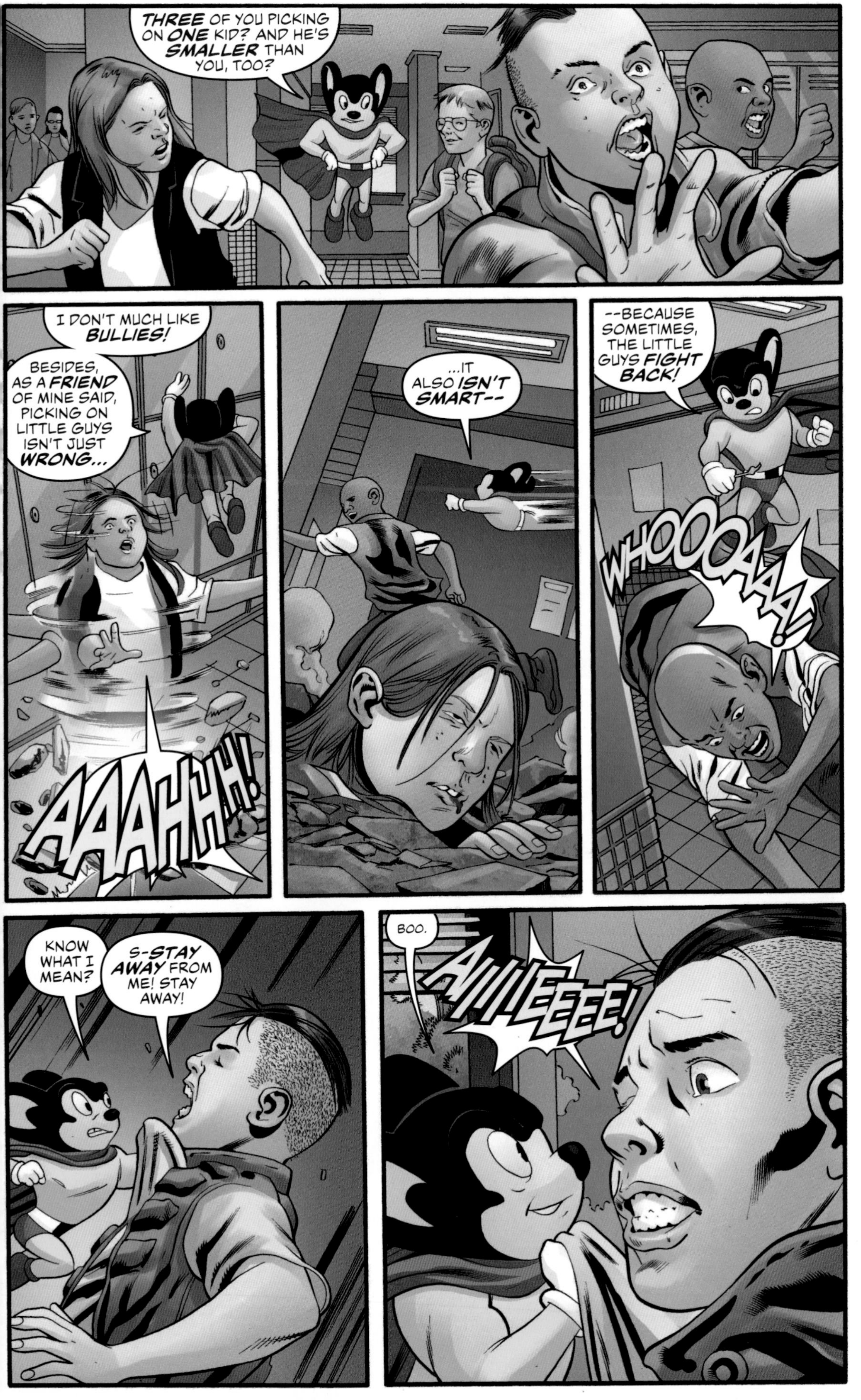

THREE OF YOU PICKING ON ONE KID? AND HE'S SMALLER THAN YOU, TOO?
I DON'T MUCH LIKE BULLIES!
BESIDES, AS A FRIEND OF MINE SAID, PICKING ON LITTLE GUYS ISN'T JUST WRONG...
AAAHHH!
...IT ALSO ISN'T SMART--
--BECAUSE SOMETIMES, THE LITTLE GUYS FIGHT BACK!
WHOOOAAA!
KNOW WHAT I MEAN?
S-STAY AWAY FROM ME! STAY AWAY!
BOO.
AIIIEEEE!

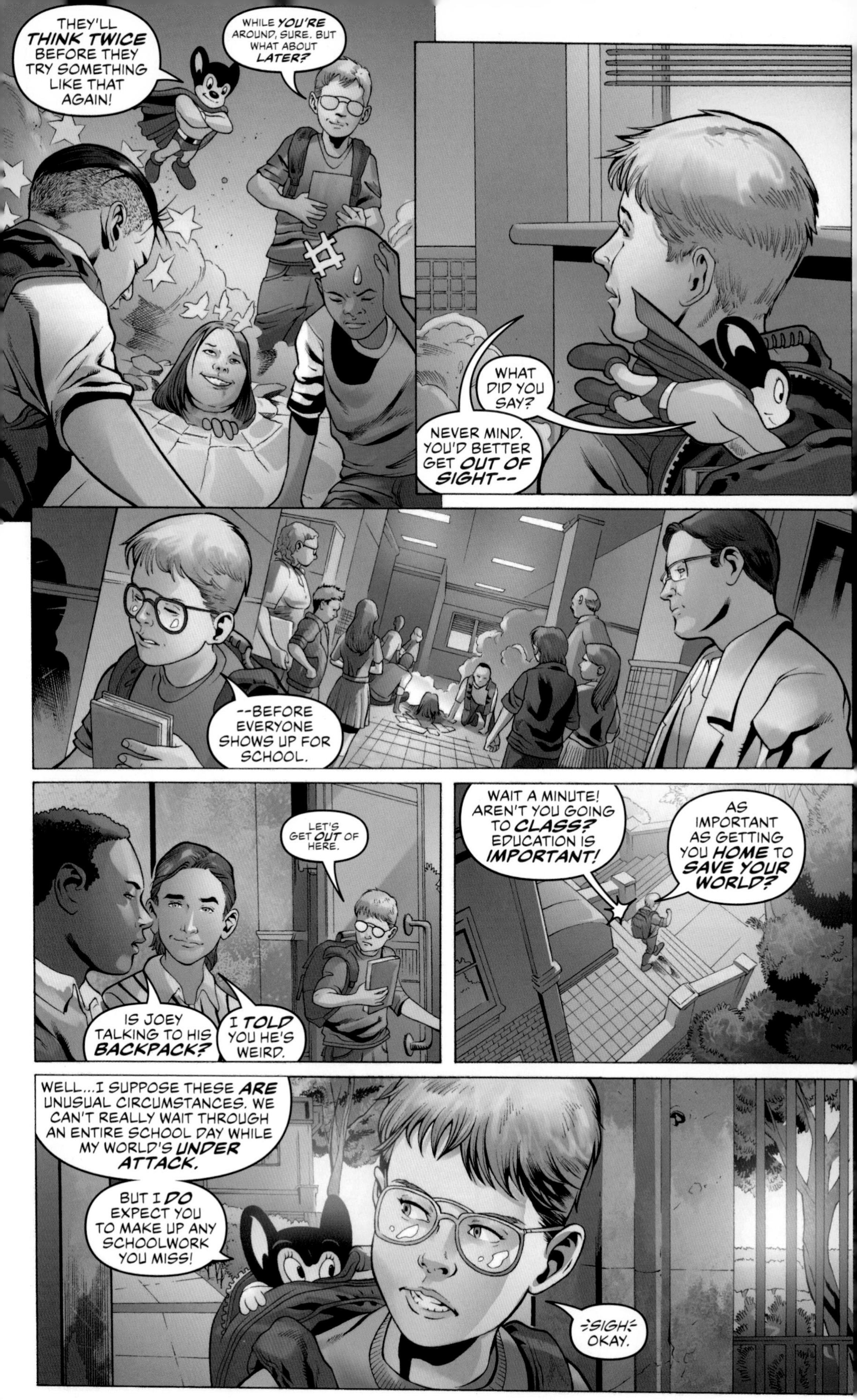
THEY'LL THINK TWICE BEFORE THEY TRY SOMETHING LIKE THAT AGAIN!
WHILE YOU'RE AROUND, SURE. BUT WHAT ABOUT LATER?
WHAT DID YOU SAY?
NEVER MIND. YOU'D BETTER GET OUT OF SIGHT--
--BEFORE EVERYONE SHOWS UP FOR SCHOOL.
LET'S GET OUT OF HERE.
IS JOEY TALKING TO HIS BACKPACK?
I TOLD YOU HE'S WEIRD.
WAIT A MINUTE! AREN'T YOU GOING TO CLASS? EDUCATION IS IMPORTANT!
AS IMPORTANT AS GETTING YOU HOME TO SAVE YOUR WORLD?
WELL...I SUPPOSE THESE ARE UNUSUAL CIRCUMSTANCES. WE CAN'T REALLY WAIT THROUGH AN ENTIRE SCHOOL DAY WHILE MY WORLD'S UNDER ATTACK.
BUT I DO EXPECT YOU TO MAKE UP ANY SCHOOLWORK YOU MISS!
SIGH OKAY.

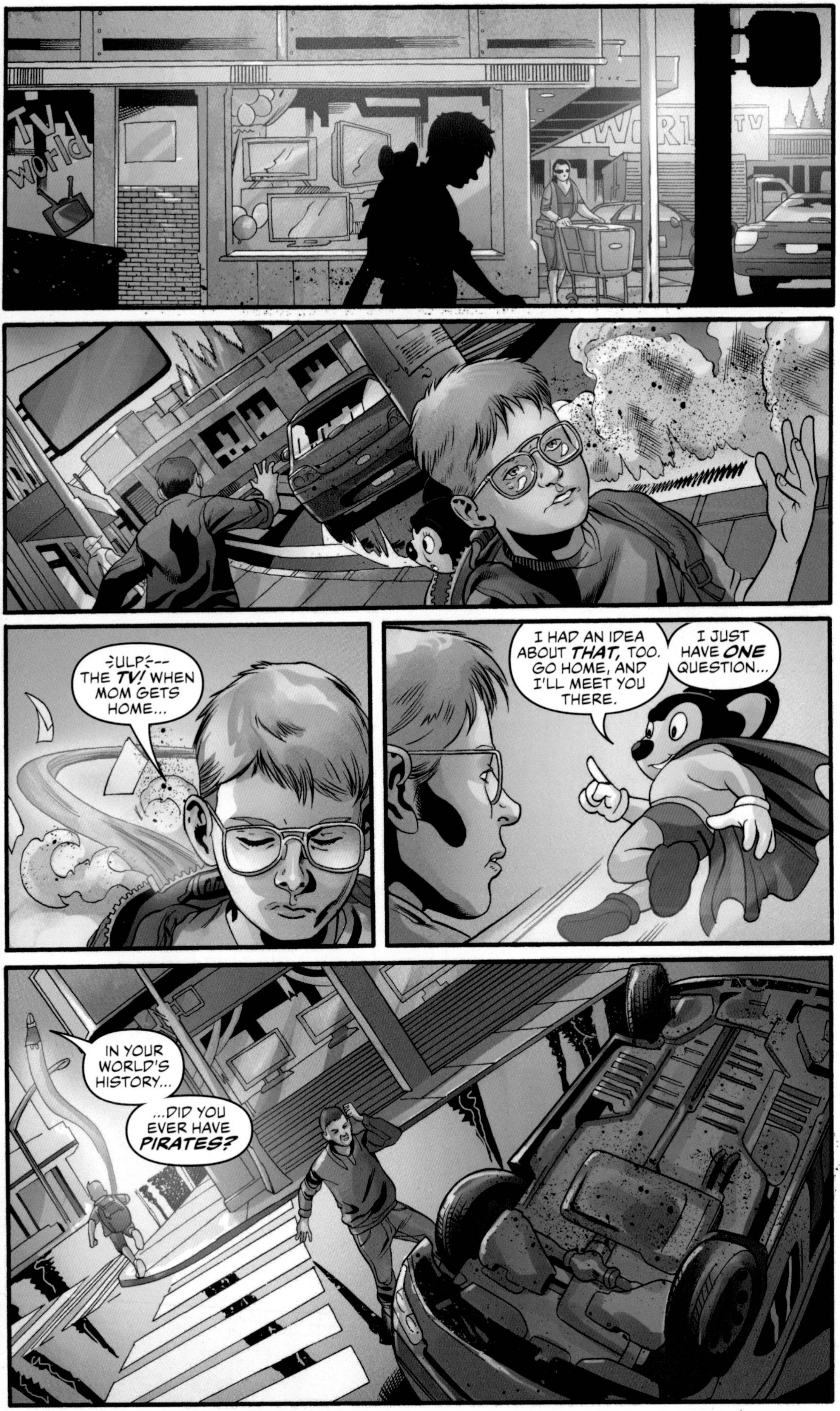
TV world
WORLD TV
-ULP- --
THE TV! WHEN MOM GETS HOME...
I HAD AN IDEA ABOUT THAT, TOO. GO HOME, AND I'LL MEET YOU THERE.
I JUST HAVE ONE QUESTION...
IN YOUR WORLD'S HISTORY...
...DID YOU EVER HAVE PIRATES?

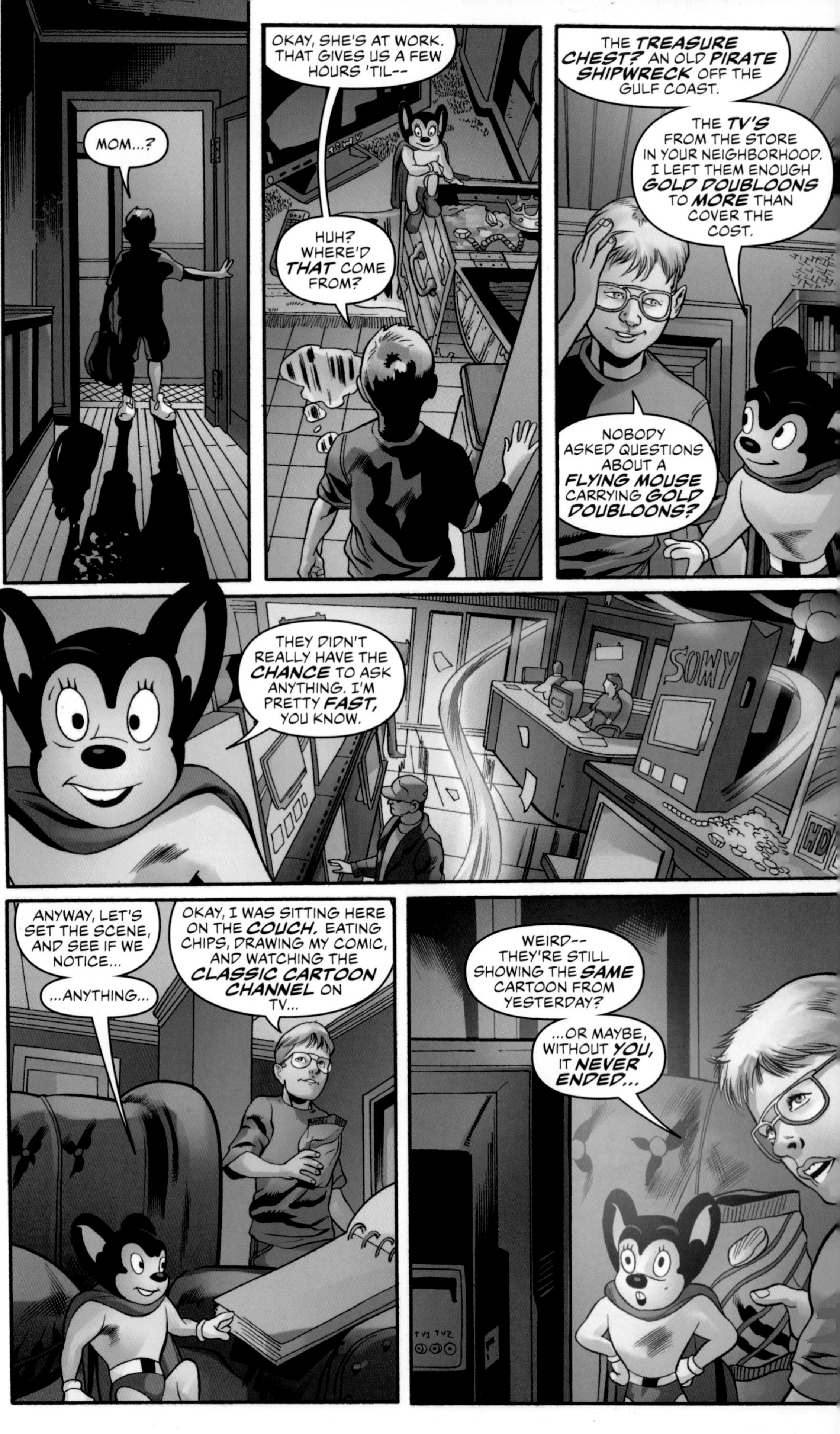
MOM...?
OKAY, SHE'S AT WORK. THAT GIVES US A FEW HOURS 'TIL--
HUH? WHERE'D THAT COME FROM?
THE TREASURE CHEST? AN OLD PIRATE SHIPWRECK OFF THE GULF COAST.
THE TV'S FROM THE STORE IN YOUR NEIGHBORHOOD. I LEFT THEM ENOUGH GOLD DOUBLOONS TO MORE THAN COVER THE COST.
NOBODY ASKED QUESTIONS ABOUT A FLYING MOUSE CARRYING GOLD DOUBLOONS?
THEY DIDN'T REALLY HAVE THE CHANCE TO ASK ANYTHING. I'M PRETTY FAST, YOU KNOW.
SOWY
ANYWAY, LET'S SET THE SCENE, AND SEE IF WE NOTICE...
...ANYTHING...
OKAY, I WAS SITTING HERE ON THE COUCH, EATING CHIPS, DRAWING MY COMIC, AND WATCHING THE CLASSIC CARTOON CHANNEL ON TV...
WEIRD-- THEY'RE STILL SHOWING THE SAME CARTOON FROM YESTERDAY?
...OR MAYBE, WITHOUT YOU, IT NEVER ENDED...

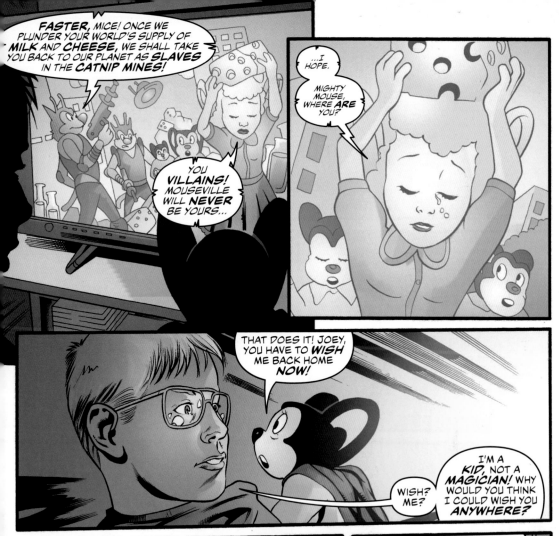

FASTER, MICE! ONCE WE PLUNDER YOUR WORLD'S SUPPLY OF **MILK** AND **CHEESE**, WE SHALL TAKE YOU BACK TO OUR PLANET AS **SLAVES** IN THE **CATNIP MINES!**

...I HOPE.

MIGHTY MOUSE, WHERE **ARE** YOU?

YOU **VILLAINS!** MOUSEVILLE WILL **NEVER** BE YOURS...

THAT DOES IT! JOEY, YOU HAVE TO **WISH** ME BACK HOME **NOW!**

WISH? ME?

I'M A **KID,** NOT A **MAGICIAN!** WHY WOULD YOU THINK I COULD WISH YOU **ANYWHERE?**

DON'T YOU SEE? JUST BEFORE THAT WEIRD FORCE **PULLED** ME TO YOUR WORLD, YOU WERE WISHING FOR US TO BE **TOGETHER**--

--TO BE **FRIENDS!** IT **CAN'T** BE A COINCIDENCE!

BUT WE ALREADY **TRIED** WISHING! IT **DIDN'T WORK!**

THEN WISH **HARDER!**

FOCUS. WISH FROM **DEEP DOWN IN YOUR HEART,** WITH **EVERY FIBER OF YOUR BEING...**

DID IT WORK?

NO.

TRY AGAIN. WISH HARDER!

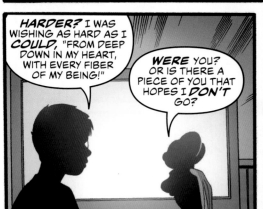

HARDER? I WAS WISHING AS HARD AS I COULD, "FROM DEEP DOWN IN MY HEART, WITH EVERY FIBER OF MY BEING!"

WERE YOU? OR IS THERE A PIECE OF YOU THAT HOPES I DON'T GO?

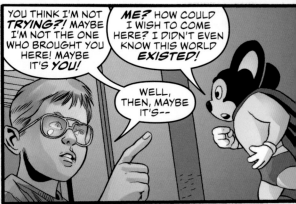

YOU THINK I'M NOT TRYING?! MAYBE I'M NOT THE ONE WHO BROUGHT YOU HERE! MAYBE IT'S YOU!

ME? HOW COULD I WISH TO COME HERE? I DIDN'T EVEN KNOW THIS WORLD EXISTED!

WELL, THEN, MAYBE IT'S--

OH.

MAYBE IT'S NOT A WISH. AND IT'S NOT JUST ME.

WHAT DO YOU MEAN?

MAYBE IT'S MORE THAN A WISH. MAYBE IT'S A... A NEED.

I NEEDED HELP WITH THOSE BULLIES, RIGHT? AND WHAT ABOUT YOU?

IT'S LIKE YOU SAID YESTERDAY: YOU'RE A HERO, AND HEROES ALWAYS COME TO HELP PEOPLE IN NEED.

SO YOU'RE SAYING IT WAS BOTH OF US?

YOU NEEDED HELP, AND I NEEDED TO HELP YOU?

MAYBE. OR AT LEAST MAYBE THAT'S PART OF IT...

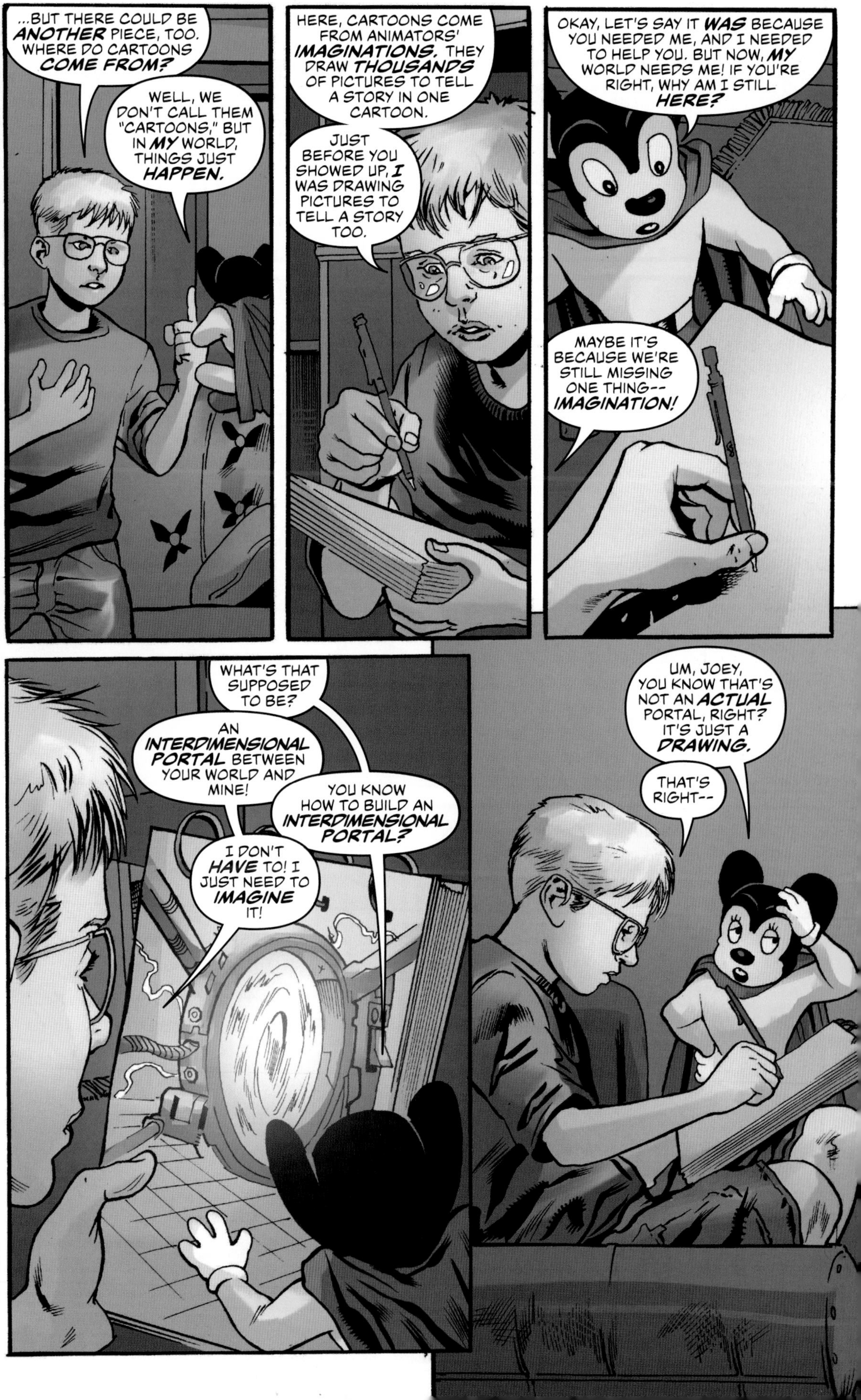
...BUT THERE COULD BE ANOTHER PIECE, TOO. WHERE DO CARTOONS COME FROM?
WELL, WE DON'T CALL THEM "CARTOONS," BUT IN MY WORLD, THINGS JUST HAPPEN.
HERE, CARTOONS COME FROM ANIMATORS' IMAGINATIONS. THEY DRAW THOUSANDS OF PICTURES TO TELL A STORY IN ONE CARTOON.
JUST BEFORE YOU SHOWED UP, I WAS DRAWING PICTURES TO TELL A STORY TOO.
OKAY, LET'S SAY IT WAS BECAUSE YOU NEEDED ME, AND I NEEDED TO HELP YOU. BUT NOW, MY WORLD NEEDS ME! IF YOU'RE RIGHT, WHY AM I STILL HERE?
MAYBE IT'S BECAUSE WE'RE STILL MISSING ONE THING-- IMAGINATION!
WHAT'S THAT SUPPOSED TO BE?
AN INTERDIMENSIONAL PORTAL BETWEEN YOUR WORLD AND MINE!
YOU KNOW HOW TO BUILD AN INTERDIMENSIONAL PORTAL?
I DON'T HAVE TO! I JUST NEED TO IMAGINE IT!
UM, JOEY, YOU KNOW THAT'S NOT AN ACTUAL PORTAL, RIGHT? IT'S JUST A DRAWING.
THAT'S RIGHT--

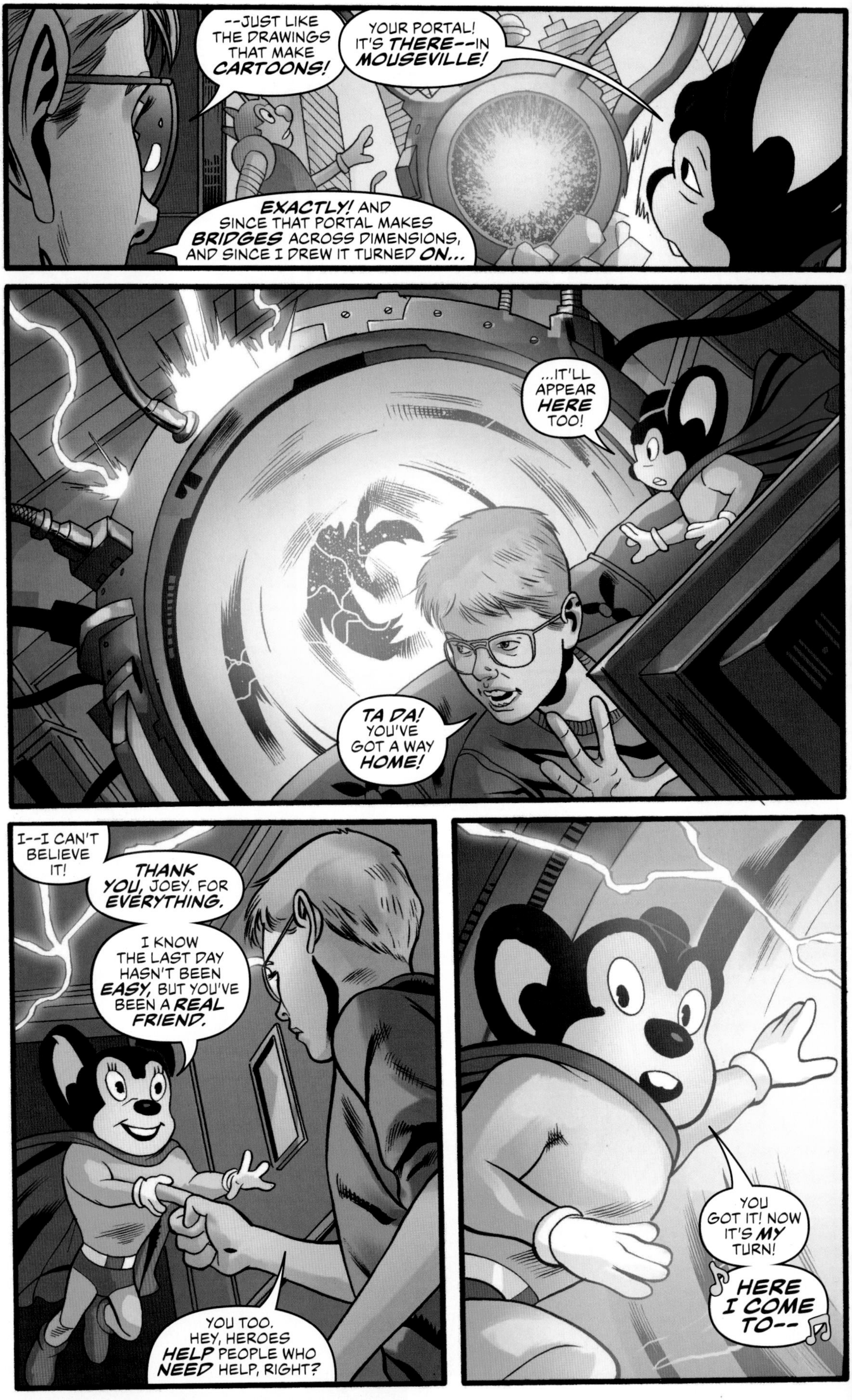
--JUST LIKE THE DRAWINGS THAT MAKE CARTOONS!
YOUR PORTAL! IT'S THERE--IN MOUSEVILLE!
EXACTLY! AND SINCE THAT PORTAL MAKES BRIDGES ACROSS DIMENSIONS, AND SINCE I DREW IT TURNED ON...
...IT'LL APPEAR HERE TOO!
TA DA! YOU'VE GOT A WAY HOME!
I--I CAN'T BELIEVE IT!
THANK YOU, JOEY. FOR EVERYTHING.
I KNOW THE LAST DAY HASN'T BEEN EASY, BUT YOU'VE BEEN A REAL FRIEND.
YOU TOO. HEY, HEROES HELP PEOPLE WHO NEED HELP, RIGHT?
YOU GOT IT! NOW IT'S MY TURN!
HERE I COME TO--

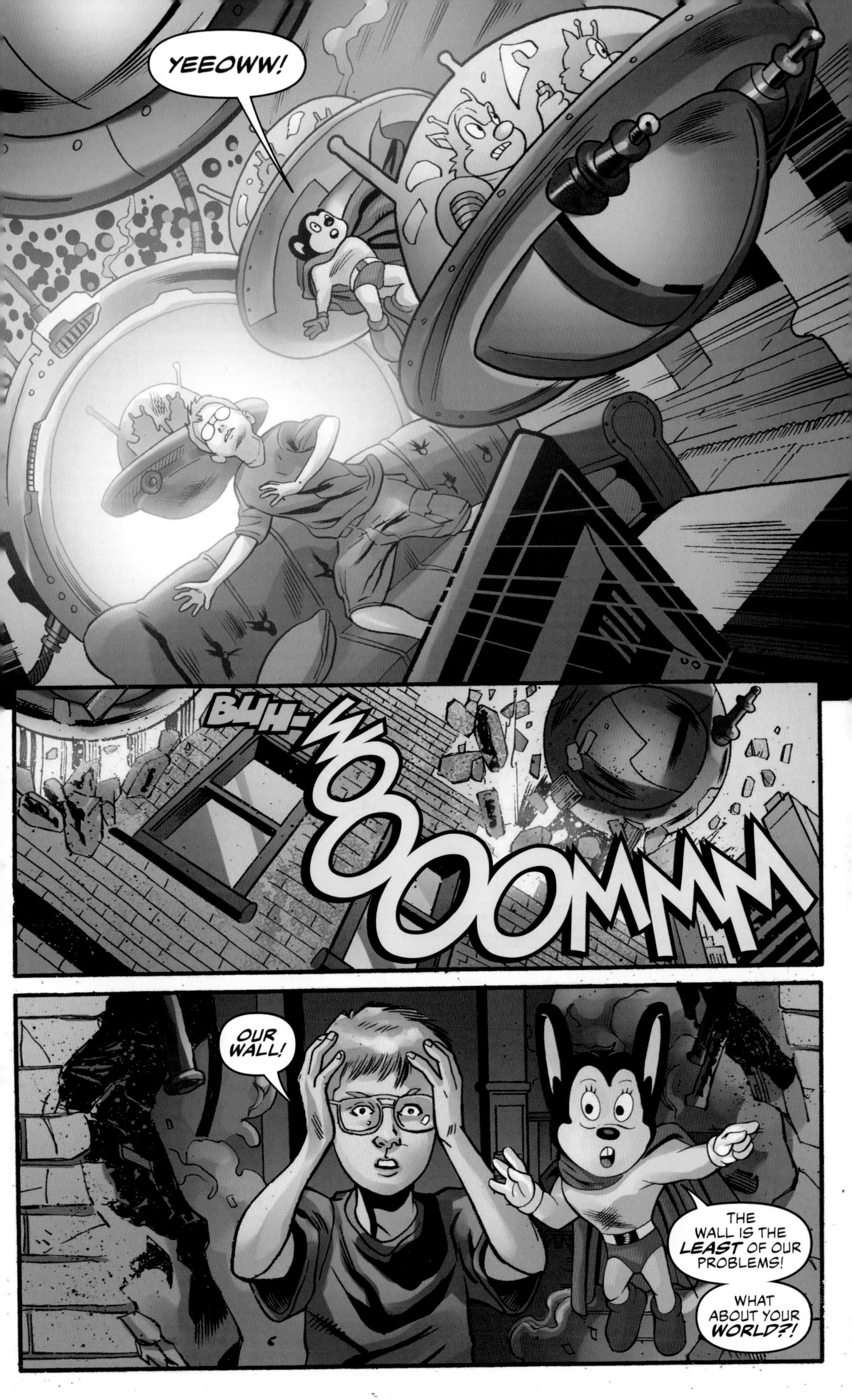
YEEOWW!
BUH-WOOOOMMMM
OUR WALL!
THE WALL IS THE LEAST OF OUR PROBLEMS!
WHAT ABOUT YOUR WORLD?!

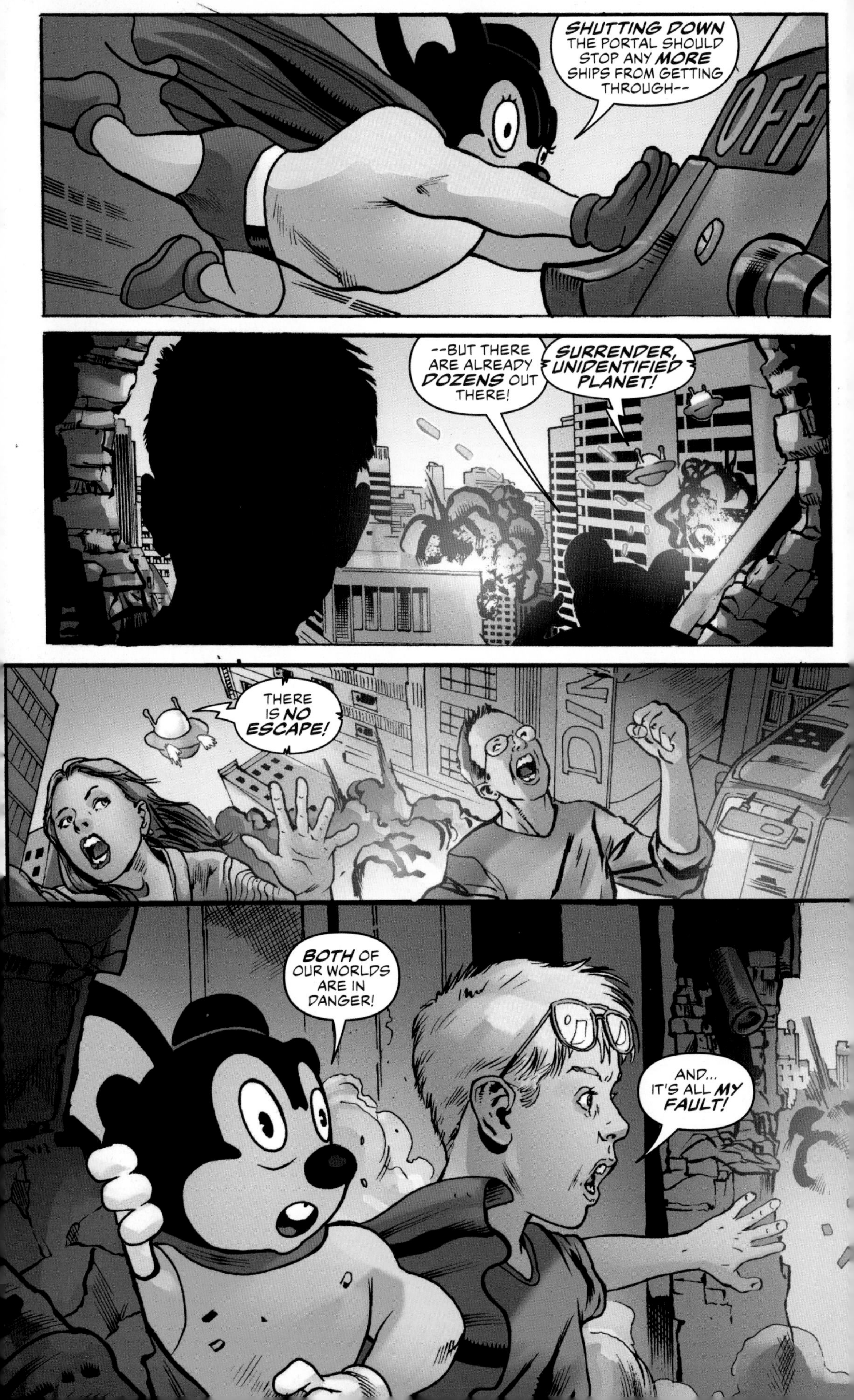
SHUTTING DOWN THE PORTAL SHOULD STOP ANY MORE SHIPS FROM GETTING THROUGH--
OFF
--BUT THERE ARE ALREADY DOZENS OUT THERE!
SURRENDER, UNIDENTIFIED PLANET!
THERE IS NO ESCAPE!
BOTH OF OUR WORLDS ARE IN DANGER!
AND... IT'S ALL MY FAULT!

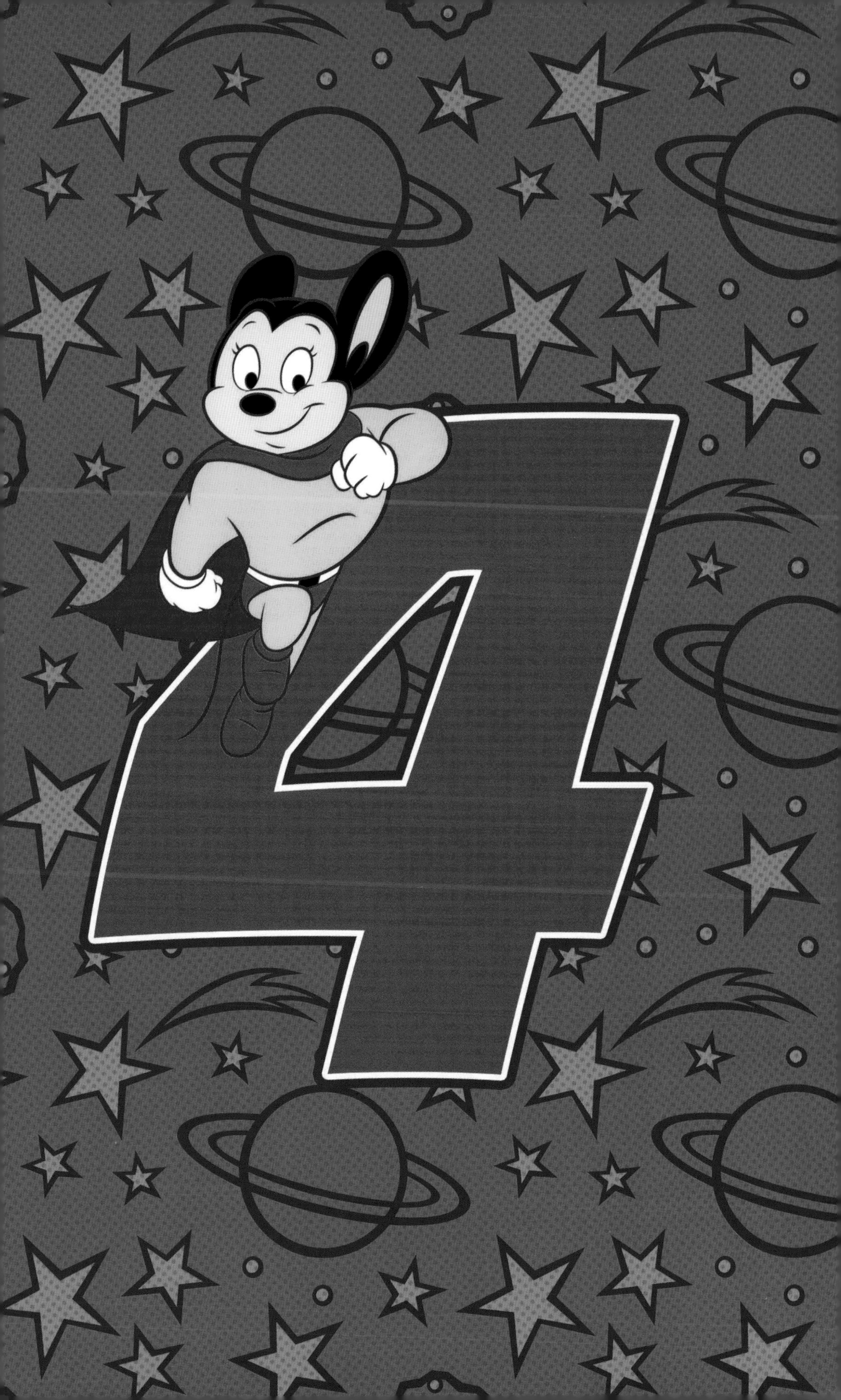

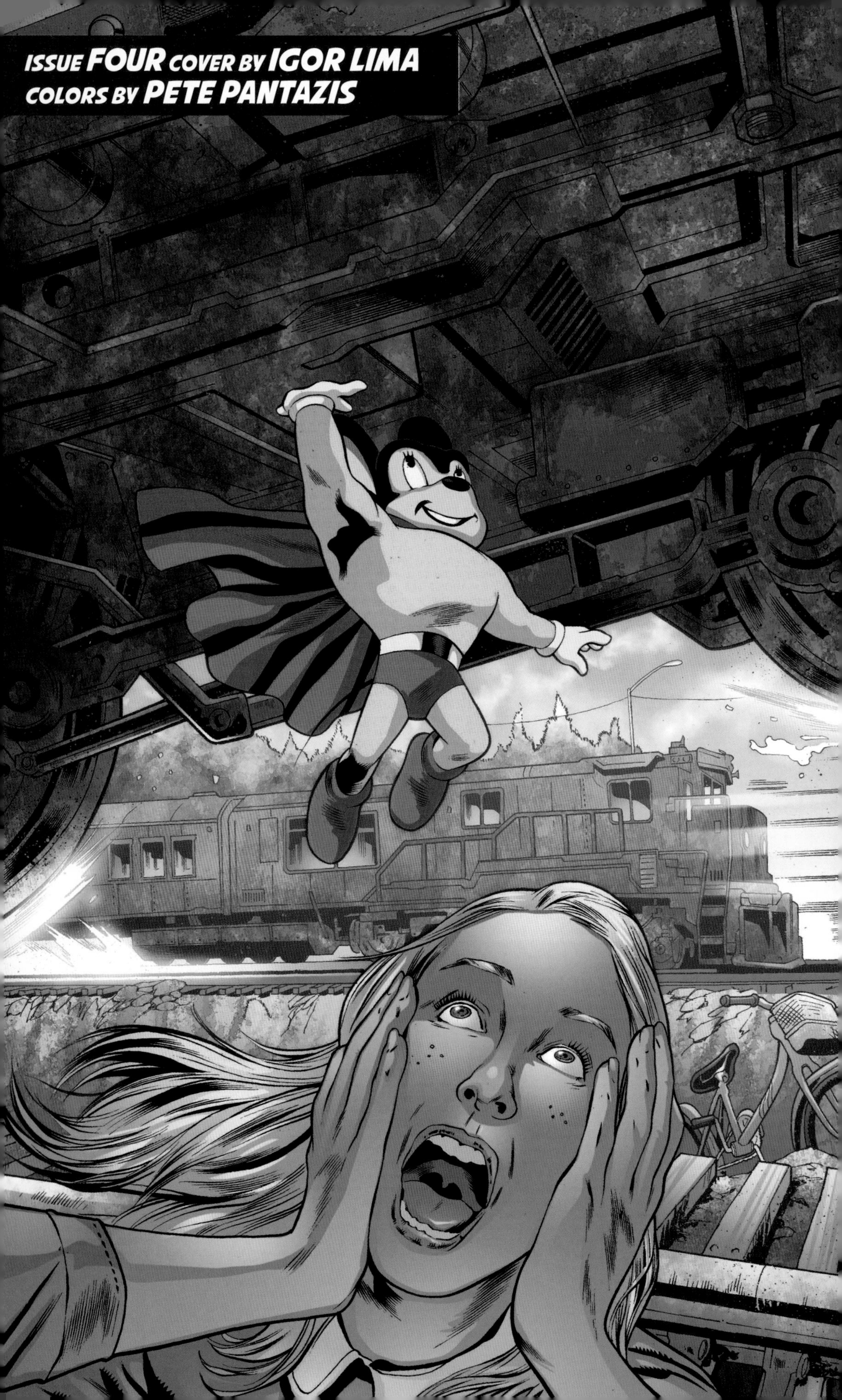

ISSUE FOUR COVER BY IGOR LIMA
COLORS BY PETE PANTAZIS

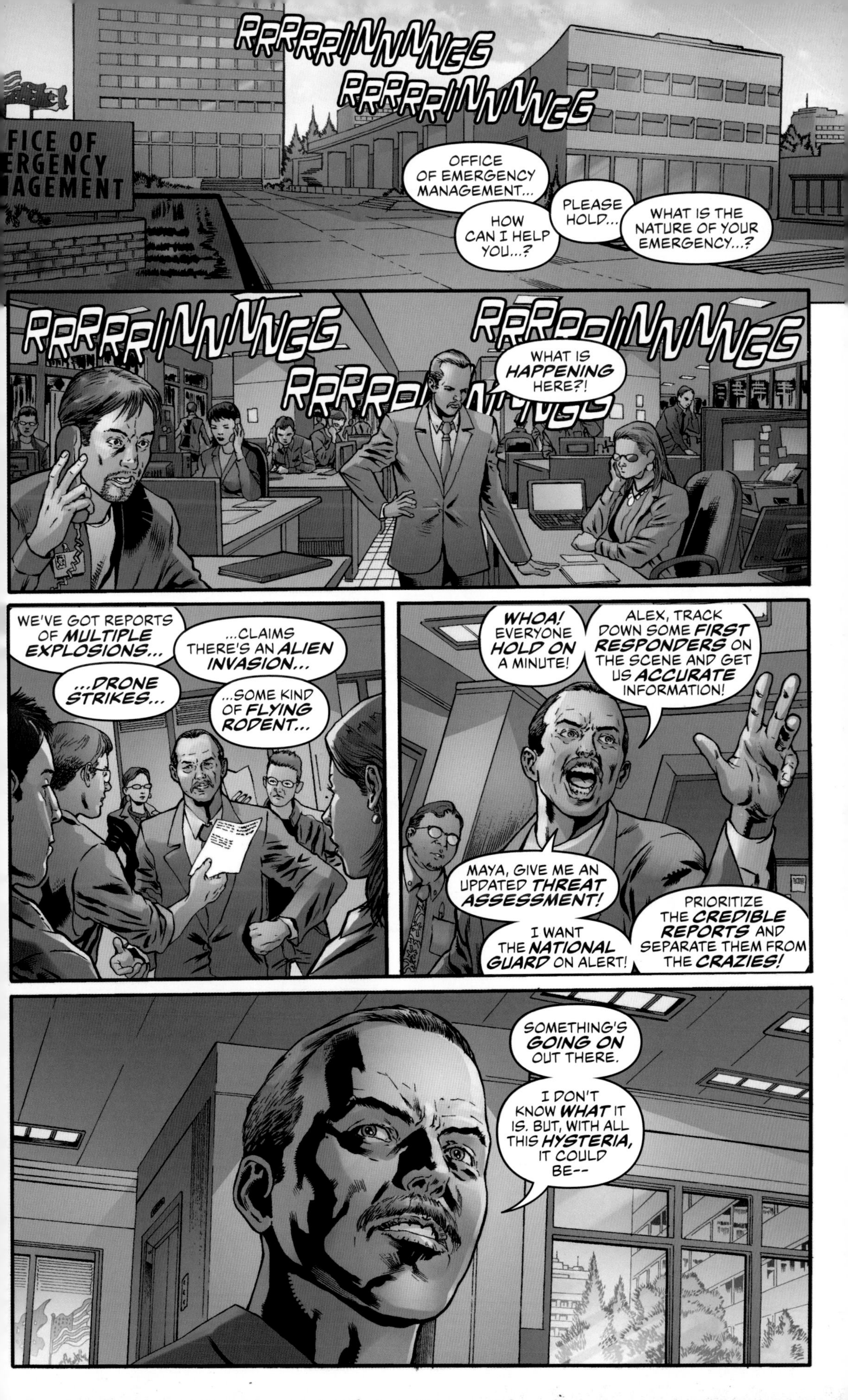
RRRRRINNNNNGG
RRRRRINNNNNGG
FICE OF
ERGENCY
AGEMENT
OFFICE OF EMERGENCY MANAGEMENT...
HOW CAN I HELP YOU...?
PLEASE HOLD...
WHAT IS THE NATURE OF YOUR EMERGENCY...?
RRRRRINNNNNGG
RRRRRINNNNNGG
WHAT IS HAPPENING HERE?!
WE'VE GOT REPORTS OF MULTIPLE EXPLOSIONS...
...DRONE STRIKES...
...CLAIMS THERE'S AN ALIEN INVASION...
...SOME KIND OF FLYING RODENT...
WHOA! EVERYONE HOLD ON A MINUTE!
ALEX, TRACK DOWN SOME FIRST RESPONDERS ON THE SCENE AND GET US ACCURATE INFORMATION!
MAYA, GIVE ME AN UPDATED THREAT ASSESSMENT!
I WANT THE NATIONAL GUARD ON ALERT!
PRIORITIZE THE CREDIBLE REPORTS AND SEPARATE THEM FROM THE CRAZIES!
SOMETHING'S GOING ON OUT THERE.
I DON'T KNOW WHAT IT IS. BUT, WITH ALL THIS HYSTERIA, IT COULD BE--

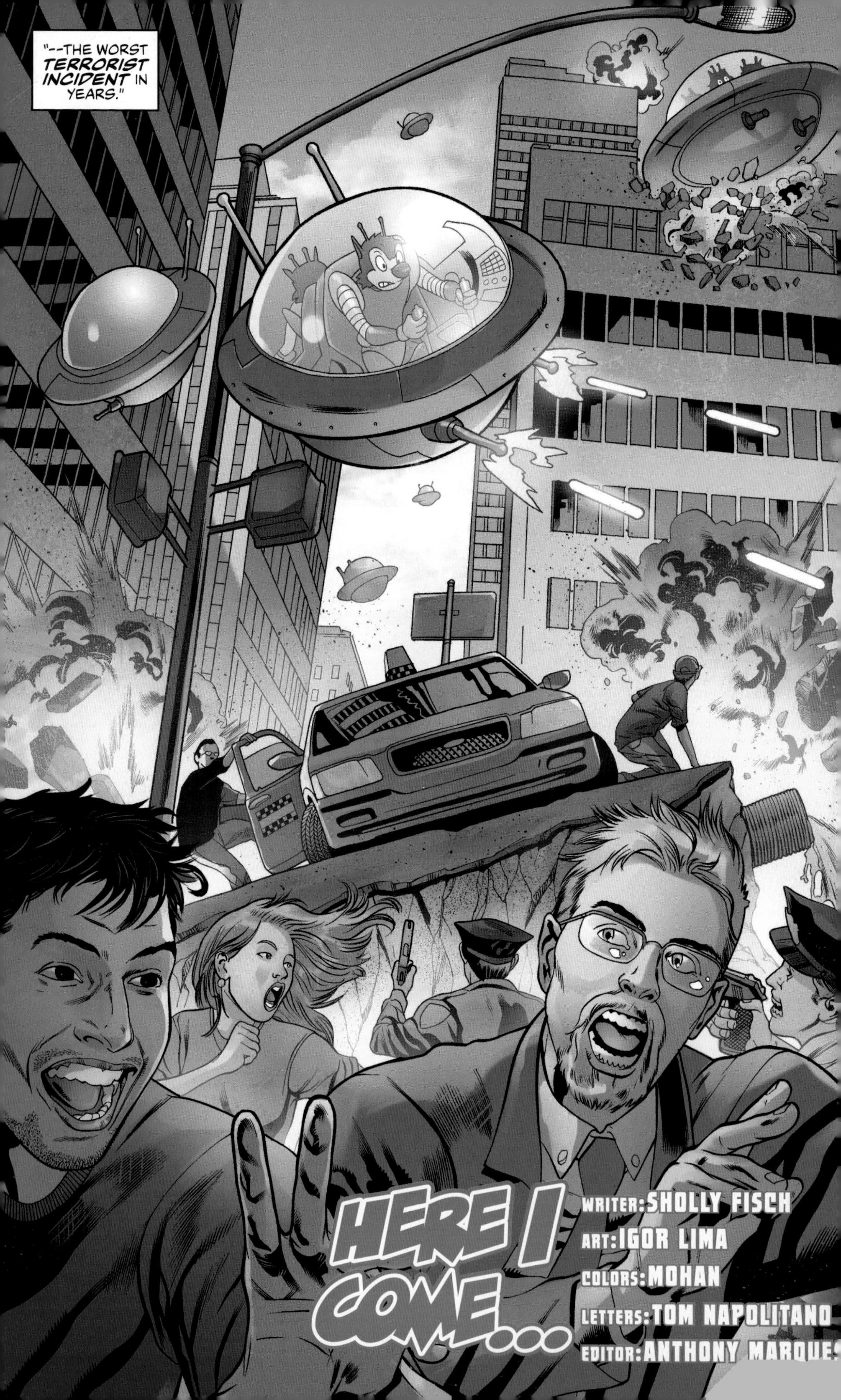

"--THE WORST TERRORIST INCIDENT IN YEARS."
HERE I COME...
WRITER:SHOLLY FISCH
ART:IGOR LIMA
COLORS:MOHAN
LETTERS:TOM NAPOLITANO
EDITOR:ANTHONY MARQUES

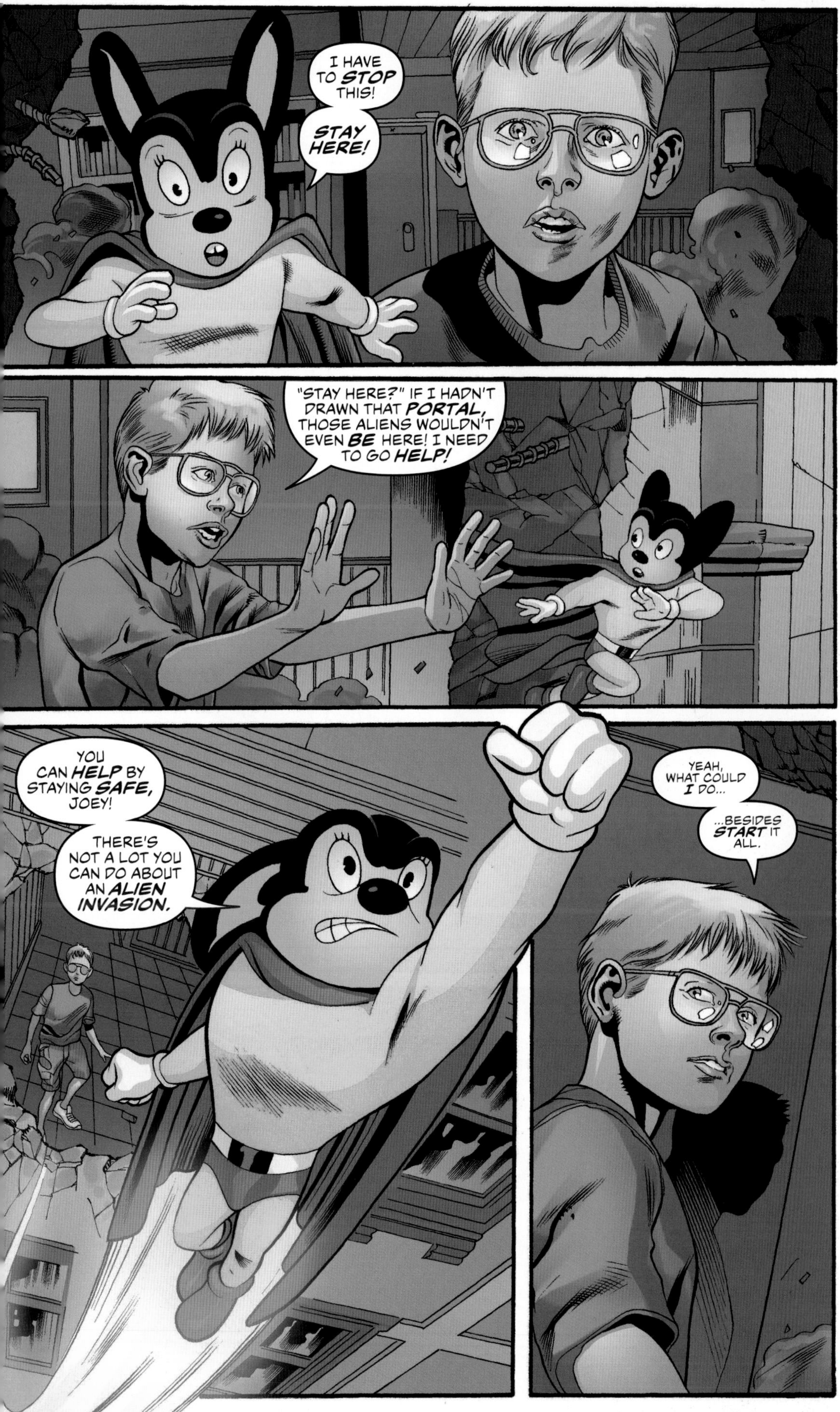
I HAVE TO STOP THIS!
STAY HERE!
"STAY HERE?" IF I HADN'T DRAWN THAT PORTAL, THOSE ALIENS WOULDN'T EVEN BE HERE! I NEED TO GO HELP!
YOU CAN HELP BY STAYING SAFE, JOEY!
THERE'S NOT A LOT YOU CAN DO ABOUT AN ALIEN INVASION.
YEAH, WHAT COULD I DO...
...BESIDES START IT ALL.

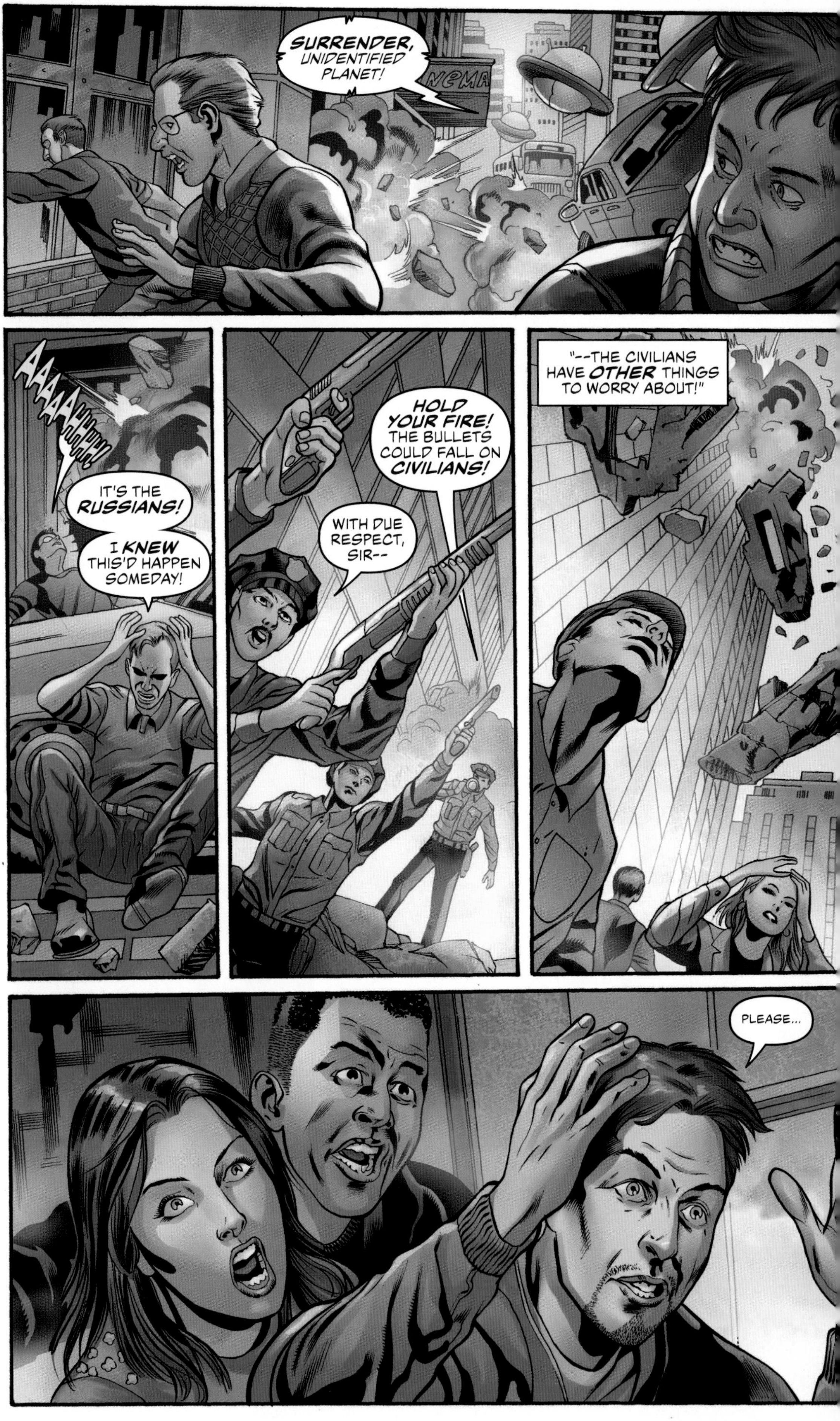
SURRENDER, UNIDENTIFIED PLANET!
NEMA
AAAAAHHH!
IT'S THE RUSSIANS!
I KNEW THIS'D HAPPEN SOMEDAY!
HOLD YOUR FIRE! THE BULLETS COULD FALL ON CIVILIANS!
WITH DUE RESPECT, SIR--
"--THE CIVILIANS HAVE OTHER THINGS TO WORRY ABOUT!"
PLEASE...

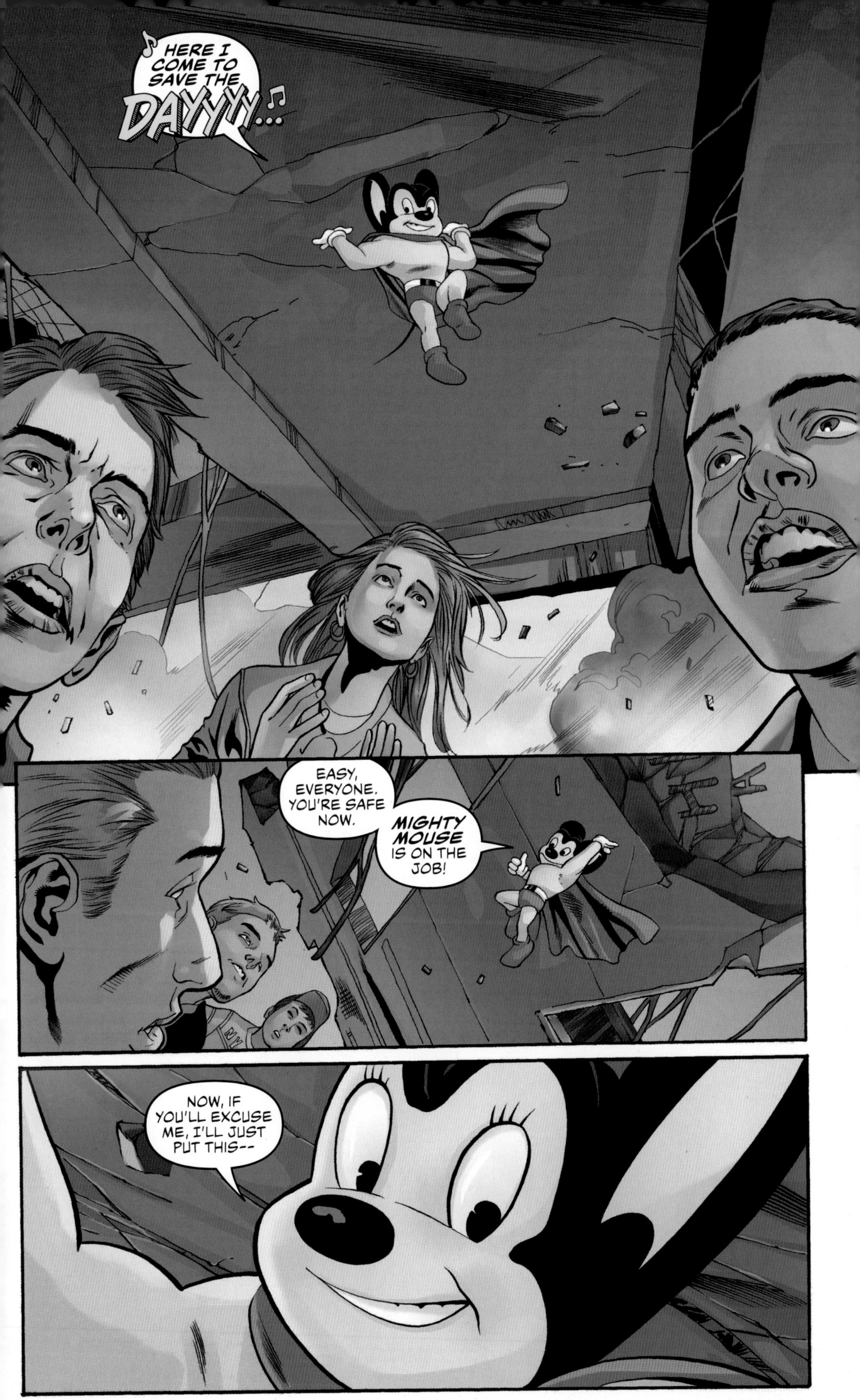

♪ HERE I COME TO SAVE THE DAYYYY... ♪
EASY, EVERYONE. YOU'RE SAFE NOW.
MIGHTY MOUSE IS ON THE JOB!
NOW, IF YOU'LL EXCUSE ME, I'LL JUST PUT THIS--

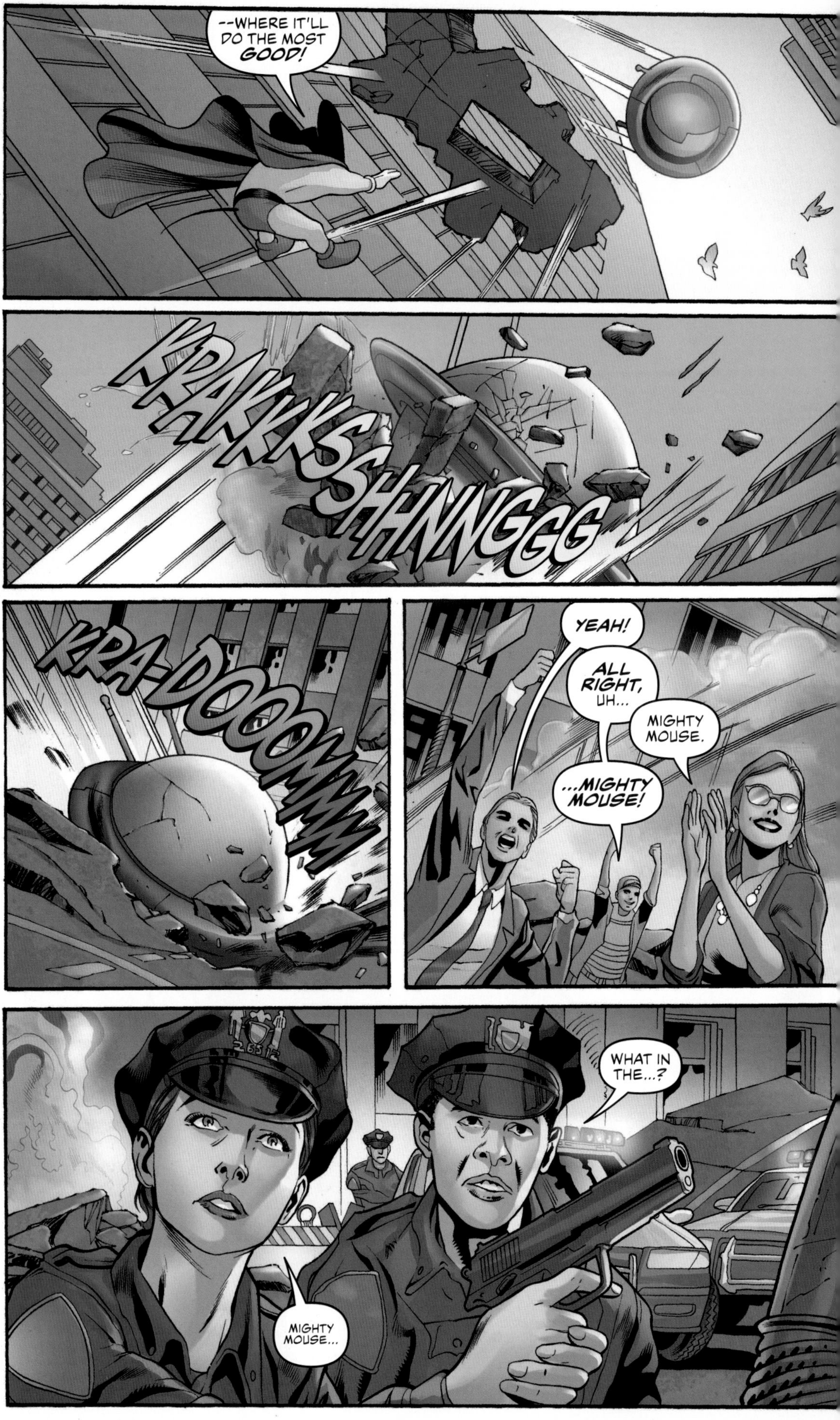
--WHERE IT'LL DO THE MOST GOOD!
KRAKKKSHHNNGGG
KRA-DOOOOMMM
YEAH!
ALL RIGHT, UH...
MIGHTY MOUSE.
...MIGHTY MOUSE!
WHAT IN THE...?
MIGHTY MOUSE...

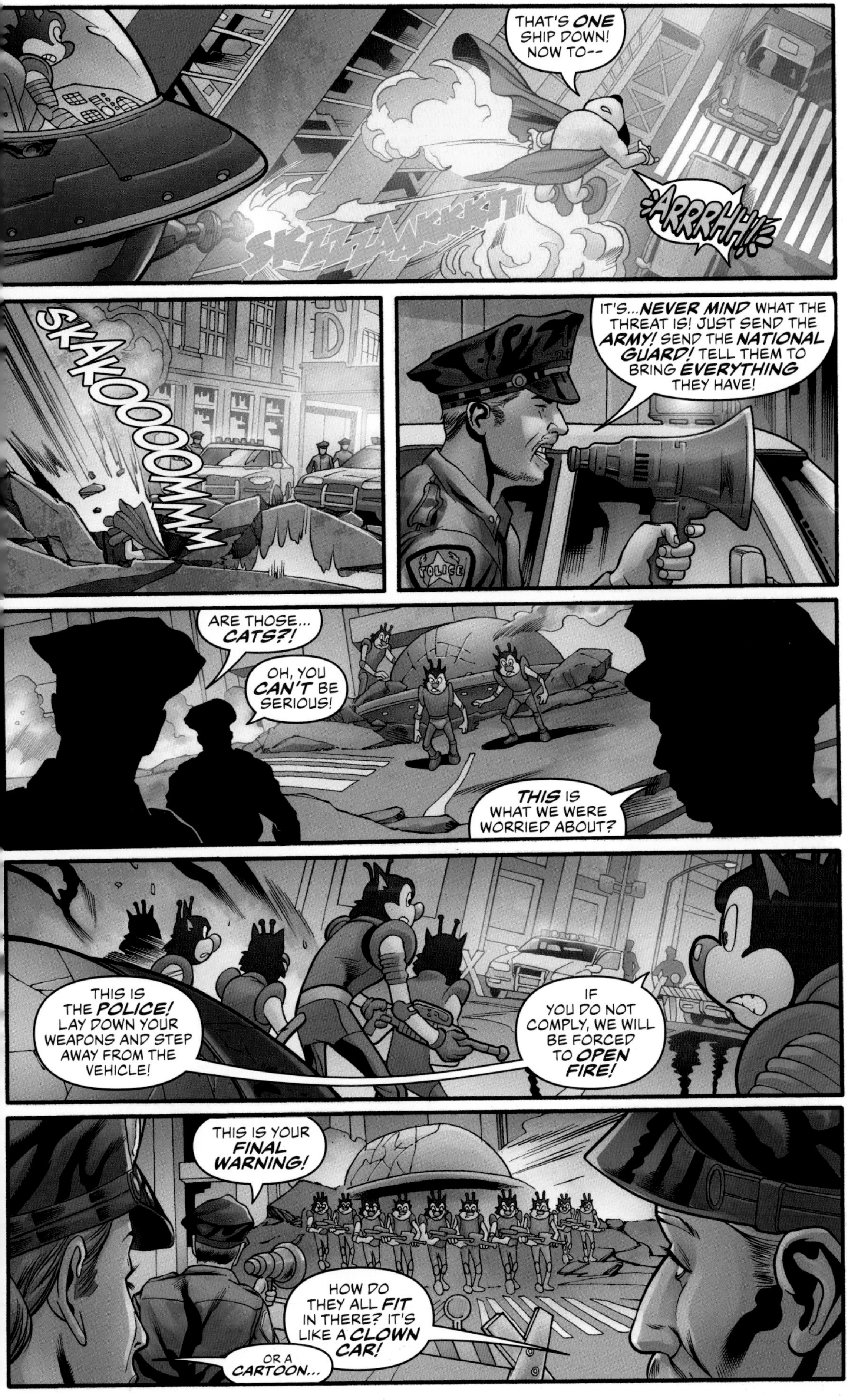

THAT'S ONE SHIP DOWN! NOW TO--
SKIZZZAAKKKTT
ARRRHH!!
SKAKOOOOOMMM
IT'S...NEVER MIND WHAT THE THREAT IS! JUST SEND THE ARMY! SEND THE NATIONAL GUARD! TELL THEM TO BRING EVERYTHING THEY HAVE!
POLICE
ARE THOSE... CATS?!
OH, YOU CAN'T BE SERIOUS!
THIS IS WHAT WE WERE WORRIED ABOUT?
THIS IS THE POLICE! LAY DOWN YOUR WEAPONS AND STEP AWAY FROM THE VEHICLE!
IF YOU DO NOT COMPLY, WE WILL BE FORCED TO OPEN FIRE!
THIS IS YOUR FINAL WARNING!
HOW DO THEY ALL FIT IN THERE? IT'S LIKE A CLOWN CAR!
OR A CARTOON...

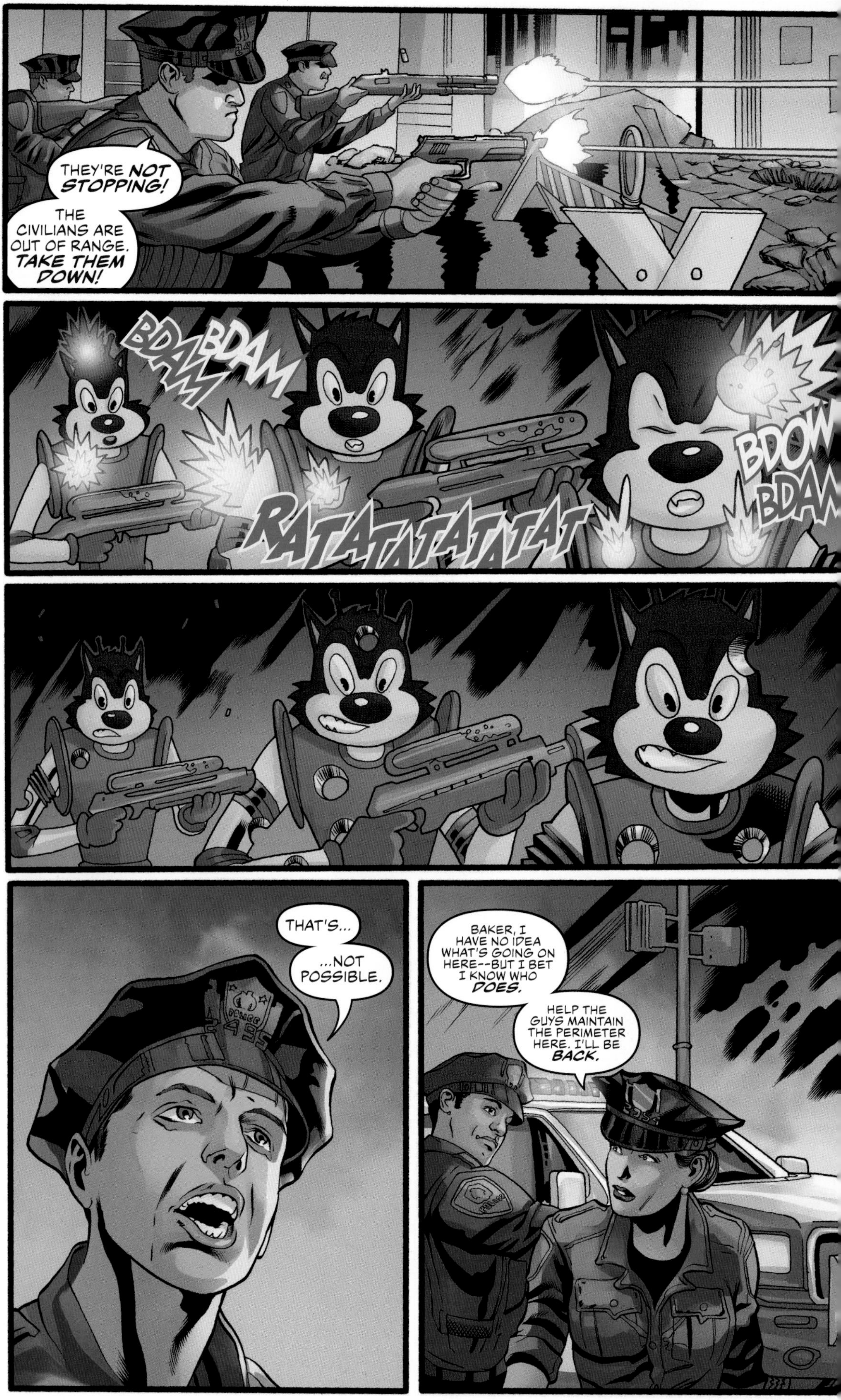
THEY'RE NOT STOPPING!
THE CIVILIANS ARE OUT OF RANGE. TAKE THEM DOWN!
BDAM BDAM
RATATATATATAT
BDOW
BDAM
THAT'S...
...NOT POSSIBLE.
BAKER, I HAVE NO IDEA WHAT'S GOING ON HERE--BUT I BET I KNOW WHO DOES.
HELP THE GUYS MAINTAIN THE PERIMETER HERE. I'LL BE BACK.

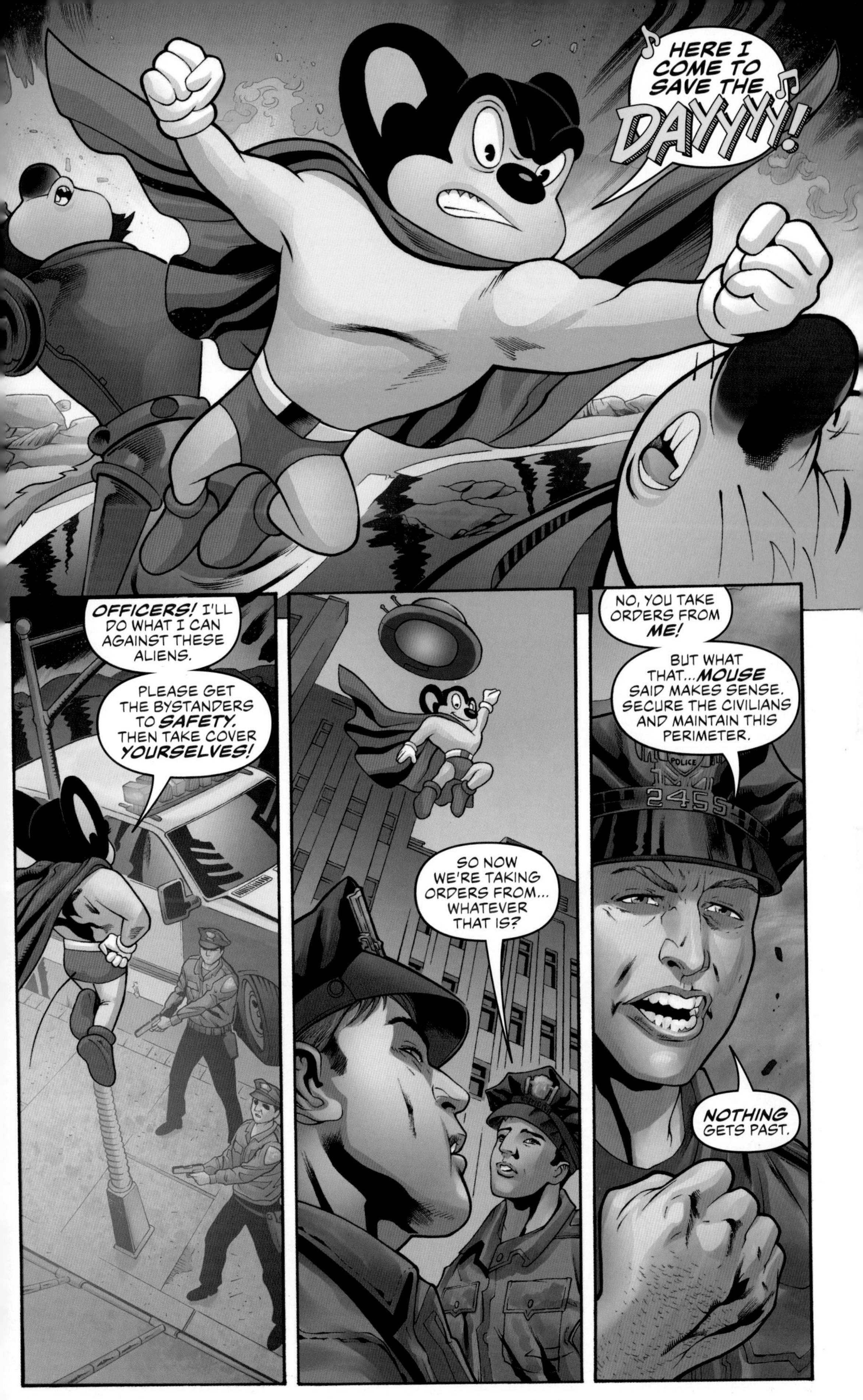

HERE I COME TO SAVE THE DAYYY!
OFFICERS! I'LL DO WHAT I CAN AGAINST THESE ALIENS.
PLEASE GET THE BYSTANDERS TO SAFETY. THEN TAKE COVER YOURSELVES!
SO NOW WE'RE TAKING ORDERS FROM... WHATEVER THAT IS?
NO, YOU TAKE ORDERS FROM ME!
BUT WHAT THAT...MOUSE SAID MAKES SENSE. SECURE THE CIVILIANS AND MAINTAIN THIS PERIMETER.
POLICE
2455
NOTHING GETS PAST.

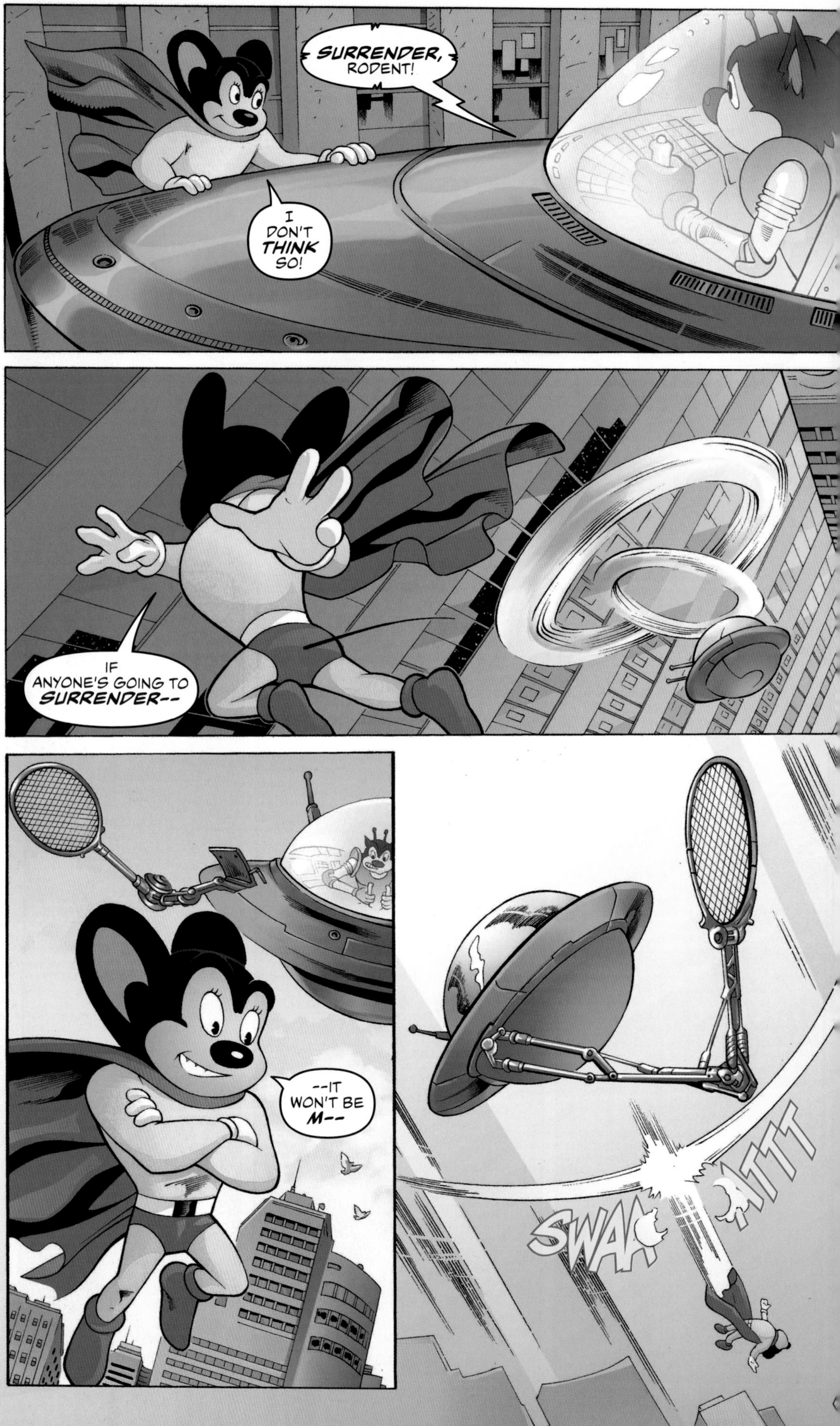

SURRENDER, RODENT!
I DON'T THINK SO!
IF ANYONE'S GOING TO SURRENDER--
--IT WON'T BE M--
SWAAATTT

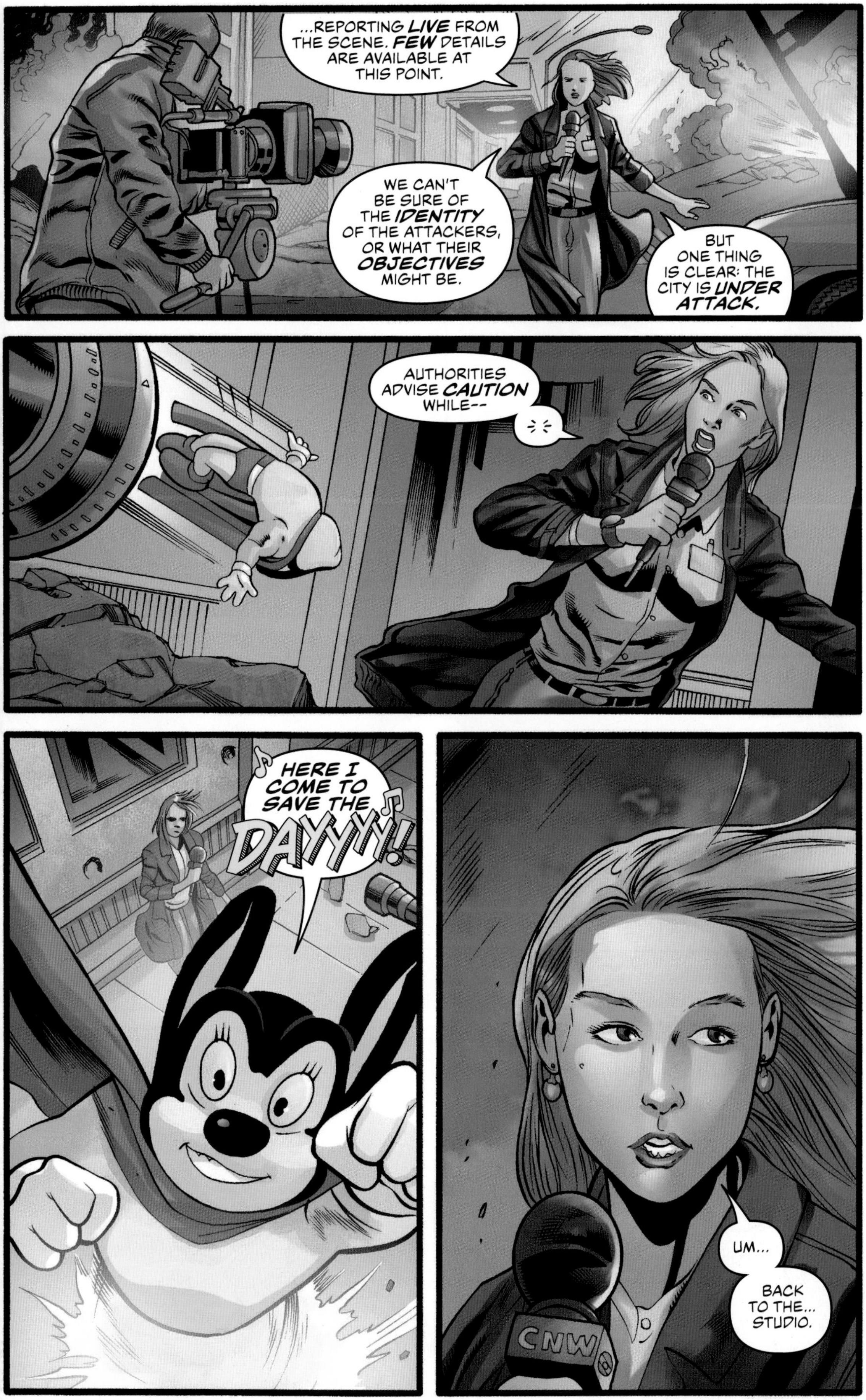
...REPORTING LIVE FROM THE SCENE. FEW DETAILS ARE AVAILABLE AT THIS POINT.
WE CAN'T BE SURE OF THE IDENTITY OF THE ATTACKERS, OR WHAT THEIR OBJECTIVES MIGHT BE.
BUT ONE THING IS CLEAR: THE CITY IS UNDER ATTACK.
AUTHORITIES ADVISE CAUTION WHILE--
HERE I COME TO SAVE THE DAYYYY!
UM...
BACK TO THE... STUDIO.
CNW

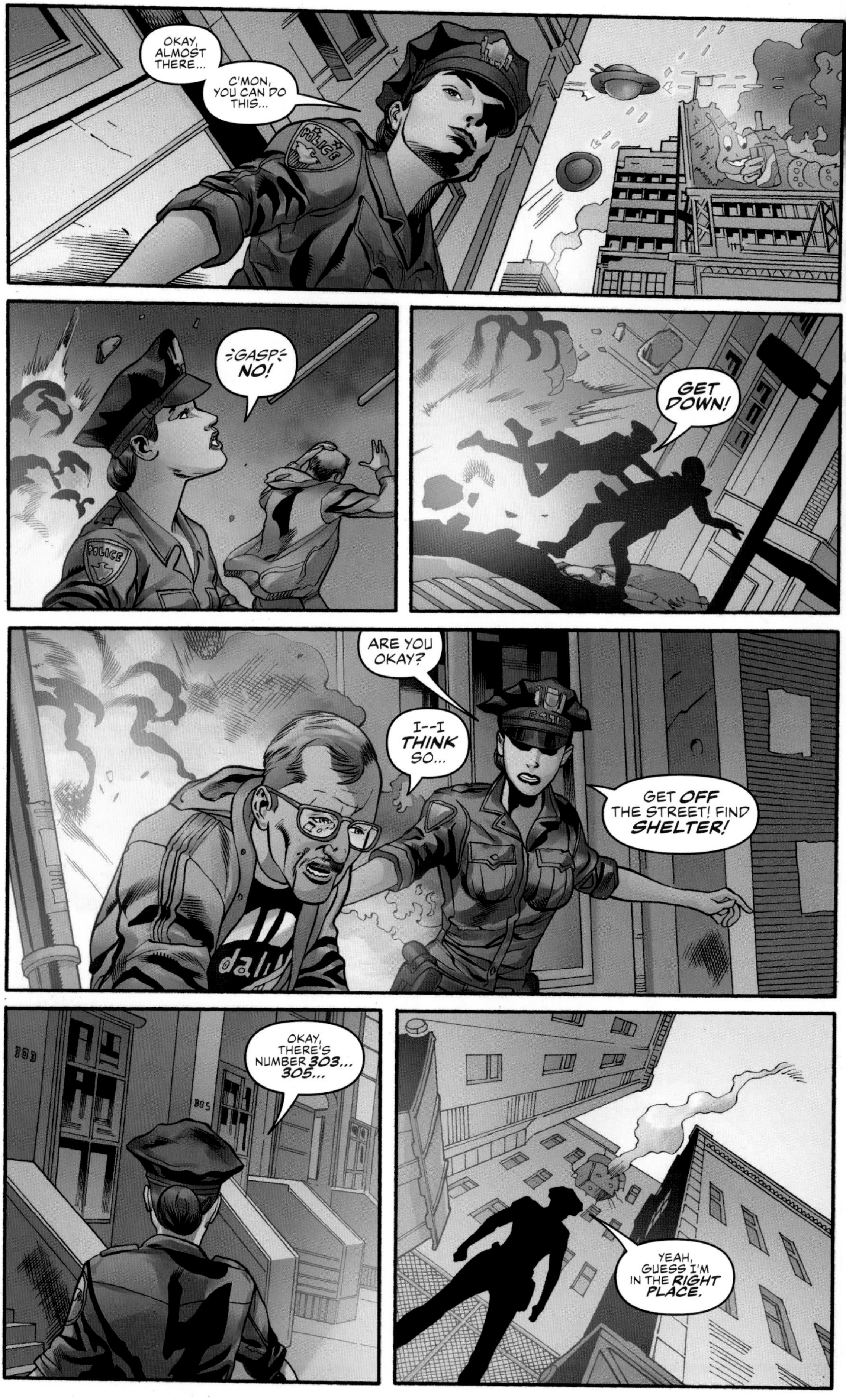

OKAY, ALMOST THERE...
C'MON, YOU CAN DO THIS...
GASP NO!
GET DOWN!
ARE YOU OKAY?
I--I THINK SO...
GET OFF THE STREET! FIND SHELTER!
OKAY, THERE'S NUMBER 303... 305...
YEAH, GUESS I'M IN THE RIGHT PLACE.

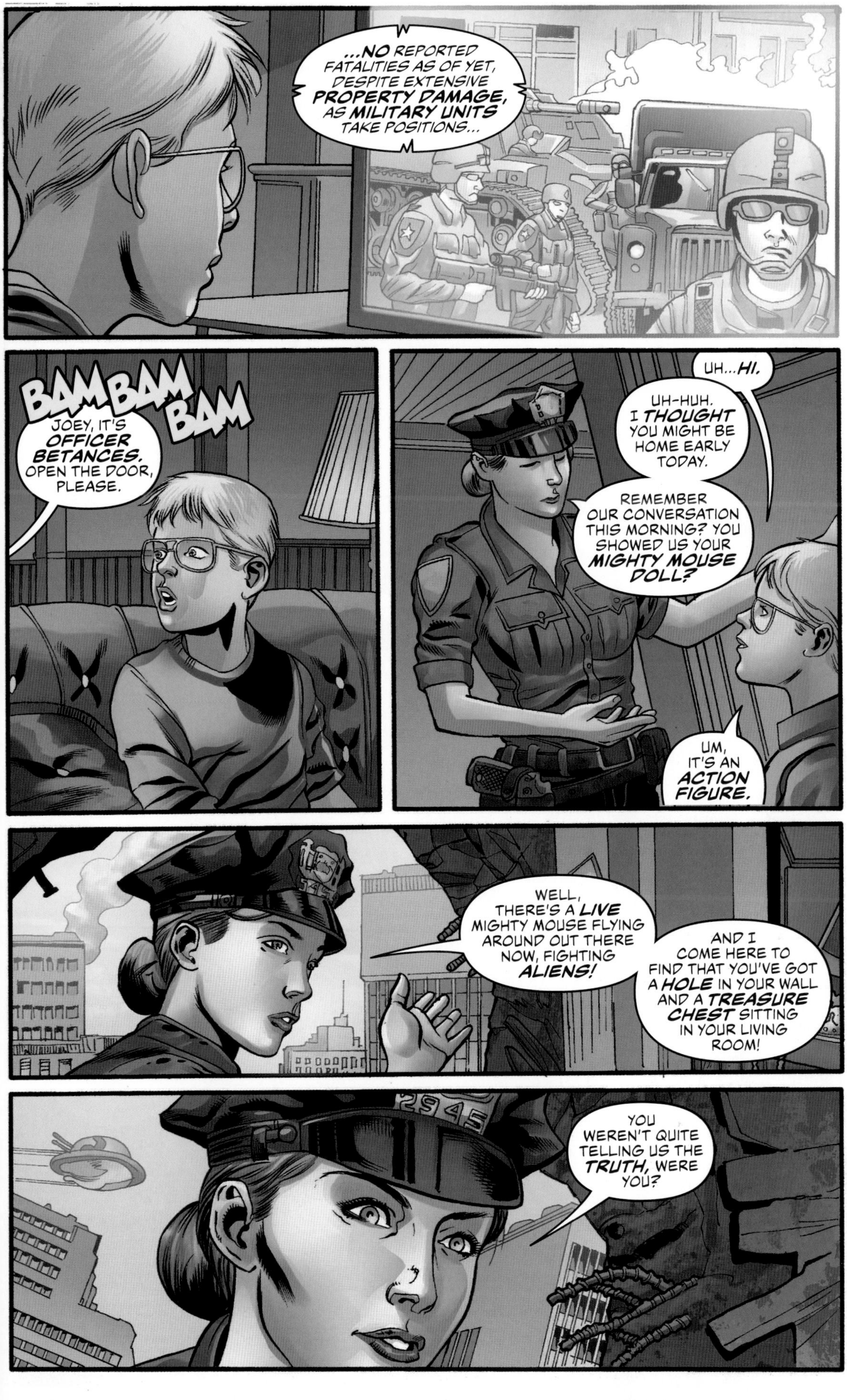

...NO REPORTED FATALITIES AS OF YET, DESPITE EXTENSIVE PROPERTY DAMAGE, AS MILITARY UNITS TAKE POSITIONS...
BAM BAM BAM
JOEY, IT'S OFFICER BETANCES. OPEN THE DOOR, PLEASE.
UH...HI.
UH-HUH. I THOUGHT YOU MIGHT BE HOME EARLY TODAY.
REMEMBER OUR CONVERSATION THIS MORNING? YOU SHOWED US YOUR MIGHTY MOUSE DOLL?
UM, IT'S AN ACTION FIGURE.
WELL, THERE'S A LIVE MIGHTY MOUSE FLYING AROUND OUT THERE NOW, FIGHTING ALIENS!
AND I COME HERE TO FIND THAT YOU'VE GOT A HOLE IN YOUR WALL AND A TREASURE CHEST SITTING IN YOUR LIVING ROOM!
YOU WEREN'T QUITE TELLING US THE TRUTH, WERE YOU?

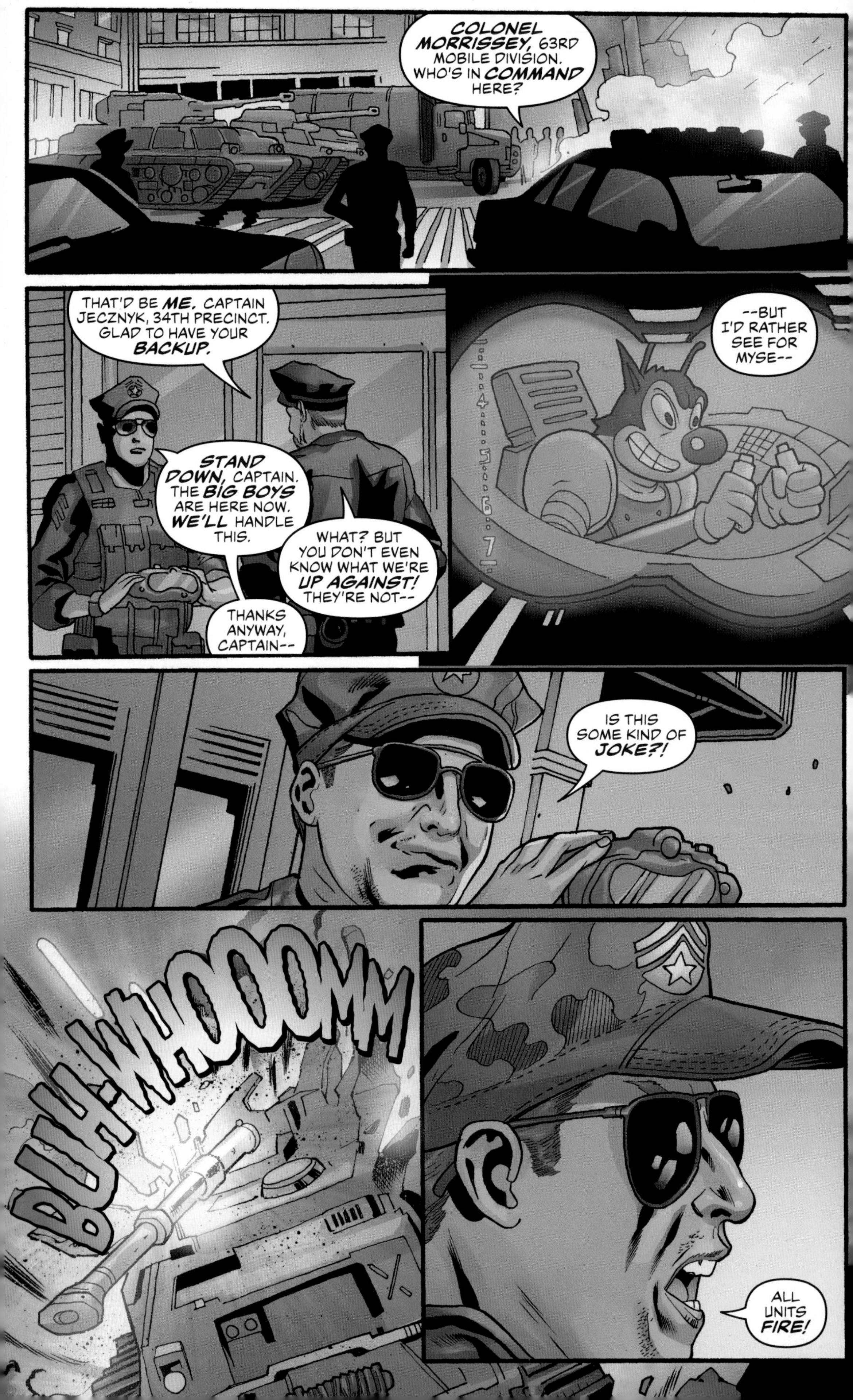
COLONEL MORRISSEY, 63RD MOBILE DIVISION. WHO'S IN COMMAND HERE?
THAT'D BE ME. CAPTAIN JECZNYK, 34TH PRECINCT. GLAD TO HAVE YOUR BACKUP.
STAND DOWN, CAPTAIN. THE BIG BOYS ARE HERE NOW. WE'LL HANDLE THIS.
WHAT? BUT YOU DON'T EVEN KNOW WHAT WE'RE UP AGAINST! THEY'RE NOT--
THANKS ANYWAY, CAPTAIN--
--BUT I'D RATHER SEE FOR MYSE--
4
5
6
7
IS THIS SOME KIND OF JOKE?!
BUHWHOOOMM
ALL UNITS FIRE!

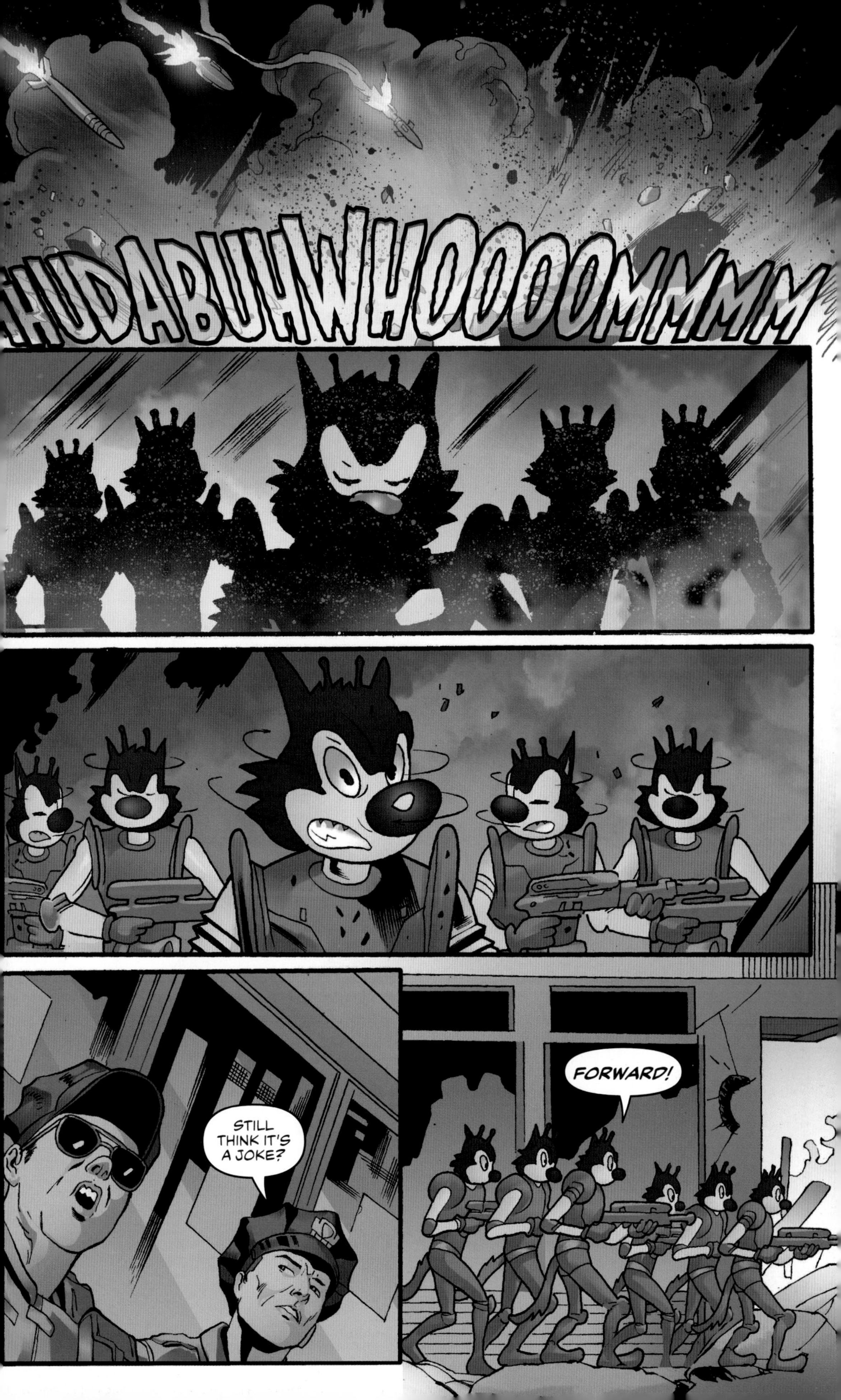
HUDABUHWHOOOOMMMM
STILL THINK IT'S A JOKE?
FORWARD!

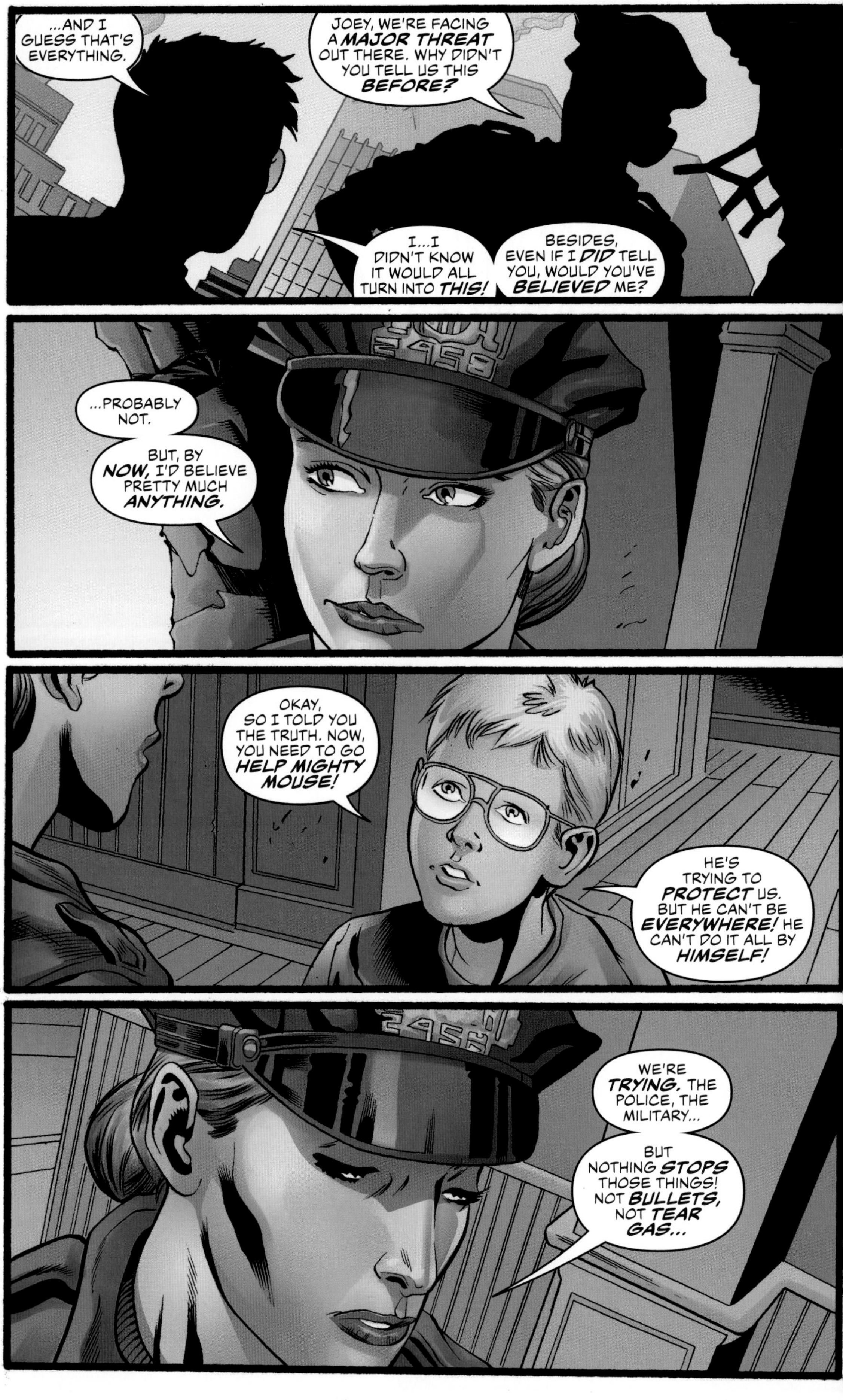
...AND I GUESS THAT'S EVERYTHING.
JOEY, WE'RE FACING A MAJOR THREAT OUT THERE. WHY DIDN'T YOU TELL US THIS BEFORE?
I...I DIDN'T KNOW IT WOULD ALL TURN INTO THIS!
BESIDES, EVEN IF I DID TELL YOU, WOULD YOU'VE BELIEVED ME?
...PROBABLY NOT.
BUT, BY NOW, I'D BELIEVE PRETTY MUCH ANYTHING.
OKAY, SO I TOLD YOU THE TRUTH. NOW, YOU NEED TO GO HELP MIGHTY MOUSE!
HE'S TRYING TO PROTECT US. BUT HE CAN'T BE EVERYWHERE! HE CAN'T DO IT ALL BY HIMSELF!
WE'RE TRYING. THE POLICE, THE MILITARY...
BUT NOTHING STOPS THOSE THINGS! NOT BULLETS, NOT TEAR GAS...

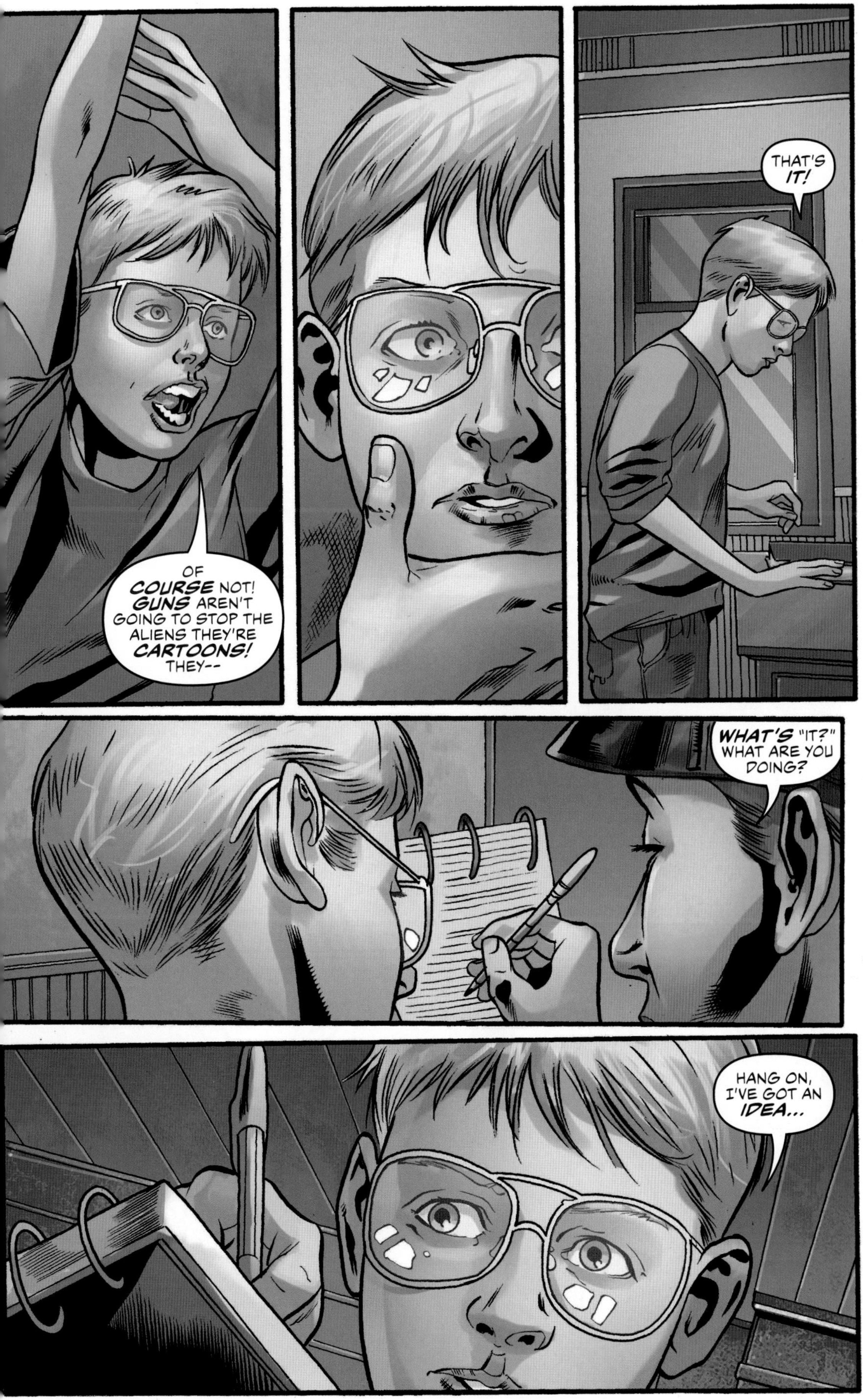
OF COURSE NOT! GUNS AREN'T GOING TO STOP THE ALIENS THEY'RE CARTOONS! THEY--
THAT'S IT!
WHAT'S "IT?" WHAT ARE YOU DOING?
HANG ON, I'VE GOT AN IDEA...

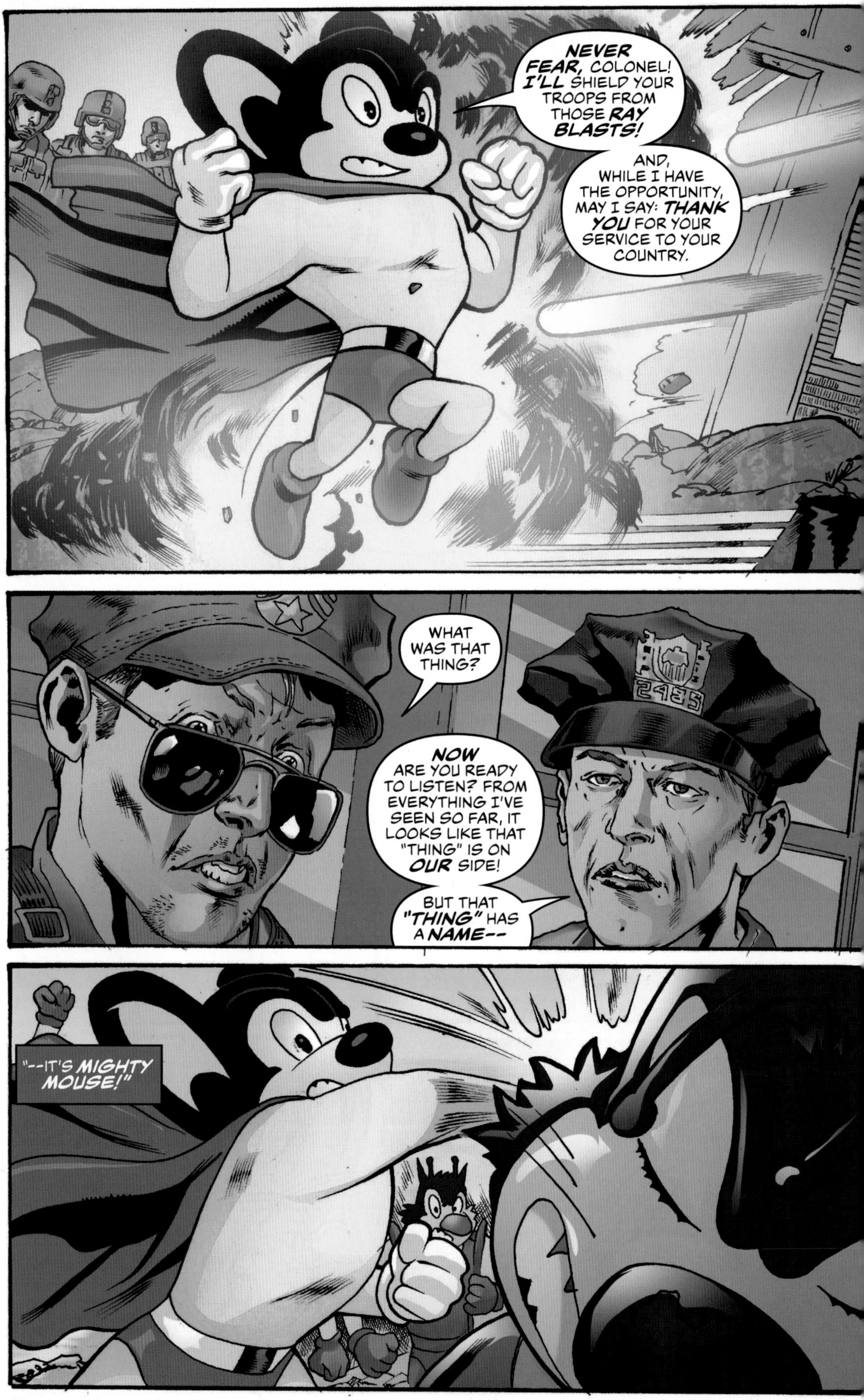

NEVER FEAR, COLONEL! I'LL SHIELD YOUR TROOPS FROM THOSE RAY BLASTS!
AND, WHILE I HAVE THE OPPORTUNITY, MAY I SAY: THANK YOU FOR YOUR SERVICE TO YOUR COUNTRY.
WHAT WAS THAT THING?
2485
NOW ARE YOU READY TO LISTEN? FROM EVERYTHING I'VE SEEN SO FAR, IT LOOKS LIKE THAT "THING" IS ON OUR SIDE!
BUT THAT "THING" HAS A NAME--
"--IT'S MIGHTY MOUSE!"

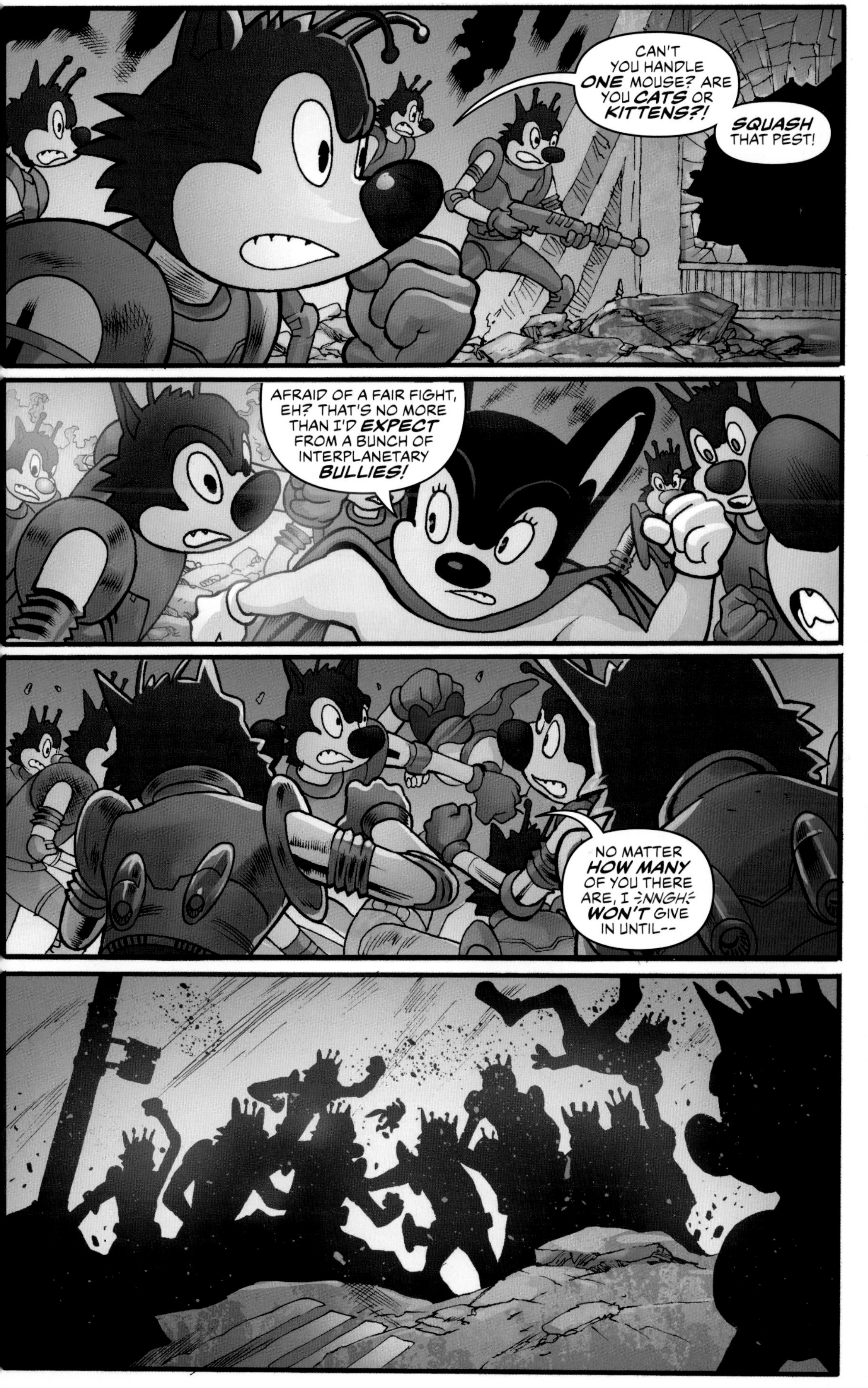
CAN'T YOU HANDLE ONE MOUSE? ARE YOU CATS OR KITTENS?!
SQUASH THAT PEST!
AFRAID OF A FAIR FIGHT, EH? THAT'S NO MORE THAN I'D EXPECT FROM A BUNCH OF INTERPLANETARY BULLIES!
NO MATTER HOW MANY OF YOU THERE ARE, I ≈NNGH≈ WON'T GIVE IN UNTIL--

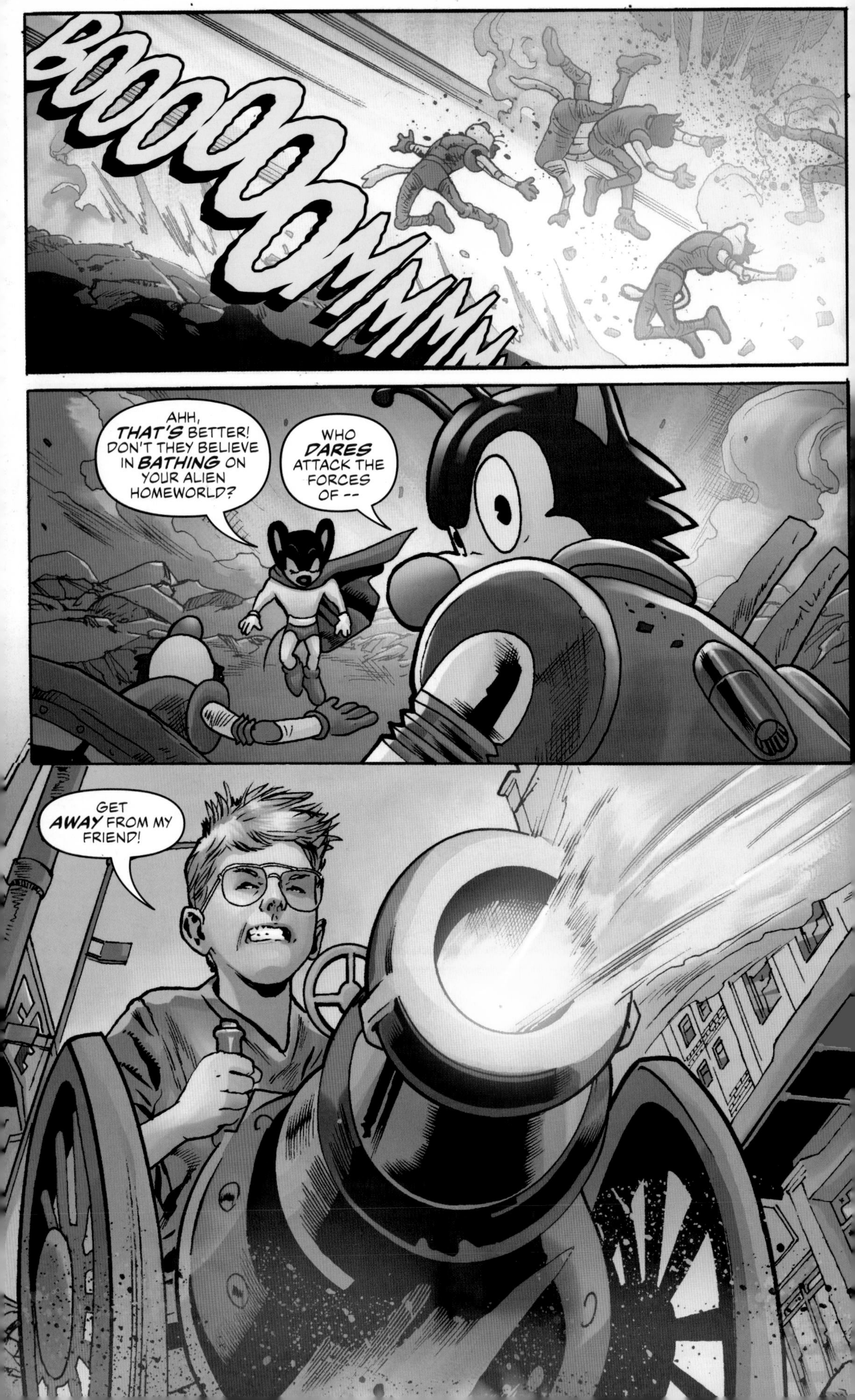
BOOOOOOMMMM
AHH, THAT'S BETTER! DON'T THEY BELIEVE IN BATHING ON YOUR ALIEN HOMEWORLD?
WHO DARES ATTACK THE FORCES OF --
GET AWAY FROM MY FRIEND!

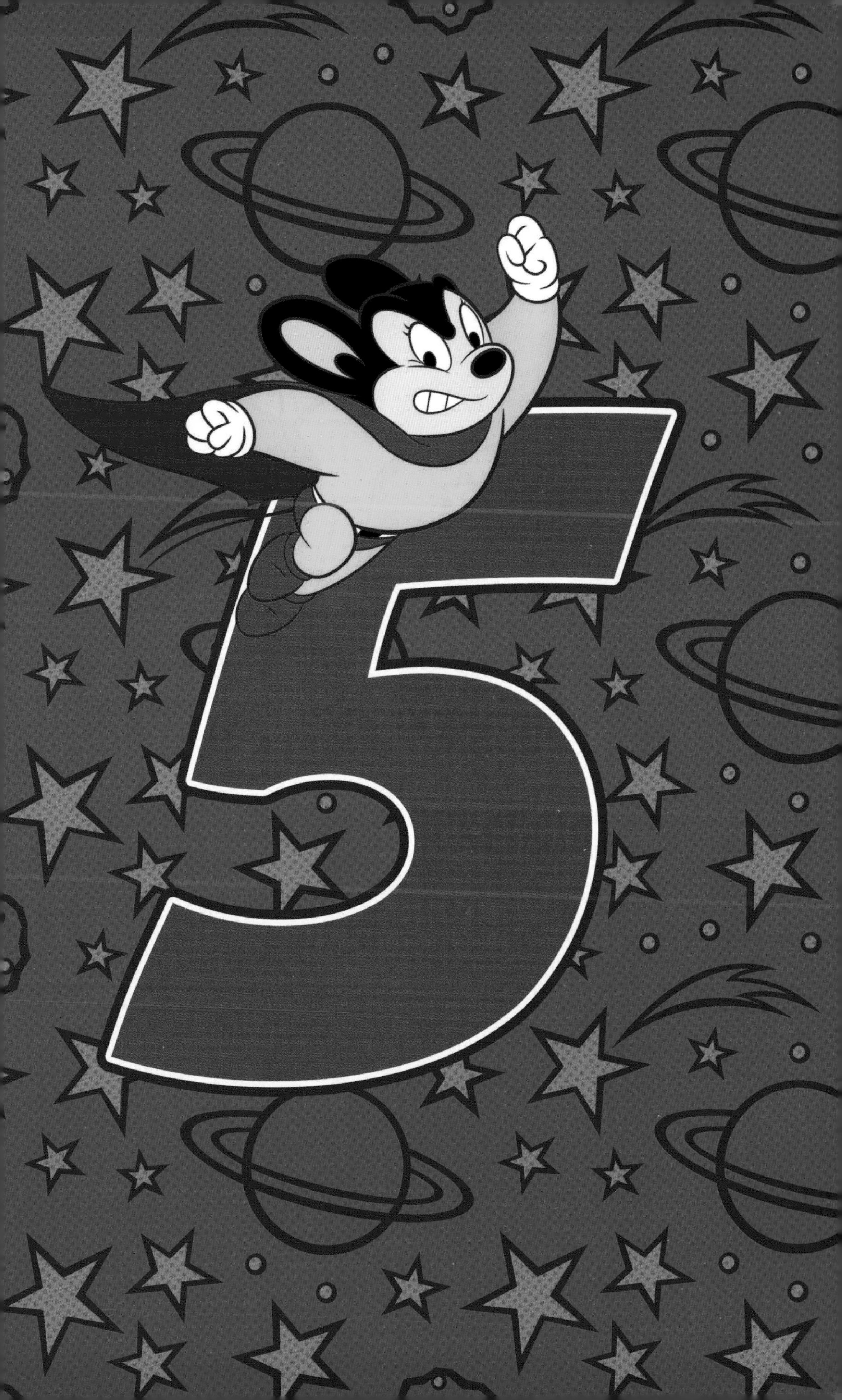
5

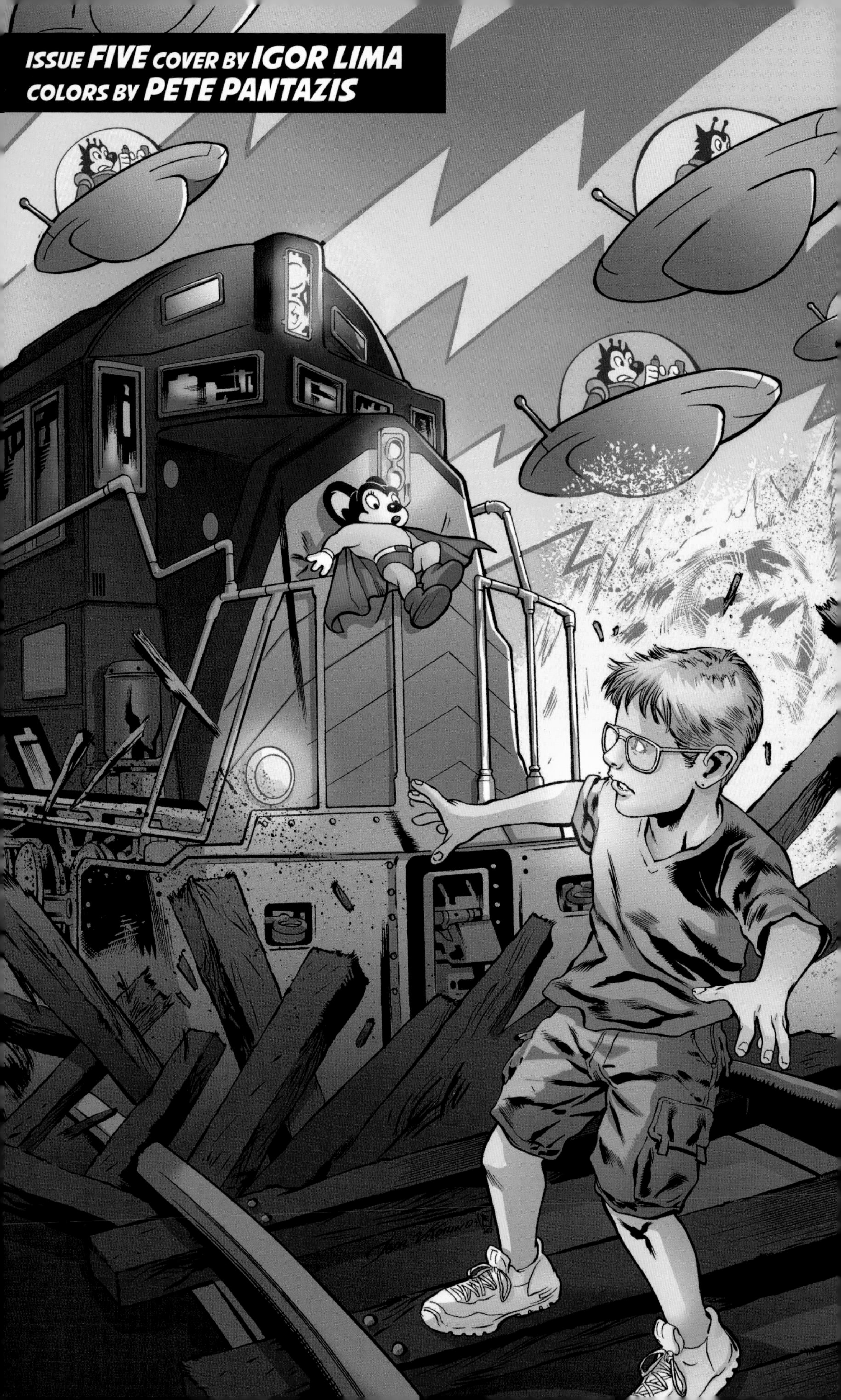

ISSUE FIVE COVER BY **IGOR LIMA**
COLORS BY **PETE PANTAZIS**

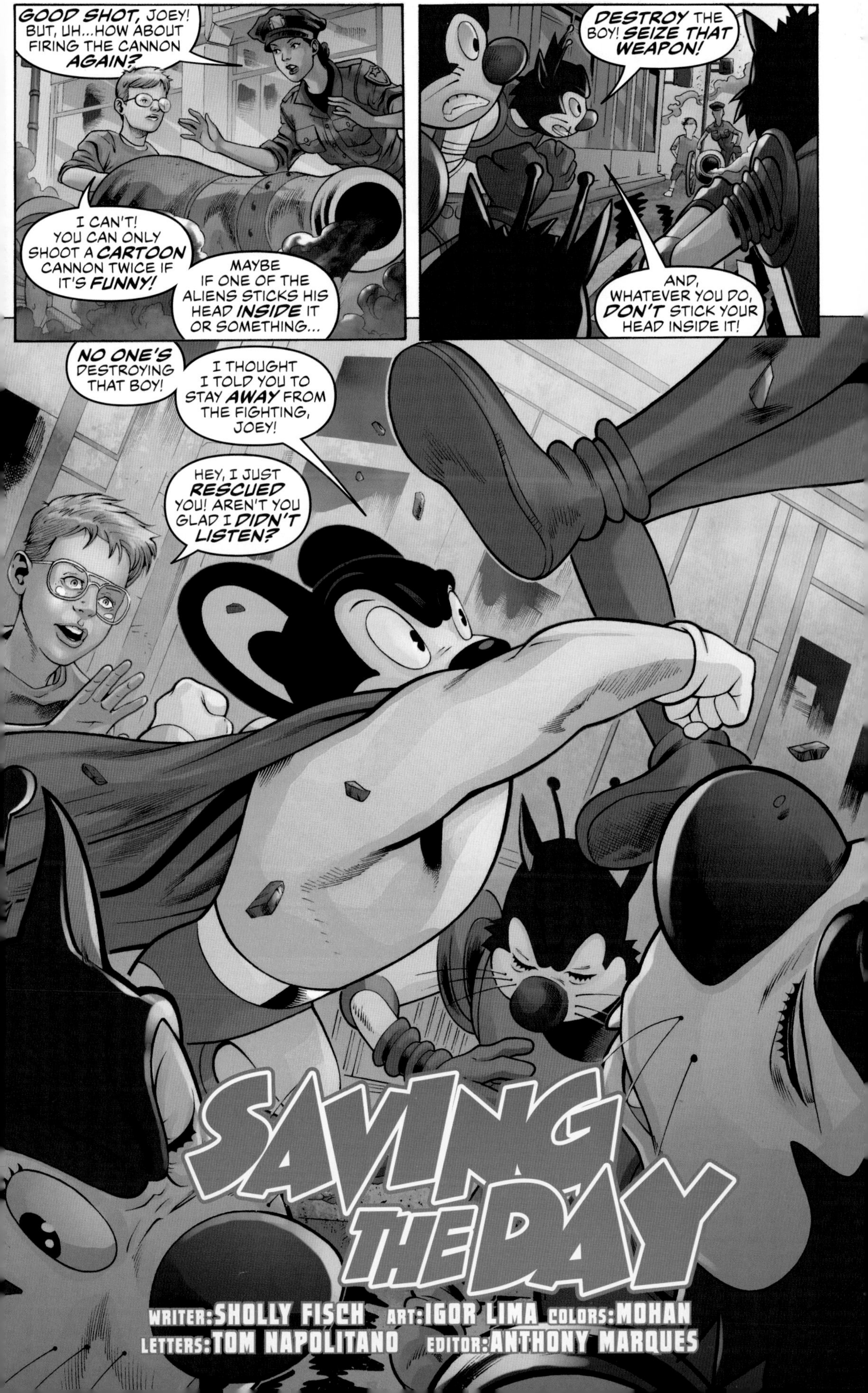
GOOD SHOT, JOEY! BUT, UH...HOW ABOUT FIRING THE CANNON AGAIN?
I CAN'T! YOU CAN ONLY SHOOT A CARTOON CANNON TWICE IF IT'S FUNNY!
MAYBE IF ONE OF THE ALIENS STICKS HIS HEAD INSIDE IT OR SOMETHING...
DESTROY THE BOY! SEIZE THAT WEAPON!
AND, WHATEVER YOU DO, DON'T STICK YOUR HEAD INSIDE IT!
NO ONE'S DESTROYING THAT BOY!
I THOUGHT I TOLD YOU TO STAY AWAY FROM THE FIGHTING, JOEY!
HEY, I JUST RESCUED YOU! AREN'T YOU GLAD I DIDN'T LISTEN?
SAVING THE DAY
WRITER: SHOLLY FISCH ART: IGOR LIMA COLORS: MOHAN
LETTERS: TOM NAPOLITANO EDITOR: ANTHONY MARQUES

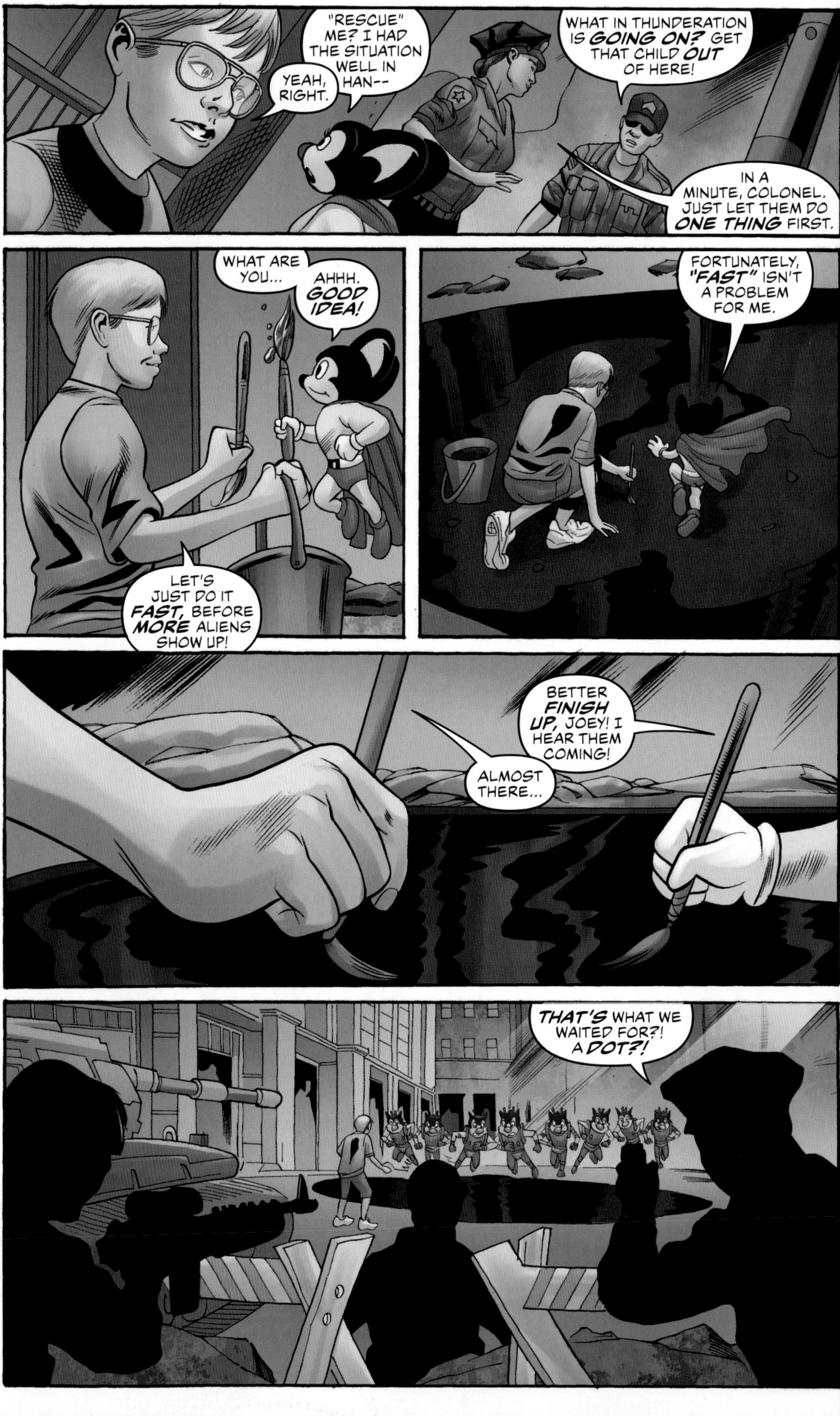

"RESCUE" ME? I HAD THE SITUATION WELL IN HAN--
YEAH, RIGHT.
WHAT IN THUNDERATION IS GOING ON? GET THAT CHILD OUT OF HERE!
IN A MINUTE, COLONEL. JUST LET THEM DO ONE THING FIRST.
WHAT ARE YOU...
AHHH. GOOD IDEA!
LET'S JUST DO IT FAST, BEFORE MORE ALIENS SHOW UP!
FORTUNATELY, "FAST" ISN'T A PROBLEM FOR ME.
BETTER FINISH UP, JOEY! I HEAR THEM COMING!
ALMOST THERE...
THAT'S WHAT WE WAITED FOR?! A DOT?!

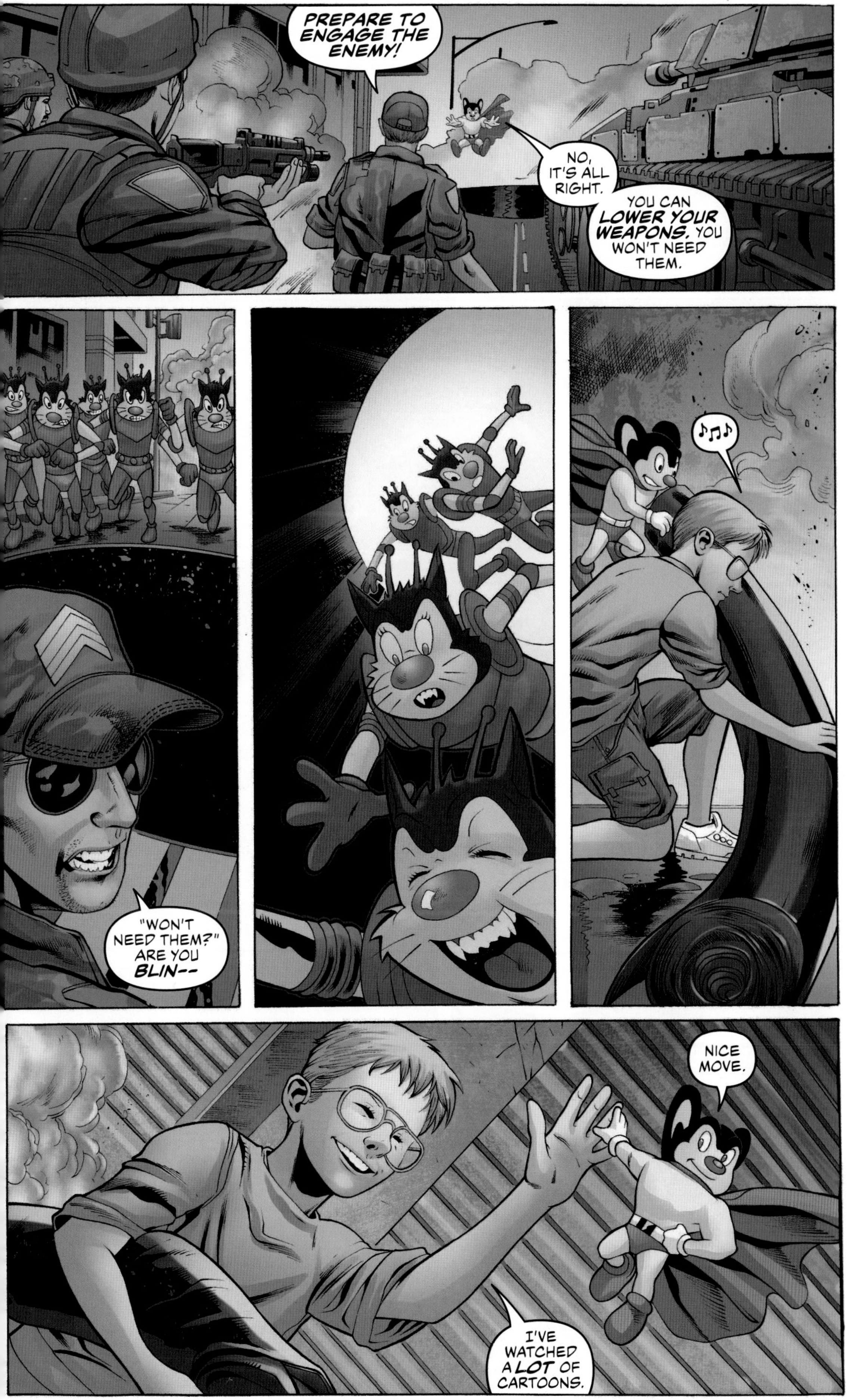
PREPARE TO ENGAGE THE ENEMY!
NO, IT'S ALL RIGHT.
YOU CAN LOWER YOUR WEAPONS. YOU WON'T NEED THEM.
"WON'T NEED THEM?" ARE YOU BLIN--
♪♫♪
NICE MOVE.
I'VE WATCHED A LOT OF CARTOONS.

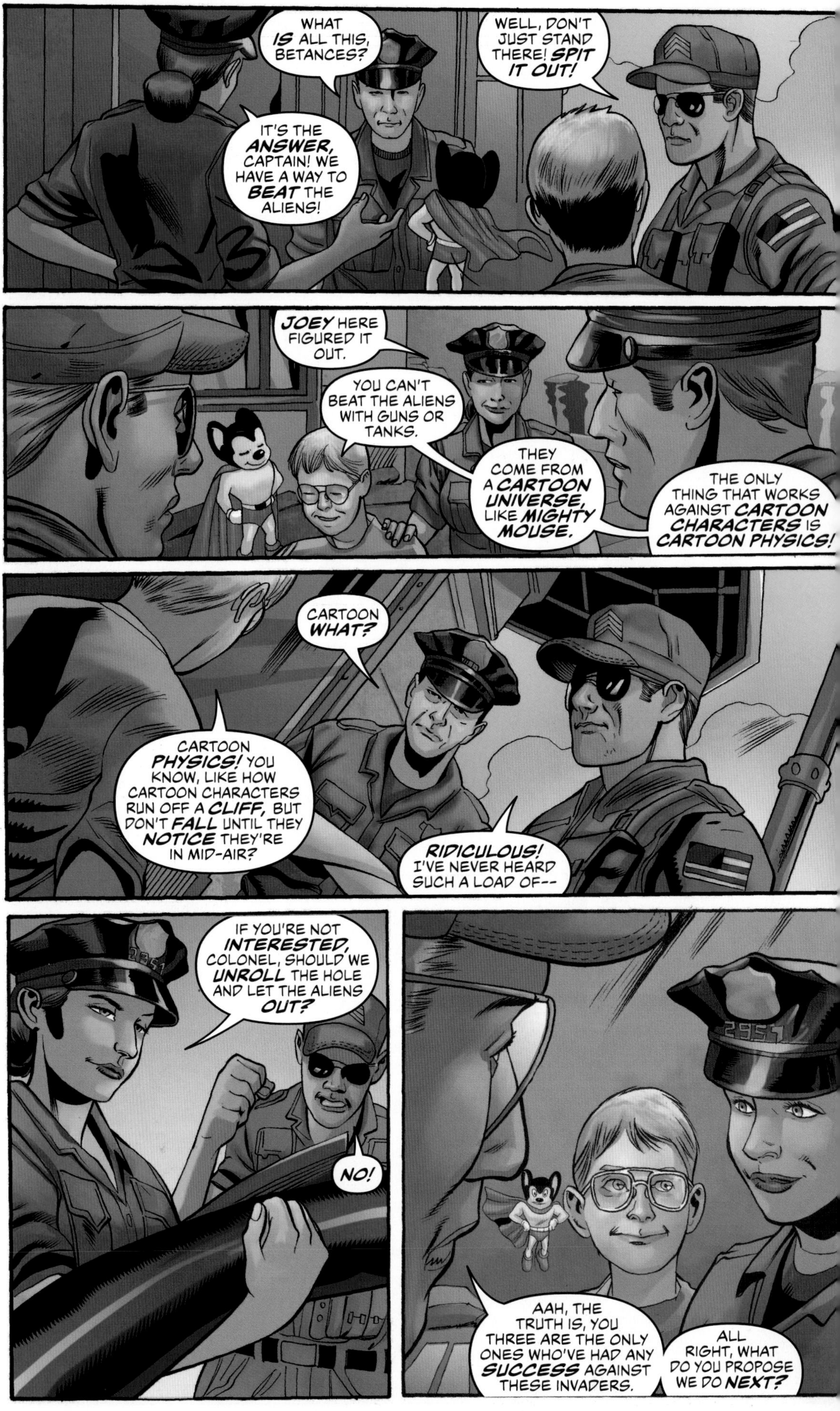
WHAT IS ALL THIS, BETANCES?
WELL, DON'T JUST STAND THERE! SPIT IT OUT!
IT'S THE ANSWER, CAPTAIN! WE HAVE A WAY TO BEAT THE ALIENS!
JOEY HERE FIGURED IT OUT.
YOU CAN'T BEAT THE ALIENS WITH GUNS OR TANKS.
THEY COME FROM A CARTOON UNIVERSE, LIKE MIGHTY MOUSE.
THE ONLY THING THAT WORKS AGAINST CARTOON CHARACTERS IS CARTOON PHYSICS!
CARTOON WHAT?
CARTOON PHYSICS! YOU KNOW, LIKE HOW CARTOON CHARACTERS RUN OFF A CLIFF, BUT DON'T FALL UNTIL THEY NOTICE THEY'RE IN MID-AIR?
RIDICULOUS! I'VE NEVER HEARD SUCH A LOAD OF--
IF YOU'RE NOT INTERESTED, COLONEL, SHOULD WE UNROLL THE HOLE AND LET THE ALIENS OUT?
NO!
AAH, THE TRUTH IS, YOU THREE ARE THE ONLY ONES WHO'VE HAD ANY SUCCESS AGAINST THESE INVADERS.
ALL RIGHT, WHAT DO YOU PROPOSE WE DO NEXT?

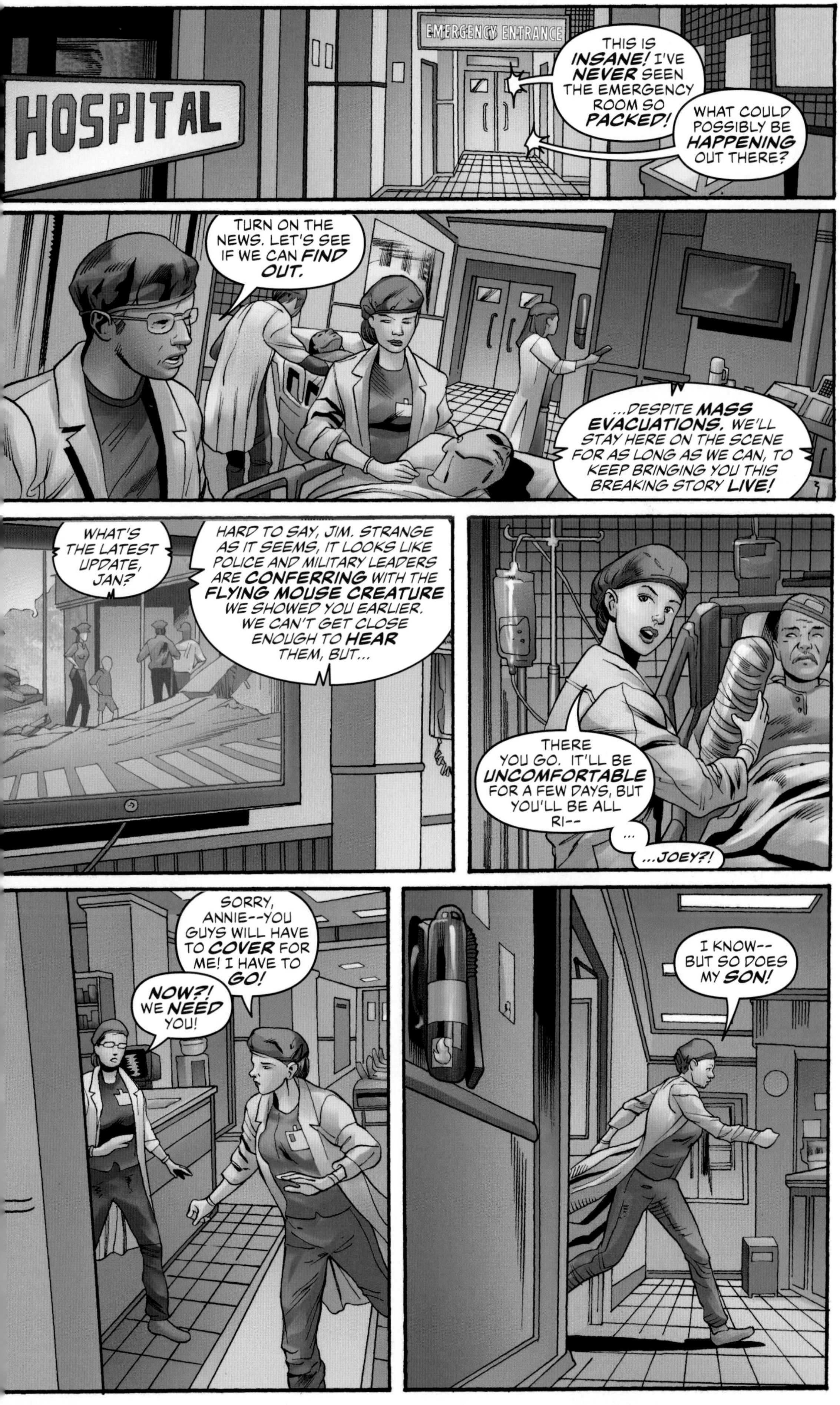
HOSPITAL
EMERGENCY ENTRANCE
THIS IS INSANE! I'VE NEVER SEEN THE EMERGENCY ROOM SO PACKED!
WHAT COULD POSSIBLY BE HAPPENING OUT THERE?
TURN ON THE NEWS. LET'S SEE IF WE CAN FIND OUT.
...DESPITE MASS EVACUATIONS. WE'LL STAY HERE ON THE SCENE FOR AS LONG AS WE CAN, TO KEEP BRINGING YOU THIS BREAKING STORY LIVE!
WHAT'S THE LATEST UPDATE, JAN?
HARD TO SAY, JIM. STRANGE AS IT SEEMS, IT LOOKS LIKE POLICE AND MILITARY LEADERS ARE CONFERRING WITH THE FLYING MOUSE CREATURE WE SHOWED YOU EARLIER. WE CAN'T GET CLOSE ENOUGH TO HEAR THEM, BUT...
THERE YOU GO. IT'LL BE UNCOMFORTABLE FOR A FEW DAYS, BUT YOU'LL BE ALL RI--
...
...JOEY?!
SORRY, ANNIE--YOU GUYS WILL HAVE TO COVER FOR ME! I HAVE TO GO!
NOW?! WE NEED YOU!
I KNOW-- BUT SO DOES MY SON!

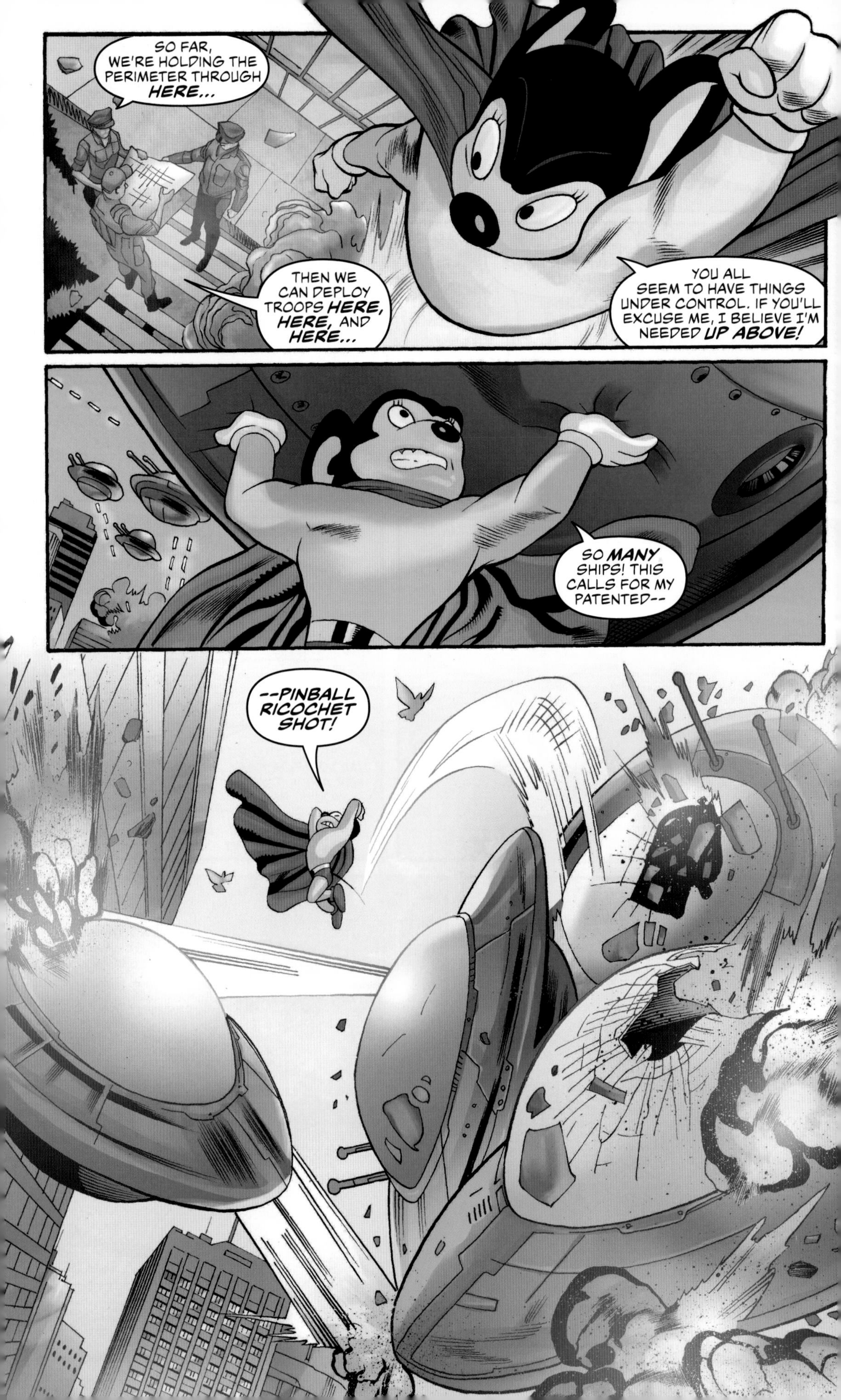

SO FAR, WE'RE HOLDING THE PERIMETER THROUGH HERE...
THEN WE CAN DEPLOY TROOPS HERE, HERE, AND HERE...
YOU ALL SEEM TO HAVE THINGS UNDER CONTROL. IF YOU'LL EXCUSE ME, I BELIEVE I'M NEEDED UP ABOVE!
SO MANY SHIPS! THIS CALLS FOR MY PATENTED--
--PINBALL RICOCHET SHOT!

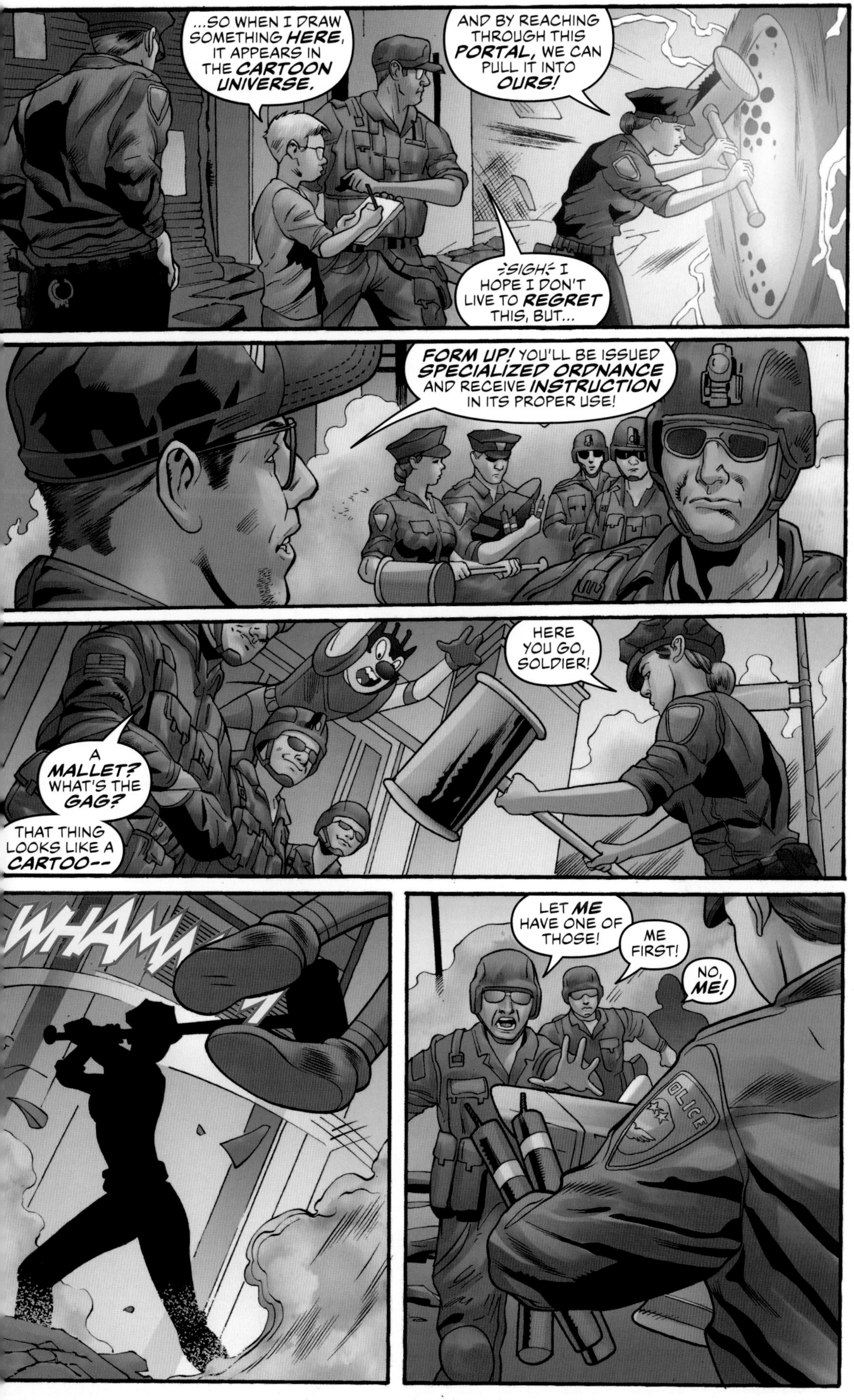
...SO WHEN I DRAW SOMETHING HERE, IT APPEARS IN THE CARTOON UNIVERSE.
AND BY REACHING THROUGH THIS PORTAL, WE CAN PULL IT INTO OURS!
SIGH I HOPE I DON'T LIVE TO REGRET THIS, BUT...
FORM UP! YOU'LL BE ISSUED SPECIALIZED ORDNANCE AND RECEIVE INSTRUCTION IN ITS PROPER USE!
HERE YOU GO, SOLDIER!
A MALLET? WHAT'S THE GAG?
THAT THING LOOKS LIKE A CARTOO--
WHAM
LET ME HAVE ONE OF THOSE!
ME FIRST!
NO, ME!
POLICE

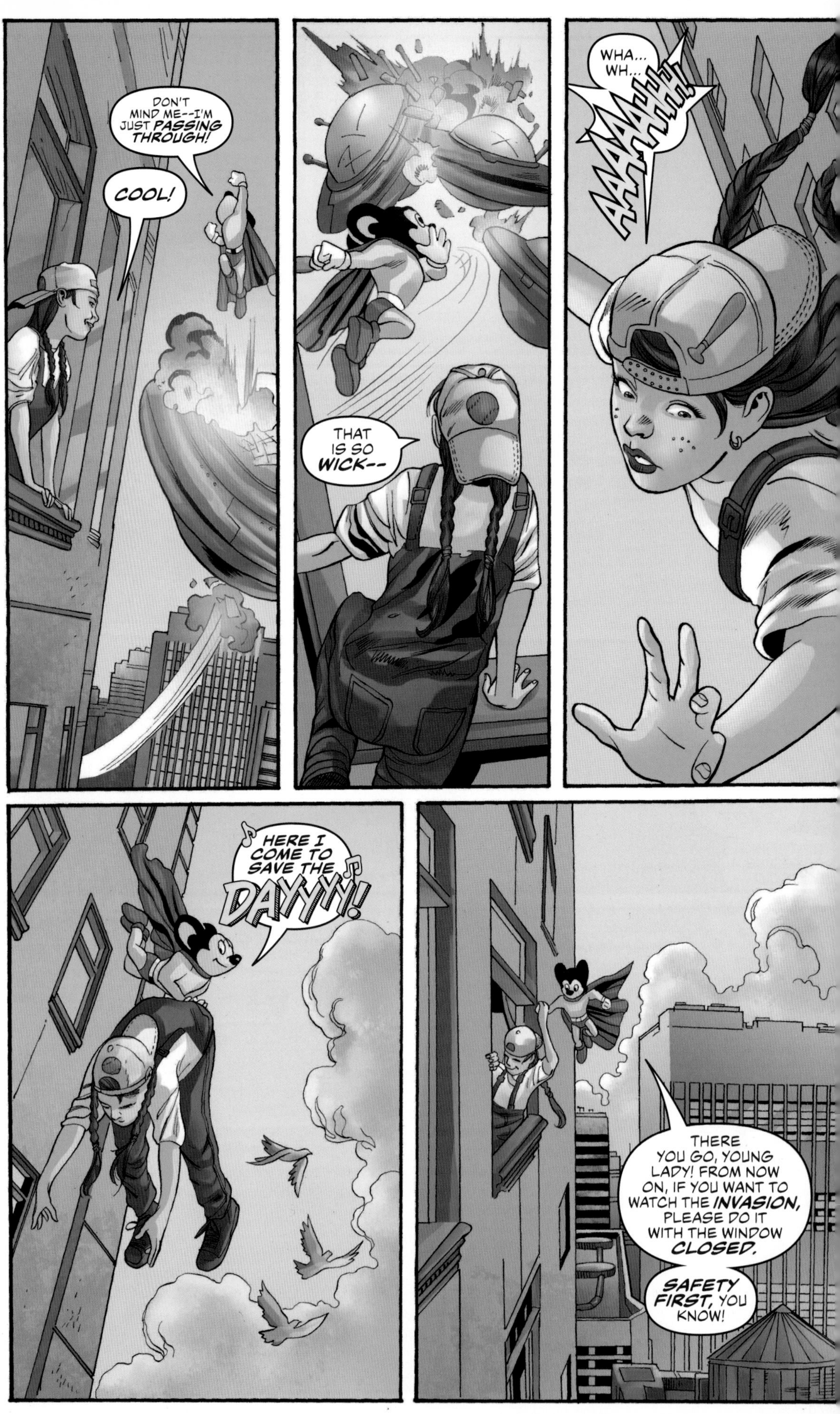
DON'T MIND ME--I'M JUST PASSING THROUGH!
COOL!
THAT IS SO WICK--
WHA... WH...
AAAAAHHH!
HERE I COME TO SAVE THE DAYYY!
THERE YOU GO, YOUNG LADY! FROM NOW ON, IF YOU WANT TO WATCH THE INVASION, PLEASE DO IT WITH THE WINDOW CLOSED.
SAFETY FIRST, YOU KNOW!

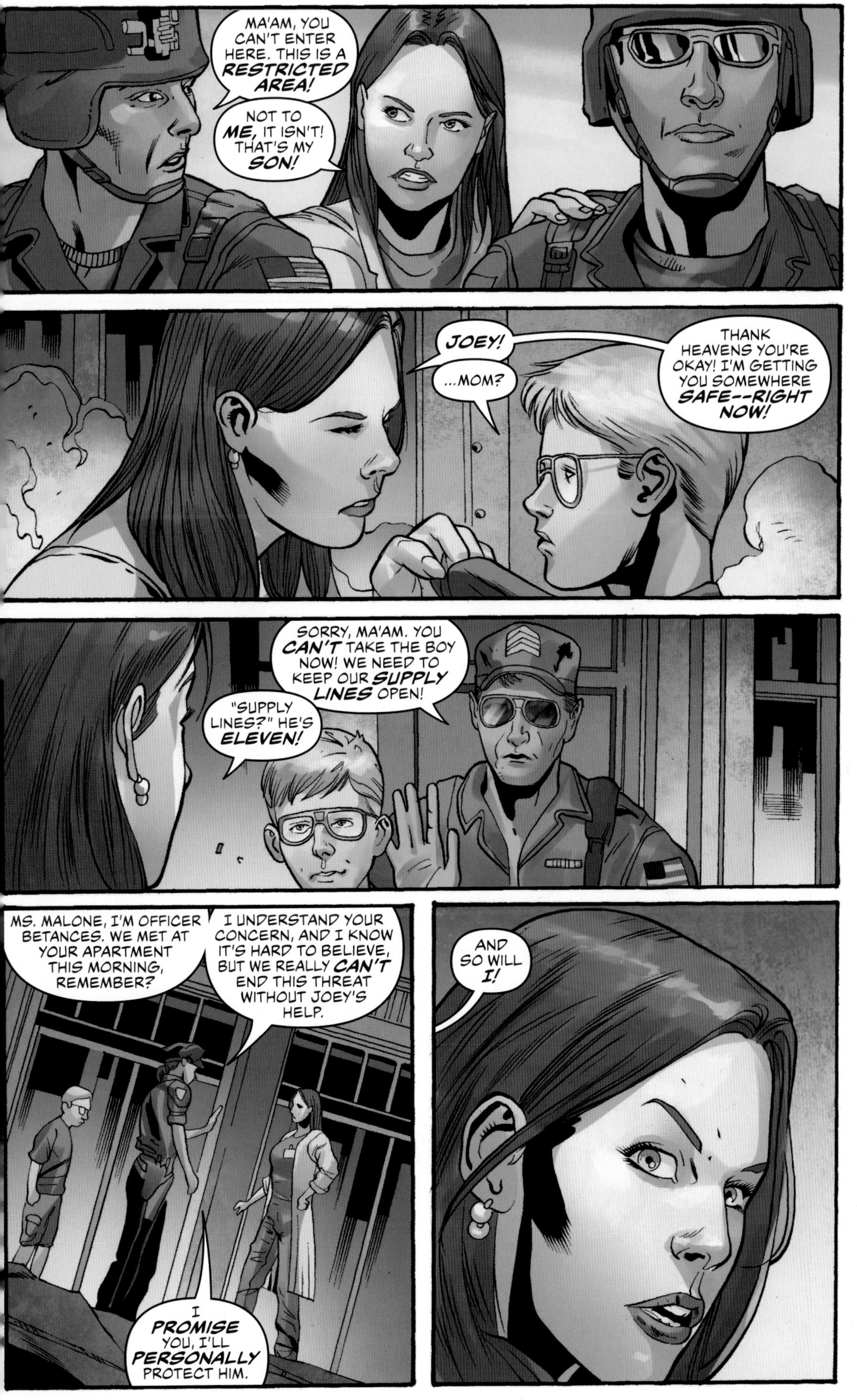
MA'AM, YOU CAN'T ENTER HERE. THIS IS A RESTRICTED AREA!
NOT TO ME, IT ISN'T! THAT'S MY SON!
JOEY!
...MOM?
THANK HEAVENS YOU'RE OKAY! I'M GETTING YOU SOMEWHERE SAFE--RIGHT NOW!
SORRY, MA'AM. YOU CAN'T TAKE THE BOY NOW! WE NEED TO KEEP OUR SUPPLY LINES OPEN!
"SUPPLY LINES?" HE'S ELEVEN!
MS. MALONE, I'M OFFICER BETANCES. WE MET AT YOUR APARTMENT THIS MORNING, REMEMBER?
I UNDERSTAND YOUR CONCERN, AND I KNOW IT'S HARD TO BELIEVE, BUT WE REALLY CAN'T END THIS THREAT WITHOUT JOEY'S HELP.
I PROMISE YOU, I'LL PERSONALLY PROTECT HIM.
AND SO WILL I!

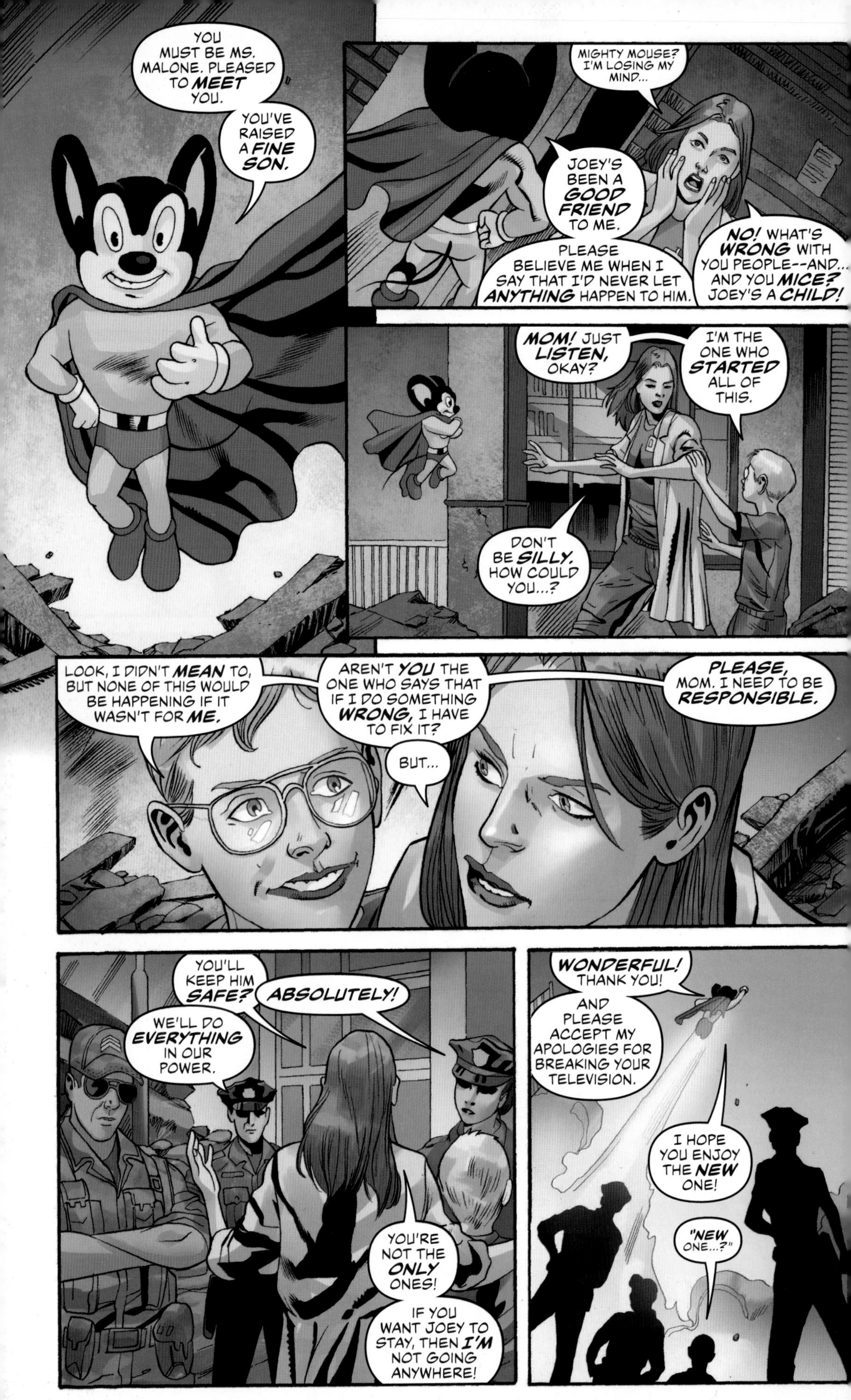

YOU MUST BE MS. MALONE. PLEASED TO MEET YOU.
YOU'VE RAISED A FINE SON.
MIGHTY MOUSE? I'M LOSING MY MIND...
JOEY'S BEEN A GOOD FRIEND TO ME.
PLEASE BELIEVE ME WHEN I SAY THAT I'D NEVER LET ANYTHING HAPPEN TO HIM.
NO! WHAT'S WRONG WITH YOU PEOPLE--AND... AND YOU MICE? JOEY'S A CHILD!
MOM! JUST LISTEN, OKAY?
I'M THE ONE WHO STARTED ALL OF THIS.
DON'T BE SILLY. HOW COULD YOU...?
LOOK, I DIDN'T MEAN TO, BUT NONE OF THIS WOULD BE HAPPENING IF IT WASN'T FOR ME.
AREN'T YOU THE ONE WHO SAYS THAT IF I DO SOMETHING WRONG, I HAVE TO FIX IT?
BUT...
PLEASE, MOM. I NEED TO BE RESPONSIBLE.
YOU'LL KEEP HIM SAFE?
ABSOLUTELY!
WE'LL DO EVERYTHING IN OUR POWER.
YOU'RE NOT THE ONLY ONES!
IF YOU WANT JOEY TO STAY, THEN I'M NOT GOING ANYWHERE!
WONDERFUL! THANK YOU!
AND PLEASE ACCEPT MY APOLOGIES FOR BREAKING YOUR TELEVISION.
I HOPE YOU ENJOY THE NEW ONE!
"NEW ONE...?"

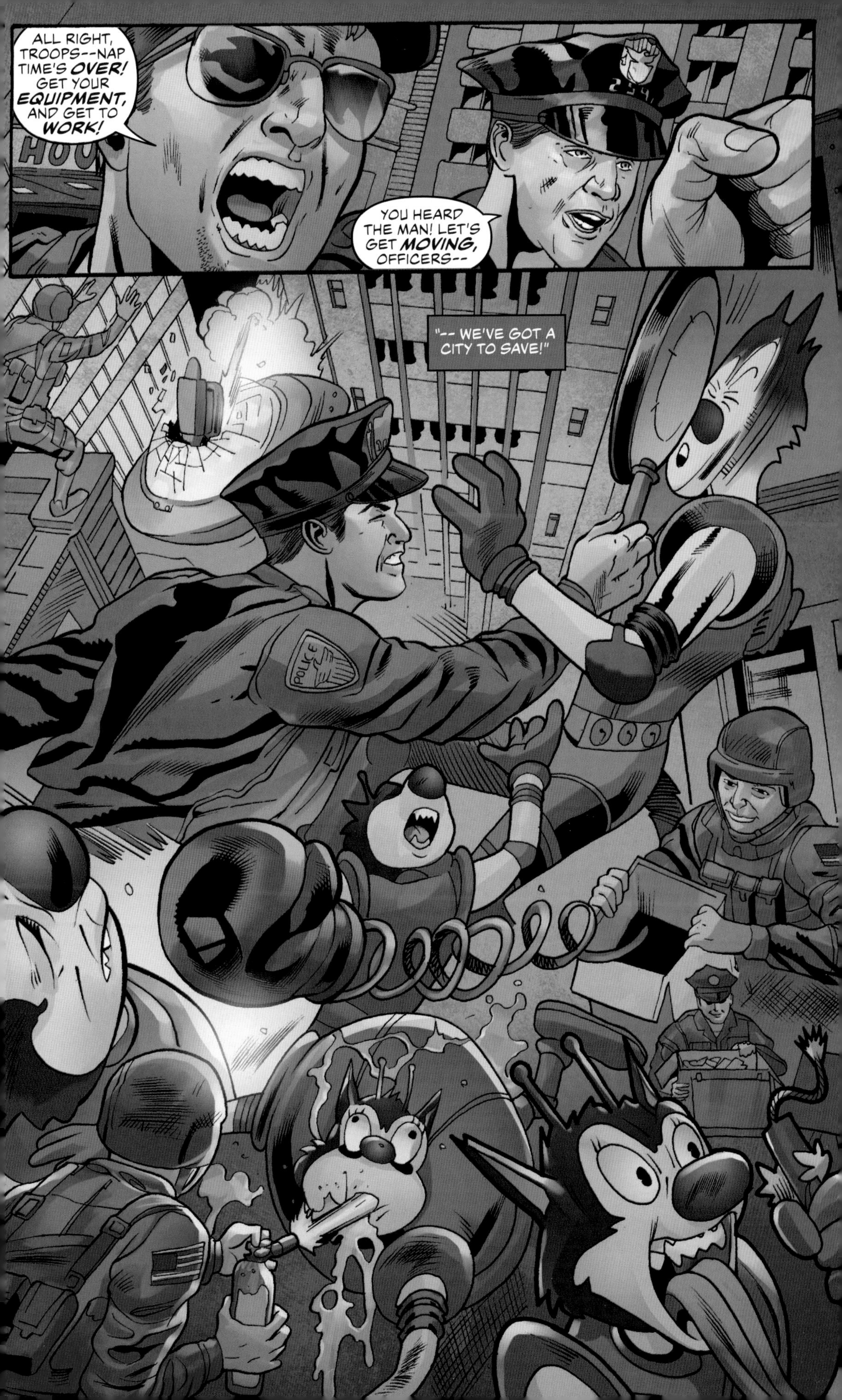
ALL RIGHT, TROOPS--NAP TIME'S OVER! GET YOUR EQUIPMENT, AND GET TO WORK!
YOU HEARD THE MAN! LET'S GET MOVING, OFFICERS--
"-- WE'VE GOT A CITY TO SAVE!"
POLICE

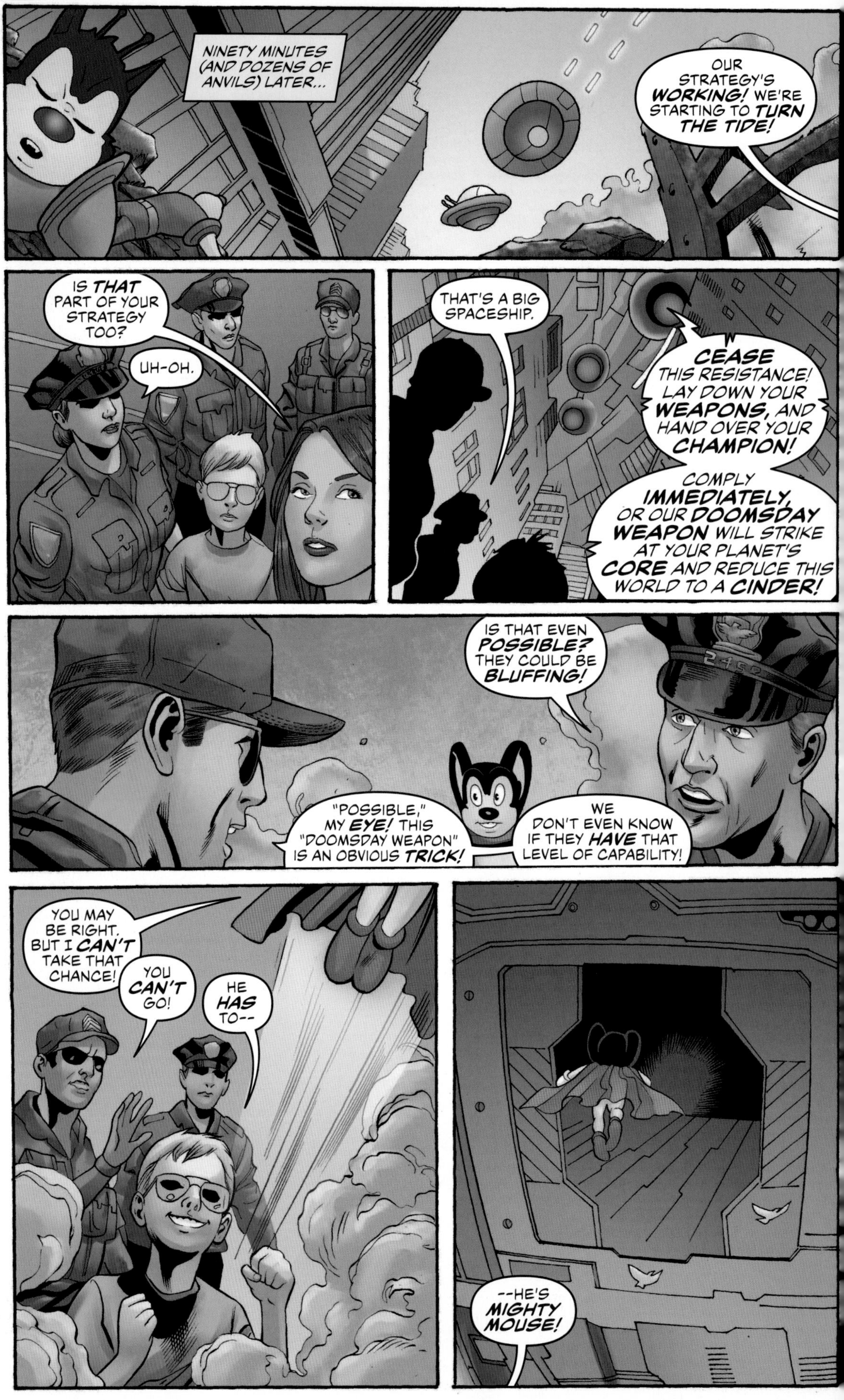
NINETY MINUTES (AND DOZENS OF ANVILS) LATER...
OUR STRATEGY'S WORKING! WE'RE STARTING TO TURN THE TIDE!
IS THAT PART OF YOUR STRATEGY TOO?
UH-OH.
THAT'S A BIG SPACESHIP.
CEASE THIS RESISTANCE! LAY DOWN YOUR WEAPONS, AND HAND OVER YOUR CHAMPION!
COMPLY IMMEDIATELY, OR OUR DOOMSDAY WEAPON WILL STRIKE AT YOUR PLANET'S CORE AND REDUCE THIS WORLD TO A CINDER!
IS THAT EVEN POSSIBLE? THEY COULD BE BLUFFING!
WE DON'T EVEN KNOW IF THEY HAVE THAT LEVEL OF CAPABILITY!
"POSSIBLE," MY EYE! THIS "DOOMSDAY WEAPON" IS AN OBVIOUS TRICK!
YOU MAY BE RIGHT. BUT I CAN'T TAKE THAT CHANCE!
YOU CAN'T GO!
HE HAS TO--
--HE'S MIGHTY MOUSE!

ORDINARILY, I TRY NOT TO LEAP TO CONCLUSIONS--

--BUT I'M GOING TO ASSUME THAT *YOU'RE* IN CHARGE HERE.

I AM THE WARLORD *FELIS REX!* MY EMPIRE SPANS A *DOZEN GALAXIES!*

MY FORCES HAVE CONQUERED *ONE HUNDRED* WORLDS!

YOU, LITTLE MOUSE, HAVE GIVEN US FAR MORE TROUBLE THAN I WOULD HAVE THOUGHT *POSSIBLE.*

HOWEVER, I AM SURE THAT WE CAN FIND A MORE *CONSTRUCTIVE* USE FOR YOUR TALENTS. NOW THAT YOU HAVE RECOGNIZED OUR *MIGHT* AND *SURRENDERED,* YOU WILL MAKE A FINE *SLAVE.*

I THINK THERE MAY HAVE BEEN A *MISUNDERSTANDING.*

I *DID* COME HERE IN RESPONSE TO YOUR THREATS --

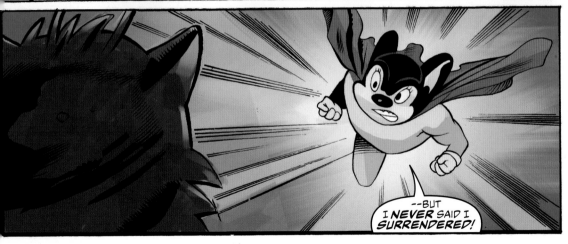

--BUT I *NEVER* SAID I *SURRENDERED!*

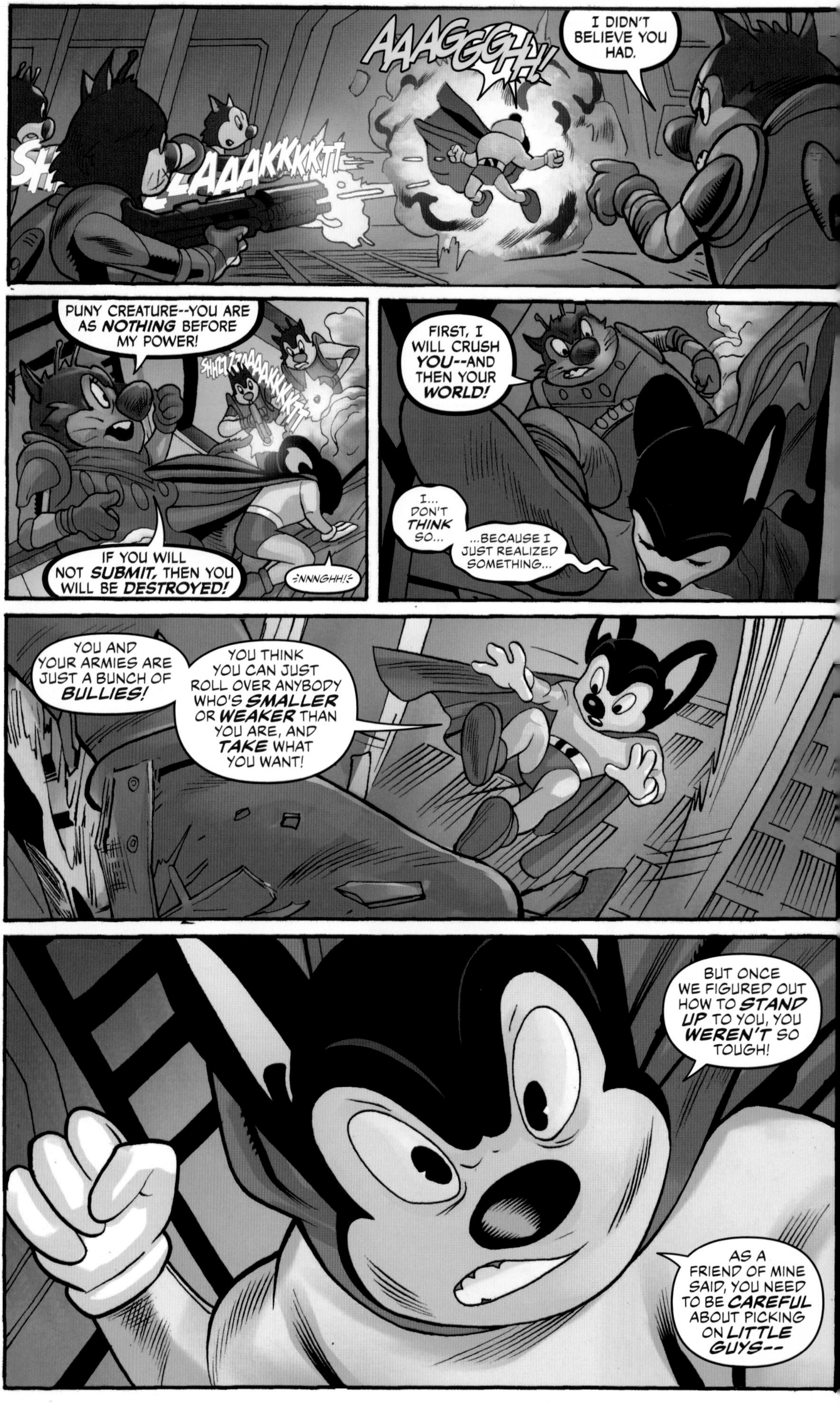

SHHH...
AAAGGGHH!
I DIDN'T BELIEVE YOU HAD.
...LAAAKKKKTT!
PUNY CREATURE--YOU ARE AS NOTHING BEFORE MY POWER!
SHHCLZZZAAAAKKKKTT!
IF YOU WILL NOT SUBMIT, THEN YOU WILL BE DESTROYED!
NNNGHH!
FIRST, I WILL CRUSH YOU--AND THEN YOUR WORLD!
I... DON'T THINK SO...
...BECAUSE I JUST REALIZED SOMETHING...
YOU AND YOUR ARMIES ARE JUST A BUNCH OF BULLIES!
YOU THINK YOU CAN JUST ROLL OVER ANYBODY WHO'S SMALLER OR WEAKER THAN YOU ARE, AND TAKE WHAT YOU WANT!
BUT ONCE WE FIGURED OUT HOW TO STAND UP TO YOU, YOU WEREN'T SO TOUGH!
AS A FRIEND OF MINE SAID, YOU NEED TO BE CAREFUL ABOUT PICKING ON LITTLE GUYS--

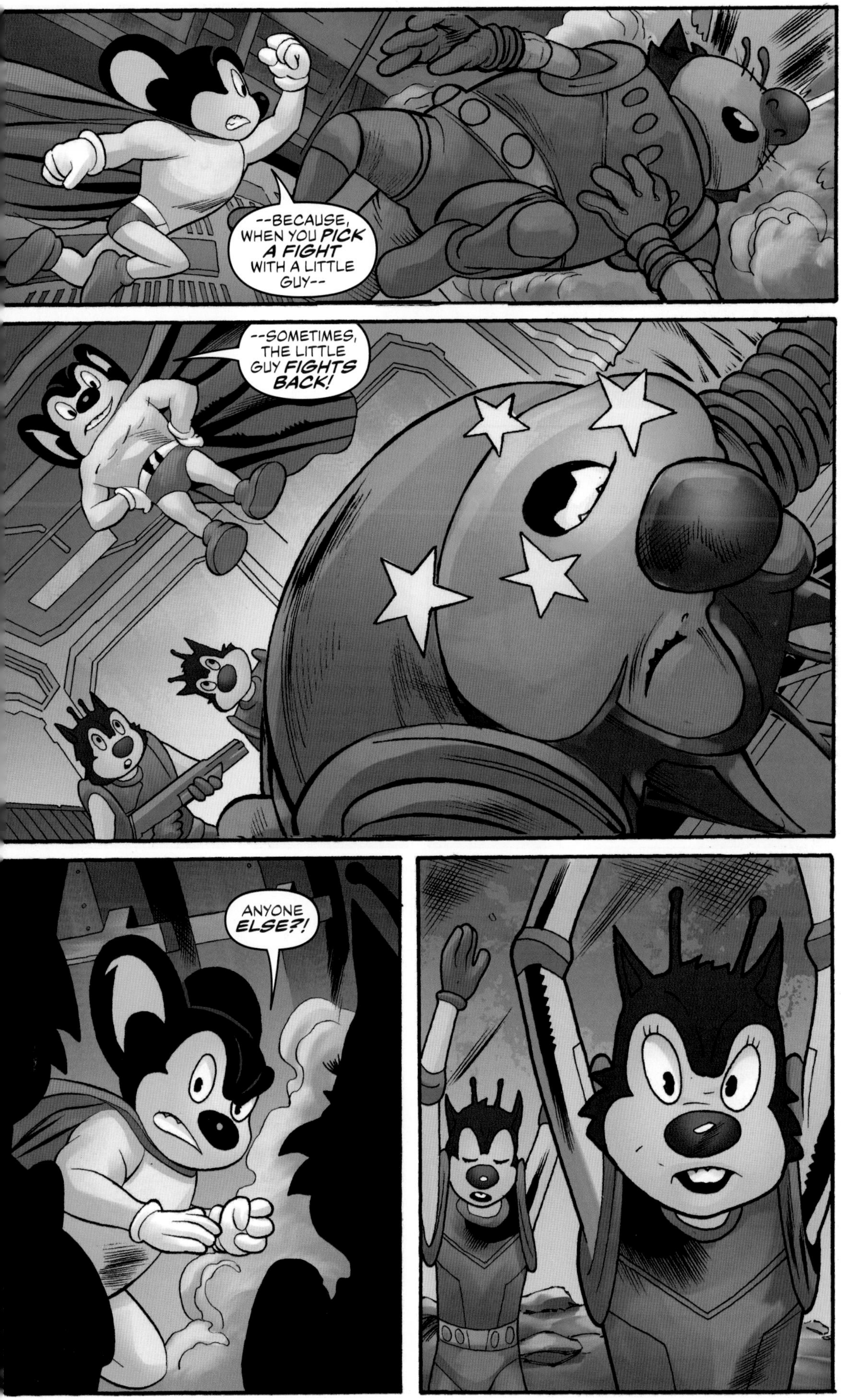
--BECAUSE, WHEN YOU PICK A FIGHT WITH A LITTLE GUY--
--SOMETIMES, THE LITTLE GUY FIGHTS BACK!
ANYONE ELSE?!

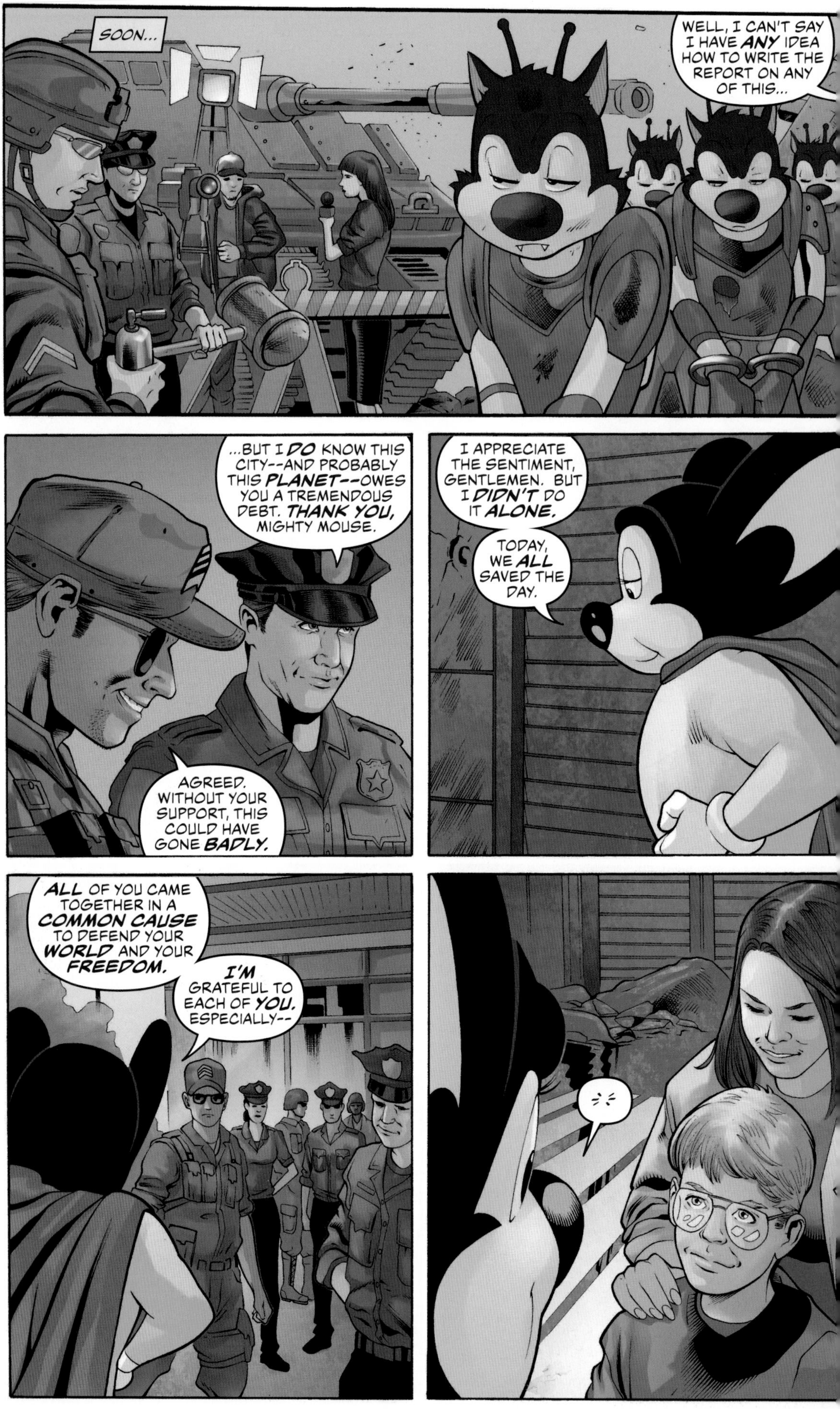
SOON...
WELL, I CAN'T SAY I HAVE ANY IDEA HOW TO WRITE THE REPORT ON ANY OF THIS...
...BUT I DO KNOW THIS CITY--AND PROBABLY THIS PLANET--OWES YOU A TREMENDOUS DEBT. THANK YOU, MIGHTY MOUSE.
AGREED. WITHOUT YOUR SUPPORT, THIS COULD HAVE GONE BADLY.
I APPRECIATE THE SENTIMENT, GENTLEMEN. BUT I DIDN'T DO IT ALONE.
TODAY, WE ALL SAVED THE DAY.
ALL OF YOU CAME TOGETHER IN A COMMON CAUSE TO DEFEND YOUR WORLD AND YOUR FREEDOM.
I'M GRATEFUL TO EACH OF YOU. ESPECIALLY--

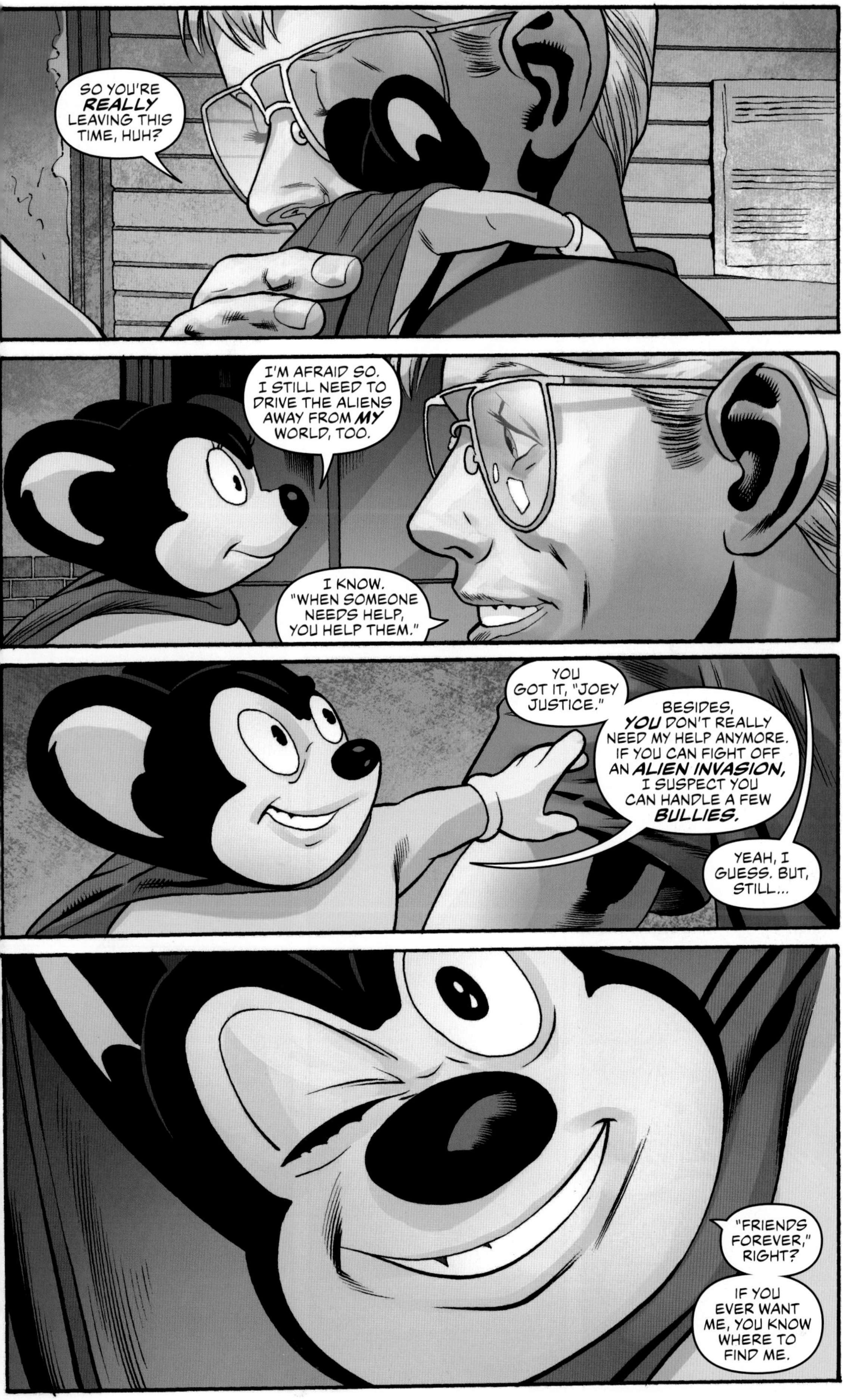
SO YOU'RE REALLY LEAVING THIS TIME, HUH?
I'M AFRAID SO. I STILL NEED TO DRIVE THE ALIENS AWAY FROM MY WORLD, TOO.
I KNOW. "WHEN SOMEONE NEEDS HELP, YOU HELP THEM."
YOU GOT IT, "JOEY JUSTICE."
BESIDES, YOU DON'T REALLY NEED MY HELP ANYMORE. IF YOU CAN FIGHT OFF AN ALIEN INVASION, I SUSPECT YOU CAN HANDLE A FEW BULLIES.
YEAH, I GUESS. BUT, STILL...
"FRIENDS FOREVER," RIGHT?
IF YOU EVER WANT ME, YOU KNOW WHERE TO FIND ME.

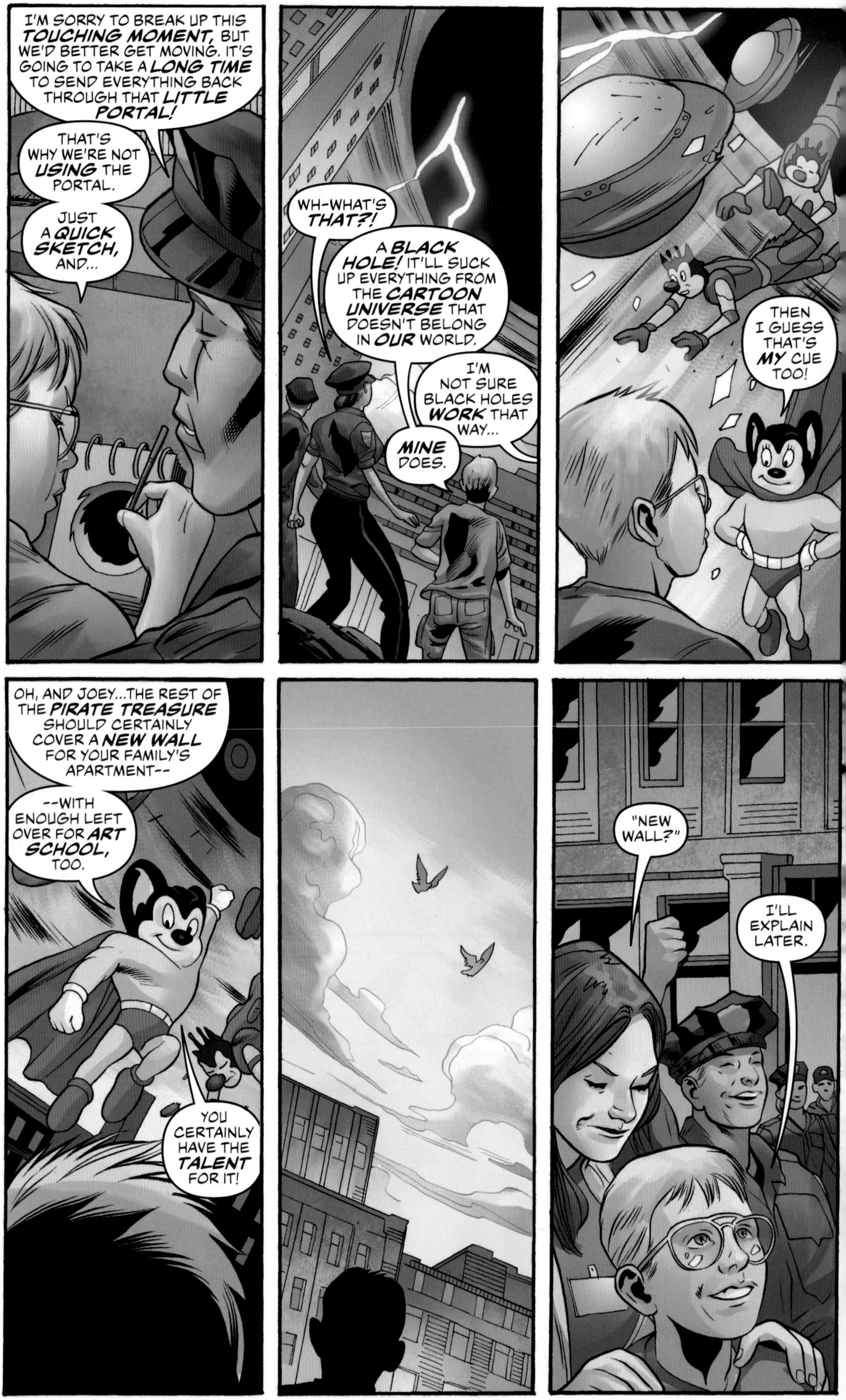

I'M SORRY TO BREAK UP THIS TOUCHING MOMENT, BUT WE'D BETTER GET MOVING. IT'S GOING TO TAKE A LONG TIME TO SEND EVERYTHING BACK THROUGH THAT LITTLE PORTAL!
THAT'S WHY WE'RE NOT USING THE PORTAL.
JUST A QUICK SKETCH, AND...
WH-WHAT'S THAT?!
A BLACK HOLE! IT'LL SUCK UP EVERYTHING FROM THE CARTOON UNIVERSE THAT DOESN'T BELONG IN OUR WORLD.
I'M NOT SURE BLACK HOLES WORK THAT WAY...
MINE DOES.
THEN I GUESS THAT'S MY CUE TOO!
OH, AND JOEY...THE REST OF THE PIRATE TREASURE SHOULD CERTAINLY COVER A NEW WALL FOR YOUR FAMILY'S APARTMENT--
--WITH ENOUGH LEFT OVER FOR ART SCHOOL, TOO.
YOU CERTAINLY HAVE THE TALENT FOR IT!
"NEW WALL?"
I'LL EXPLAIN LATER.

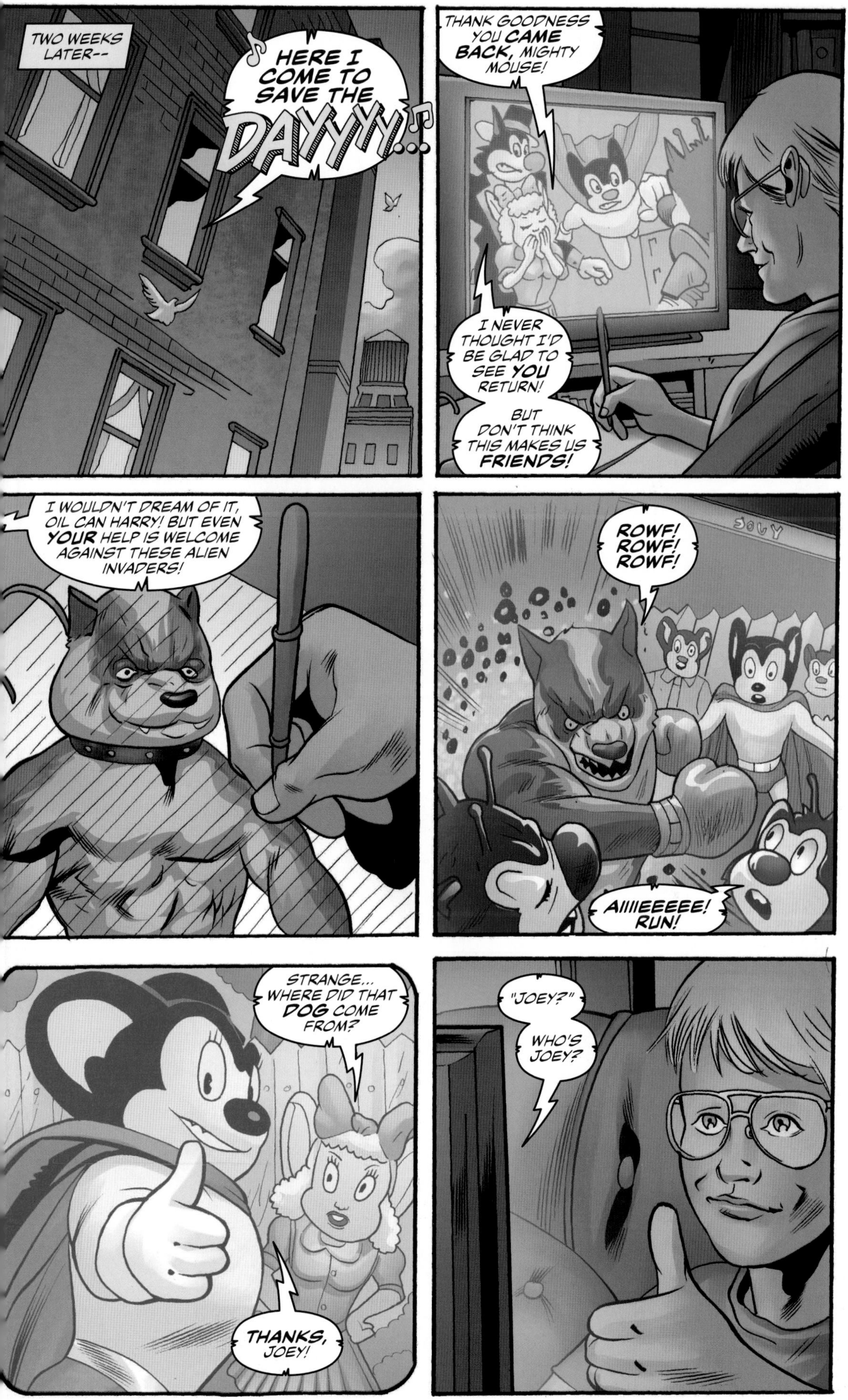

TWO WEEKS LATER--
HERE I COME TO SAVE THE DAYYY...
THANK GOODNESS YOU CAME BACK, MIGHTY MOUSE!
I NEVER THOUGHT I'D BE GLAD TO SEE YOU RETURN!
BUT DON'T THINK THIS MAKES US FRIENDS!
I WOULDN'T DREAM OF IT, OIL CAN HARRY! BUT EVEN YOUR HELP IS WELCOME AGAINST THESE ALIEN INVADERS!
JOEY
ROWF! ROWF! ROWF!
AIIIEEEEE! RUN!
STRANGE... WHERE DID THAT DOG COME FROM?
THANKS, JOEY!
"JOEY?"
WHO'S JOEY?

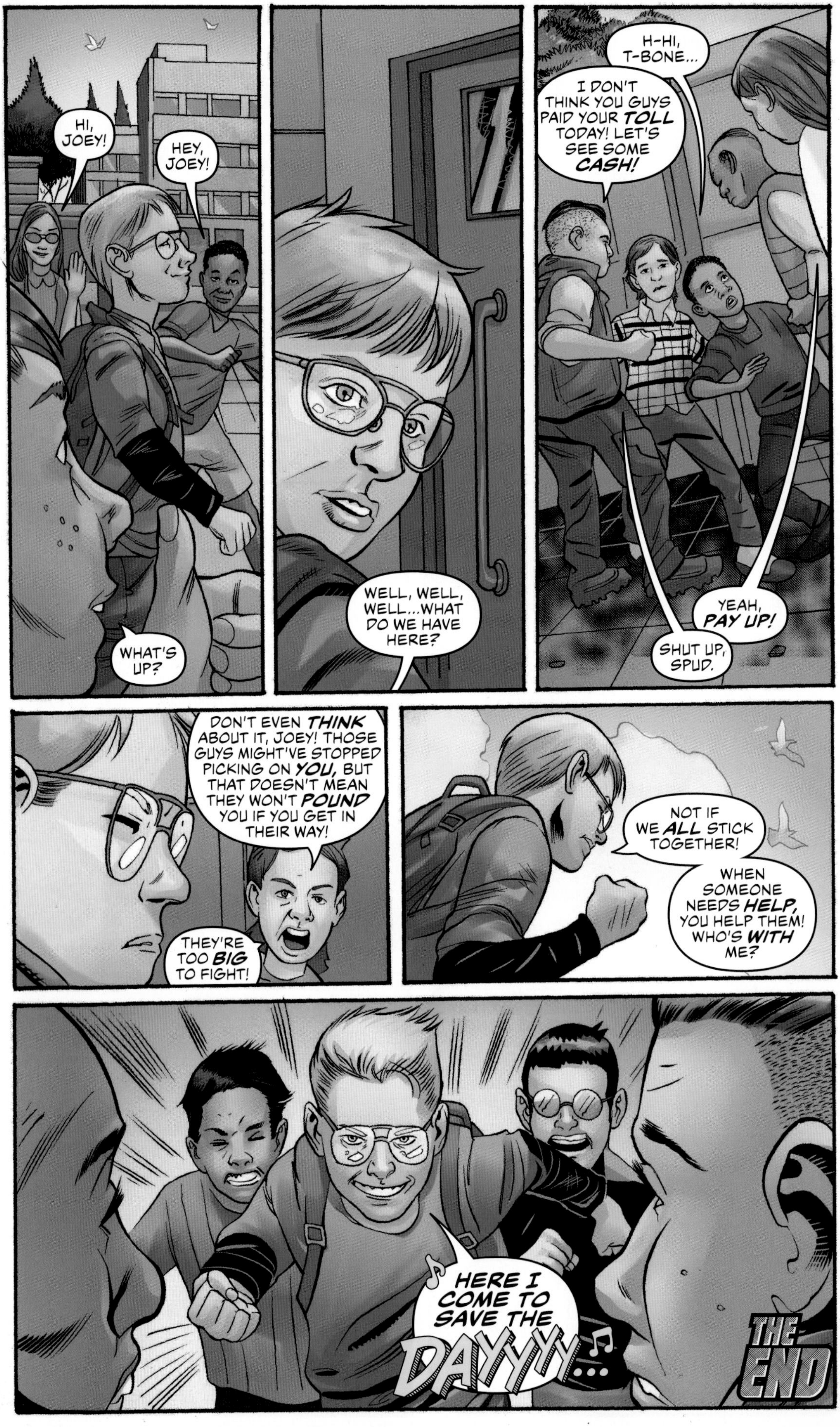
HI, JOEY!
HEY, JOEY!
WHAT'S UP?
WELL, WELL, WELL...WHAT DO WE HAVE HERE?
H-HI, T-BONE...
I DON'T THINK YOU GUYS PAID YOUR TOLL TODAY! LET'S SEE SOME CASH!
YEAH, PAY UP!
SHUT UP, SPUD.
DON'T EVEN THINK ABOUT IT, JOEY! THOSE GUYS MIGHT'VE STOPPED PICKING ON YOU, BUT THAT DOESN'T MEAN THEY WON'T POUND YOU IF YOU GET IN THEIR WAY!
THEY'RE TOO BIG TO FIGHT!
NOT IF WE ALL STICK TOGETHER!
WHEN SOMEONE NEEDS HELP, YOU HELP THEM! WHO'S WITH ME?
HERE I COME TO SAVE THE DAYYYY...
THE END

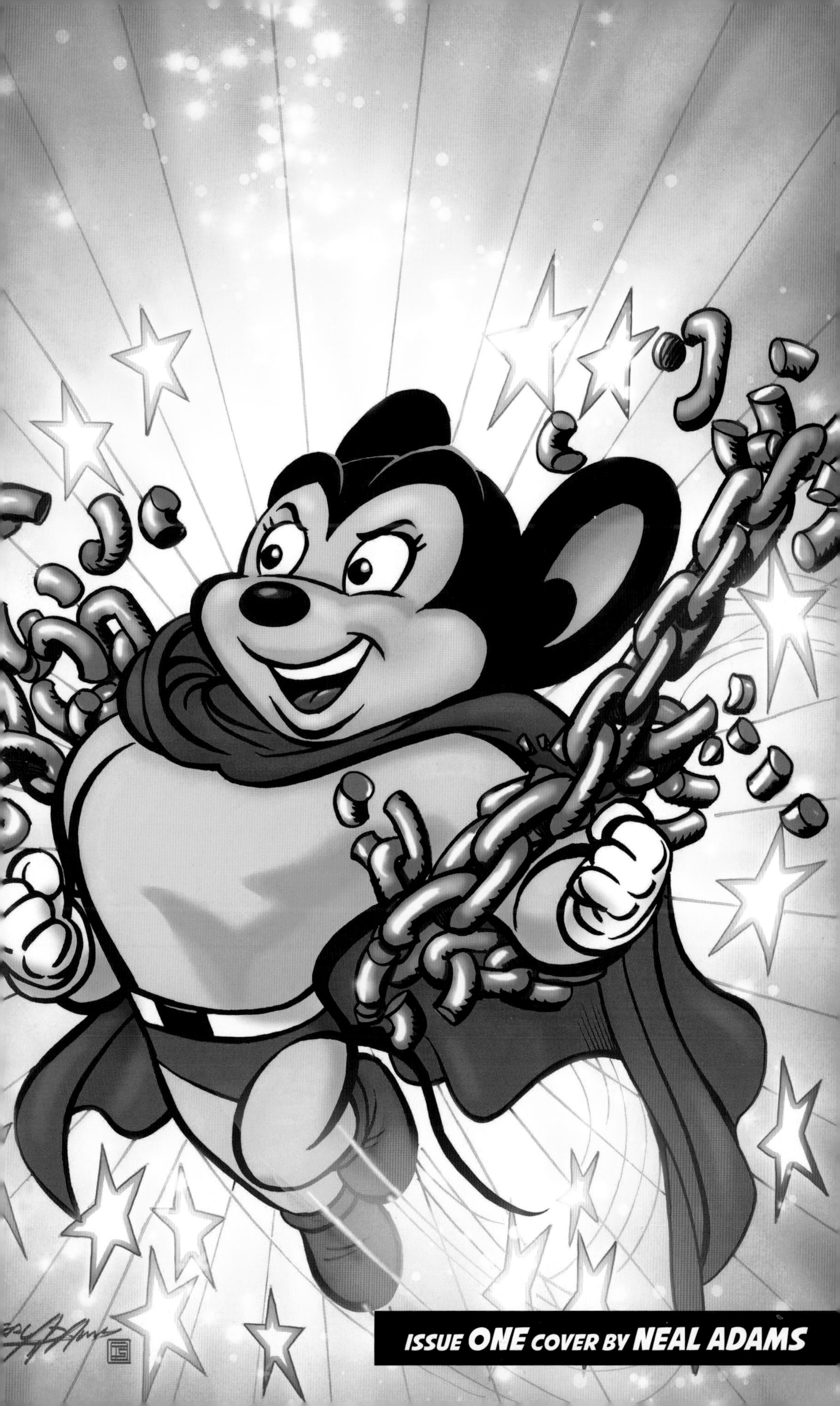

ISSUE **ONE** COVER BY **NEAL ADAMS**

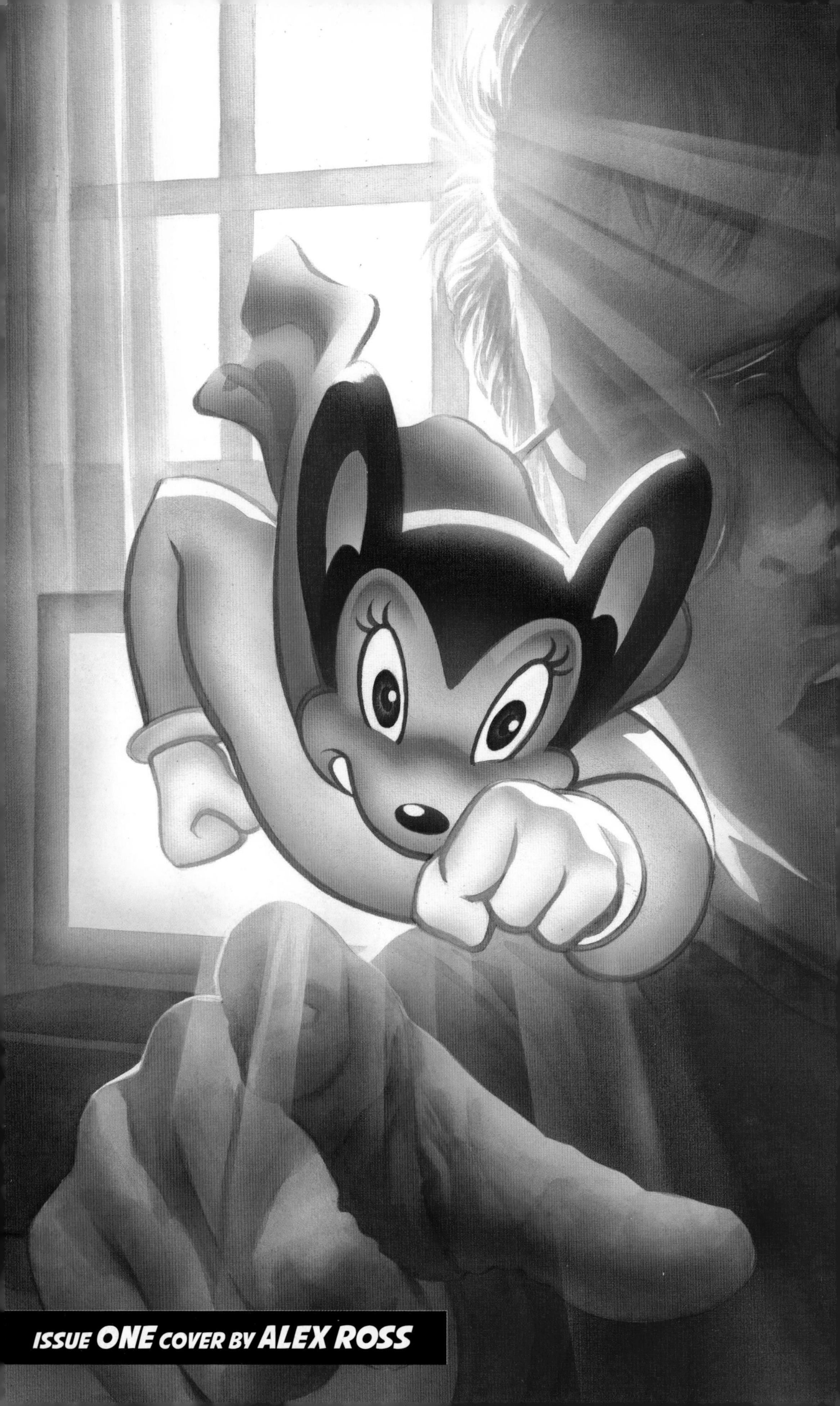

ISSUE ONE COVER BY ALEX ROSS

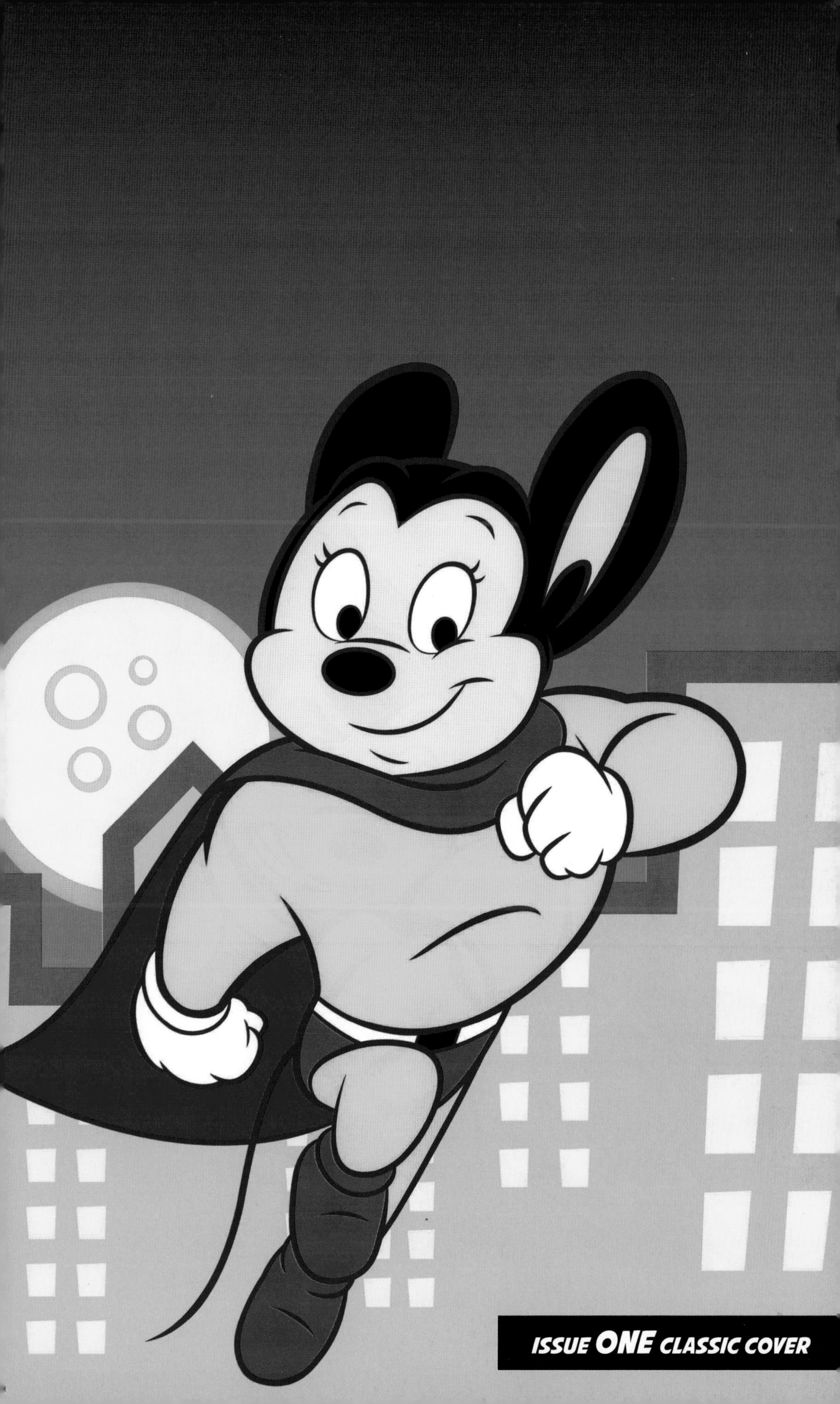
ISSUE ONE CLASSIC COVER

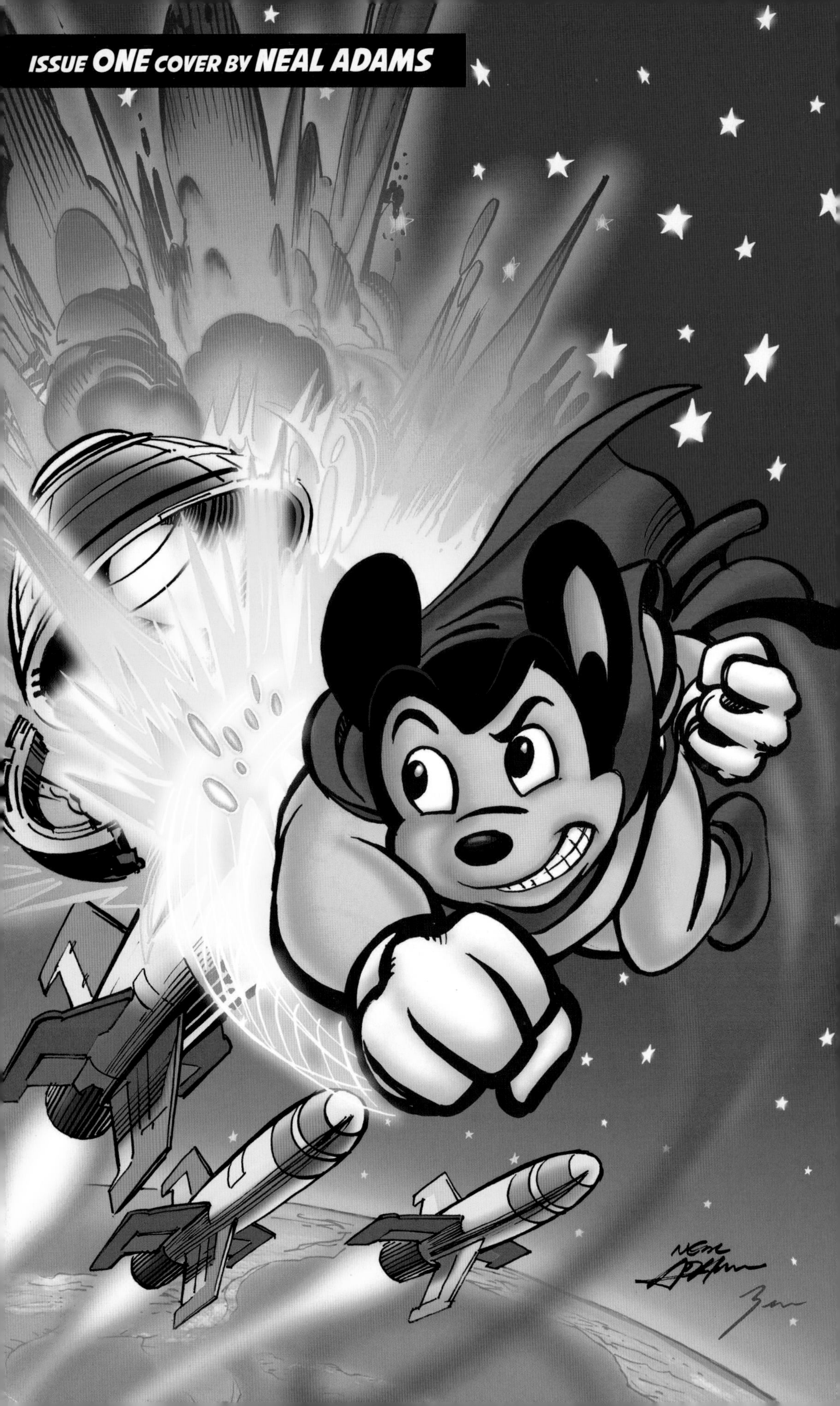

ISSUE ONE COVER BY NEAL ADAMS

ISSUE TWO COVER BY J. BONE

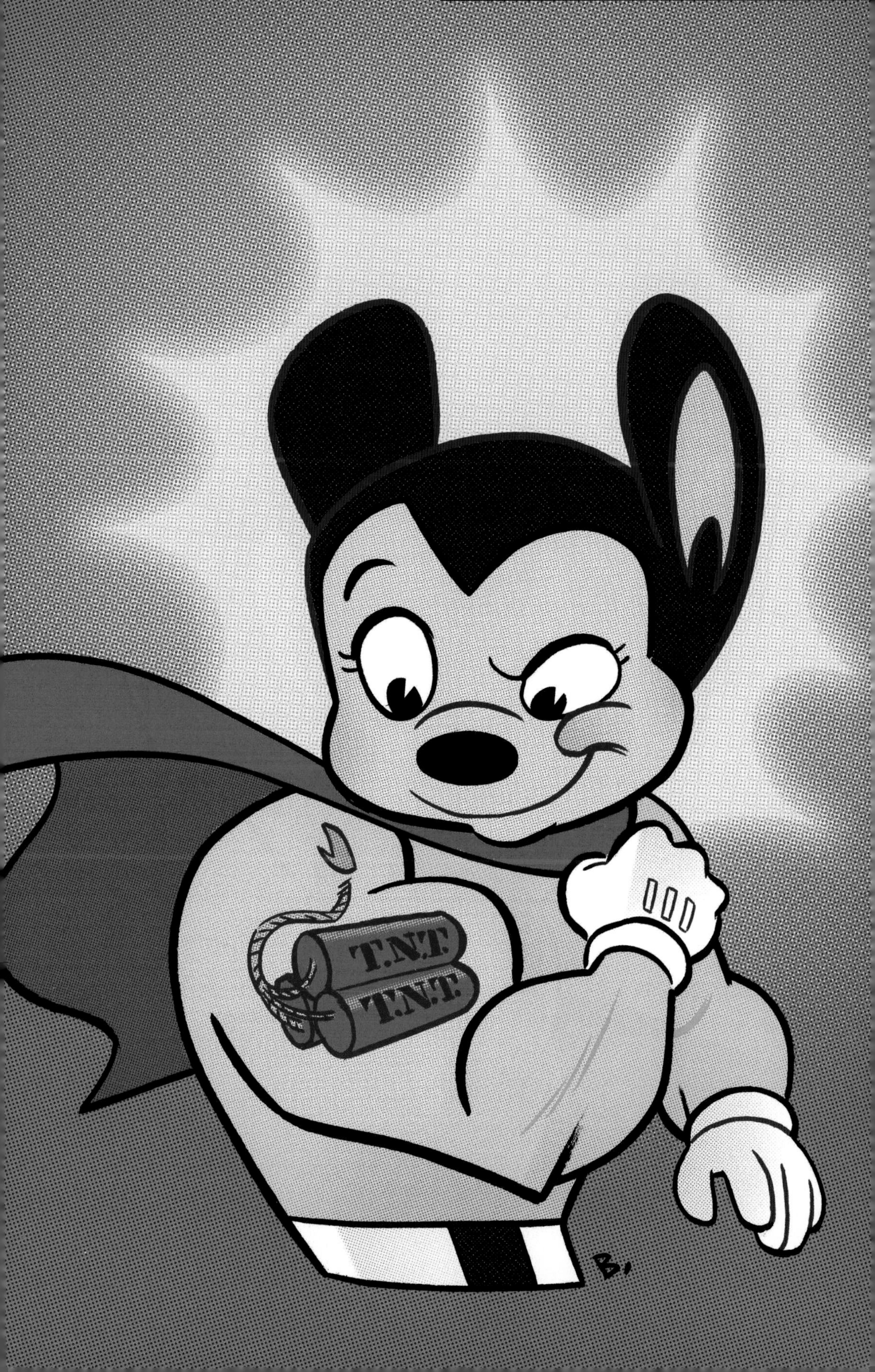

T.N.T.
T.N.T.
B.

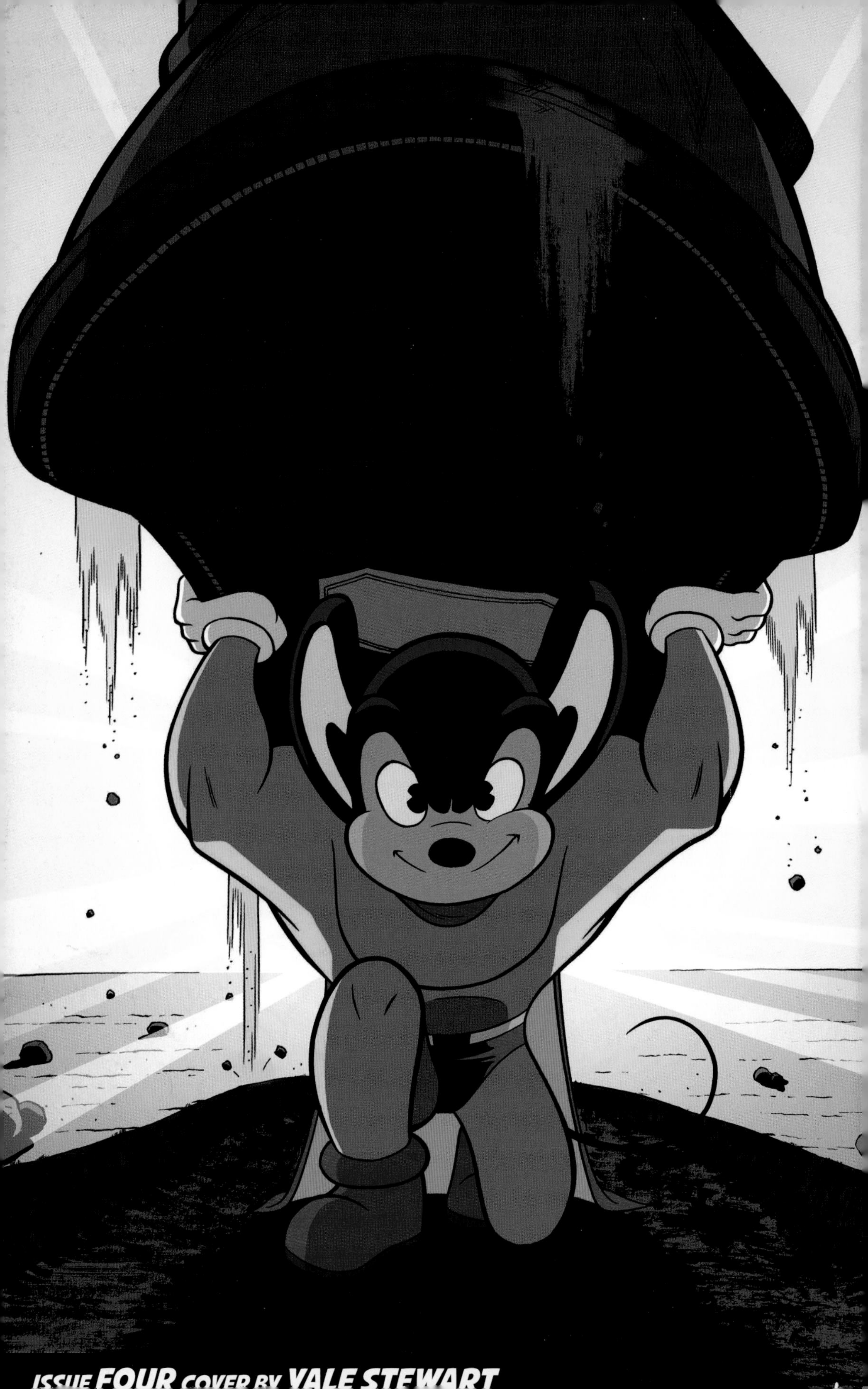

ISSUE FOUR COVER BY VALE STEWART

ISSUE FIVE COVER BY ANTHONY MARQUES
INKS BY J.BONE
COLORS BY CHRIS O'HALLORAN

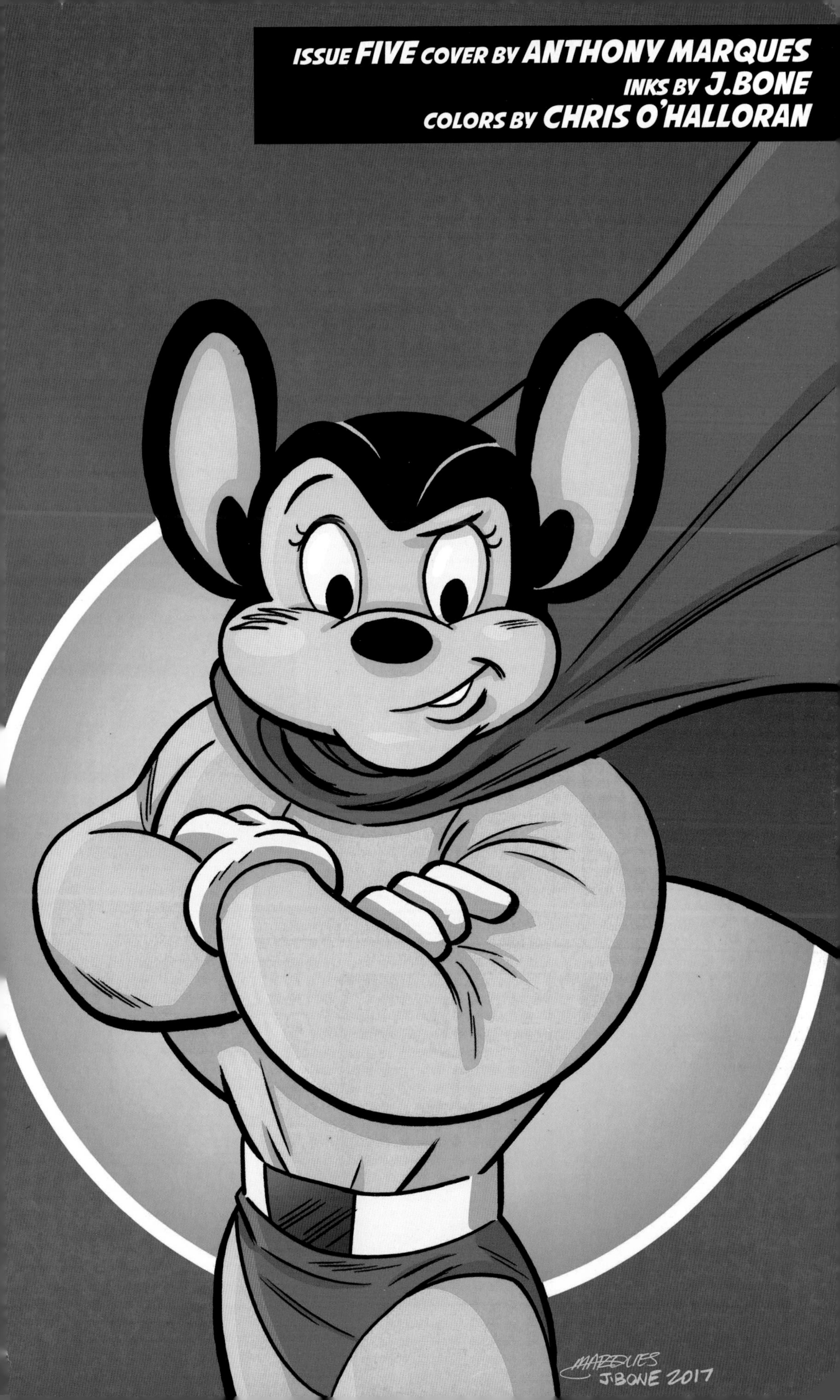
MARQUES
J.BONE 2017

FIND THESE GREAT DYNAMITE ALL-AGES BOOKS AND MORE!

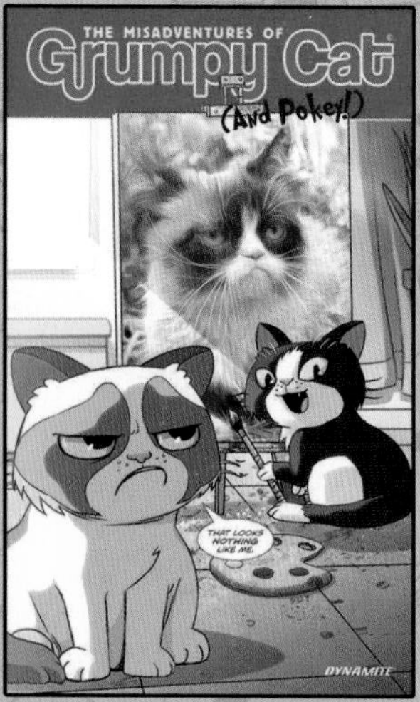
THE MISADVENTURES OF
Grumpy Cat
(And Pokey!)
THAT LOOKS NOTHING LIKE ME.
DYNAMITE

GRUMPY CAT & POKEY (VOL. 1) HARDCOVER
ISBN: 978-1-60690-796-2

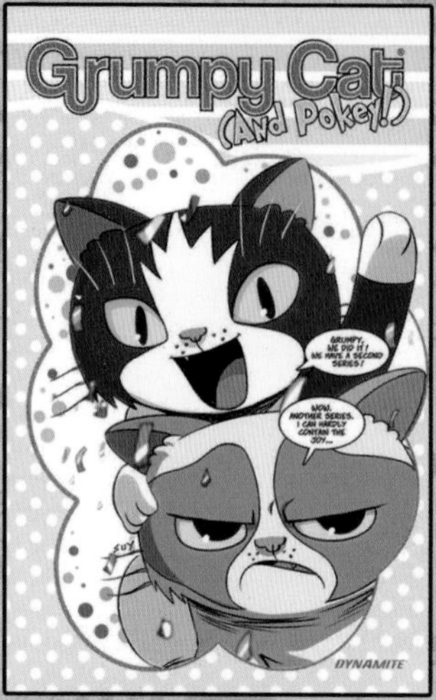
Grumpy Cat
(And Pokey!)
DYNAMITE

GRUMPY CAT & POKEY (VOL. 2) HARDCOVER
ISBN: 978-1-5241-0004-9

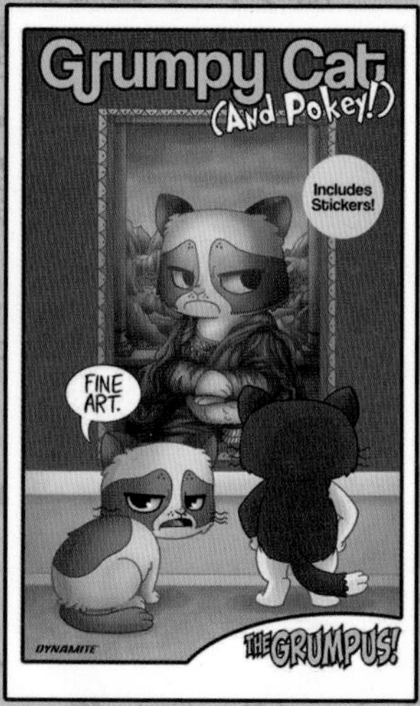
Grumpy Cat
(And Pokey!)
Includes Stickers!
FINE ART.
DYNAMITE
THE GRUMPUS!

GRUMPY CAT & POKEY: THE GRUMPUS (VOL. 3) HARDCOVER
ISBN: 978-1-5241-0246-3

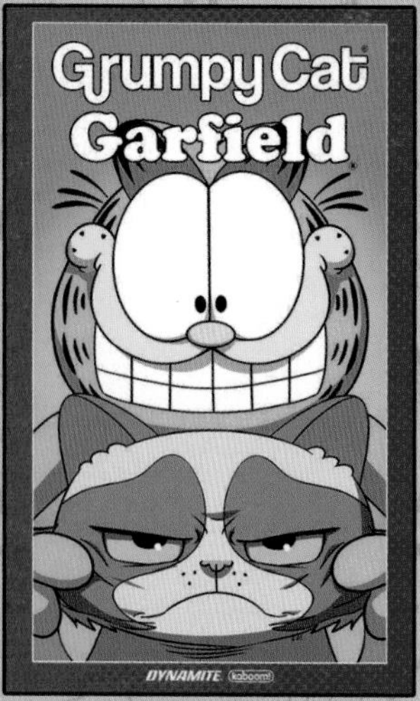
Grumpy Cat
Garfield
DYNAMITE

GRUMPY CAT GARFIELD HARDCOVER
ISBN: 978-1-5241-0496-2

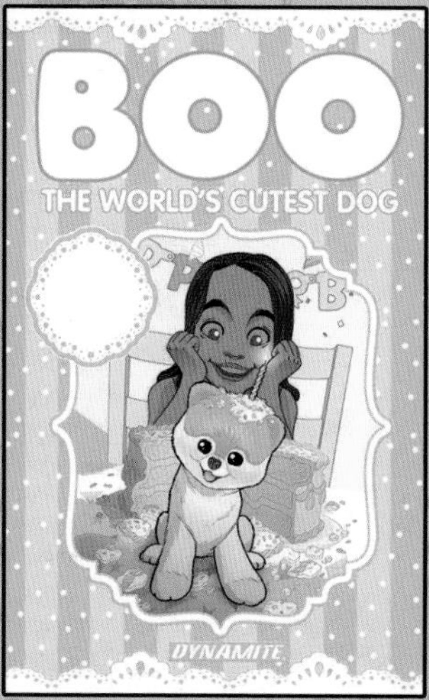
BOO
THE WORLD'S CUTEST DOG
DYNAMITE

BOO: THE WORLD'S CUTEST DOG A WALK IN THE PARK HARDCOVER
ISBN: 978-1-5241-0233-3

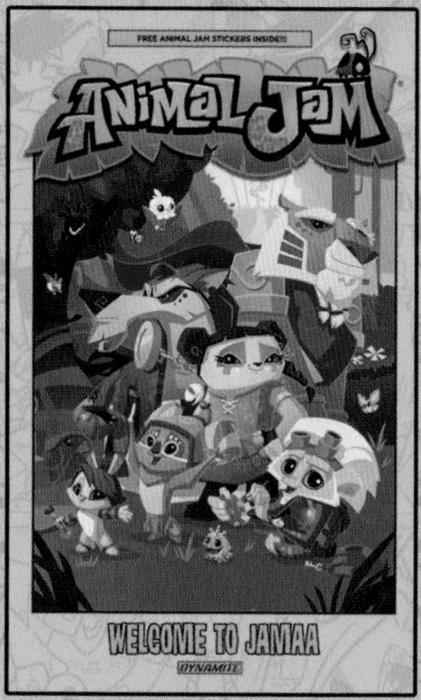
FREE ANIMAL JAM STICKERS INSIDE!!!
ANIMAL JAM
WELCOME TO JAMAA
DYNAMITE

FINAL ART PENDING LICENSOR APPROVAL

ANIMAL JAM: WELCOME TO JAMAA HARDCOVER
ISBN: 978-1-5241-0386-6

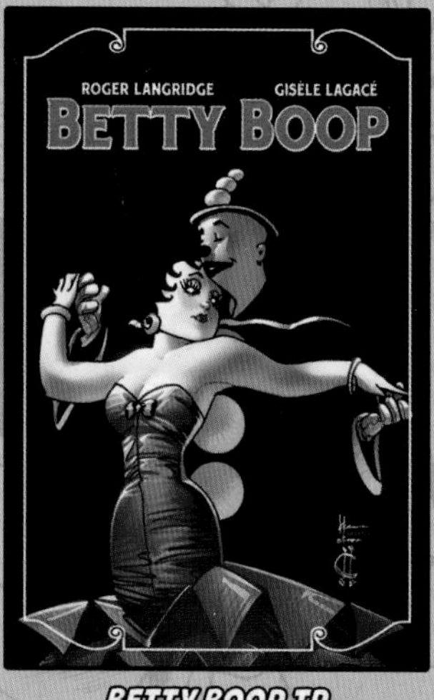
ROGER LANGRIDGE
GISÈLE LAGACÉ
BETTY BOOP

BETTY BOOP TP
ISBN: 978-1-5241-0318-7

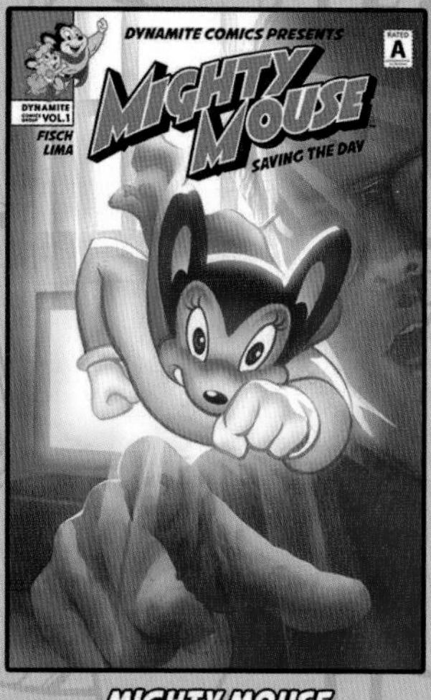
DYNAMITE COMICS PRESENTS
RATED A
DYNAMITE VOL.1
FISCH
LIMA
MIGHTY MOUSE
SAVING THE DAY

MIGHTY MOUSE SAVING THE DAY TP
ISBN: 978-1-5241-0386-6

VISIT DYNAMITE.COM OR CHECK OUT YOUR LOCAL RETAILER FOR ALL OF THESE AMAZING COLLECTIONS!

DYNAMITE

VISIT DYNAMITE.COM TO LEARN MORE

/DYNAMITECOMICS @DYNAMITECOMICS